Totalled

Totalled

Salvaging the Future from
the Wreckage of Capitalism

Colin Cremin

PlutoPress
www.plutobooks.com

First published 2015 by Pluto Press
345 Archway Road, London N6 5AA

www.plutobooks.com

Copyright © Colin Cremin 2015

The right of Colin Cremin to be identified as the author of this work
has been asserted by him in accordance with the Copyright, Designs
and Patents Act 1988.

British Library Cataloguing in Publication Data
A catalogue record for this book is available from the British Library

ISBN   978 0 7453 3438 7   Hardback
ISBN   978 0 7453 3437 0   Paperback
ISBN   978 1 7837 1267 0   PDF eBook
ISBN   978 1 7837 1268 7   Kindle eBook
ISBN   978 1 7837 1266 3   EPUB eBook

Library of Congress Cataloging in Publication Data applied for

10   9   8   7   6   5   4   3   2   1

Typeset by Stanford DTP Services, Northampton, England
Text design by Melanie Patrick
Simultaneously printed digitally by CPI Antony Rowe, Chippenham, UK
and Edwards Bros in the United States of America

Contents

Acknowledgements

First, I want to express my immense gratitude to David Castle and all the people at Pluto Press for enabling this book to happen. Thanks to the University of Auckland for grants and funds that helped me conduct research for the book. I would also like to thank Steve Matthewman, who has done so much for the department of sociology, and for me: a friend, comrade, and intellectual fellow traveller. I'd also like to offer a belated thanks to another colleague, friend – comrade – Bruce Cohen, and his partner Jessica Terruhn, for helping to make the transition to Aotearoa/New Zealand such a smooth and pleasurable one, the ever reliable Good Times Tsars. I have had the pleasure of teaching and supervising excellent students during the past couple of years. Particular mention should go to Eli Boulton, Bartek Goldman, Juliet Perano, Mediya Rangi and Dylan Taylor. A special thanks goes to Janet McAllister for her thoroughgoing and invaluable proofreading and critical commentary on the first draft of the manuscript.

Also, thanks to Tracey Sharp for the research she conducted for me. I could thank many other people here for a whole variety of reasons and can only apologise for the sake of brevity for not mentioning you by name. Finally, if anyone has more than any other borne the weight of anxieties and frustrations that go with working on a manuscript, it is Akiko, to whom in friendship and love I am indebted.

Introduction:
Year Zero

At 4.7500 degrees longitude and 155.4000 degrees latitude you will find the Carteret Islands of the South Pacific. Made up of six atolls, they are inhabited by some 2,500 people. They lack access to basic infrastructure; there are no cars, shops or phones on the islands. Seline Netoi, who lives on one of the smaller atolls, survives on coconut milk and fish. Two metres of shoreline disappear each year. In 2009, the King Tide, which comes three times a year, completely covered the island.[1] Whether this is a result of sinking tectonic plates or climatic change is moot for those forced to leave the islands. Many have already evacuated; others refuse to leave. As Rufina Moi explains, 'There is nothing better than home. Our treasure is this island. We think of our mothers and fathers and grandfathers who are buried on the island and we cannot leave them. We might as well die with them because we love our Carterets.'[2] If the intensive exploitation of natural resources and their despoliation by industrial production, waste and warfare elsewhere in the world has a role to play, then what has happened here is a dispossession of land by abstract processes far removed in culture and geography from life on the islands. There is no accumulative moment after the fact of dispossession, just ocean. Neither a year zero for a twenty-first-century Marshall plan, nor a blank slate for private contractors to build on. Rising sea levels, desertification and radioactive soils make dead zones from which people have migrated and metaphors for the total loss we are threatened with by processes most of us are only dimly aware of. *Totalled* is about those processes or, more precisely, the relationships that bind the force of human subjectivity to a more abstract and destructive force threatening life not only in the South Pacific but throughout the world generally. It is a diagnosis of our material dependencies on, ideological affinities with, and libidinal investments in the forces and relations of capitalist production, distribution, exchange and consumption. The book examines how our drives and desires, crucial to the circulation and expansion of capital, is expended in work and consumption; it traces this expenditure in order to consider how desire is made to work for capital and what this means for the whole of human society.

Capitalism encompasses the totality of societal relations, weaving ever more intricately into the fabric of all that it means to be human. It is a system that totalises and which has upended the modernity project through industrialised warfare, surveillance, commodification and control. With ever deepening crises and ecological catastrophes it threatens the total destruction of human civilisation. But in amongst this wreckage there are still functioning parts, machines to be salvaged through the collective force of the human imagination and the total mobilisation of the peoples of this earth to realise a different future to the apocalyptic endings forewarned of by scientists, prescribed by economists, accommodated by politicians and turned into spectacle by the entertainment industry. The plight of the Carteret Islanders signal one kind of year zero, one in which, as with the clocks that ticked before the Hiroshima bomb, time comes to an abrupt halt. But there is another year zero, the end of one epoch and the beginning of another – the end of class history: Germinal, the beginning of the post-revolutionary calendar.

While focused on the subject of hitherto more affluent times, the book has wider implications for how we think about capitalism, ideology and desire. It identifies in this moment utopian ideas, impulses and practices that are of central importance to a salvaging project. This is reserved for the final two chapters of the book. The preceding chapters present a grim picture of the current conjunction of forces: a diagnosis of what will here be referred to as an apocalyptic age, though one in which there remains the possibility, albeit faint, of changing the course of history.

Eros and Apocalypse

There was a time when the future seemed brighter than it does today. There were traces of optimism even in early 2007 when the banking system appeared to be, as the saying goes, 'as safe as houses'. But in truth, the times have always been apocalyptic. Lives are permanently at breaking point, subject to the contingencies of greater economic and ecological forces, subject to plagues and famines, speculative bubbles, redundancies and repossessions. The commodity is today's great destroyer, a divider and accumulator speeding through global communication networks, creating a chain reaction of fear, chauvinism, depression and a recurring apocalyptic fantasy present, as Jean Baudrillard put it, 'in homoeopathic doses, in each of us' (2010: 89). But such fantasies are opiates, a comforting drug that dulls us into thinking capital will collapse by itself under its own contradictions or that nature will have her revenge and wipe the slate clean. Business is at world's end.

Such fantasies and the fears that accompany them do not happen in a vacuum. Media obsessions with the end-of-the-world theme and the more scholarly concerns about the future – 'end times' (Žižek, 2010), 'inflection points' (Harvey, 2012) and human/nature 'metabolic rifts' (Foster, 2000) – are not merely ideological. They are echoes of economic crisis, rising carbon emissions and events from 9/11 through to Occupy, the Arab Spring and Fukushima. These events and unfolding processes characterise the first decades of what Franco Berardi (2011) pronounces the century with no future. Walter Benjamin was perhaps a little more sanguine when, between the great wars of the last century, he wrote 'all that one might have been in this world, one is in another' (2003 [1927–40]: 114). Recognising both the loss incurred to humanity by the conditions forced upon it and the impossibility of transcending those conditions, including alienation in a time of mass destruction, Benjamin felt there remained the faint possibility of renewal, if not for himself then for future generations.

Current renderings of the kind of horror and barbarism that Benjamin bore witness to are relayed to more affluent classes in the myriad of pixelated lights on flattened electronic screens; two-dimensional planes paralleling the one-dimensionality of the pseudo-politics they invite us to engage in. Brute reality in the slum regions of the world is delivered as a surreal otherworldliness to suburban enclaves. The 2008 banking crisis may not have precipitated another global war but for many who had enjoyed at least some of the fruits of incessant accumulation and expansion, the economic crisis brought the harsh realities of free-market capitalism closer to home. A financial trauma has given rise to countless other traumas as livelihoods are shattered and the prospect of a better life is reduced to a cinder. In these times of intractable, ever expanding and intensifying crises, austerity has delayed the creative moment in the economic cycle that Schumpeter famously spoke of. In this world, some 80 or so years after Benjamin imagined a non-alienated future, simply being an alienated worker with a stable job has for many become today's utopian wish.

Apocalyptic fantasies flourish in times when the prospects for political transformation appear limited. Catastrophes have communising effects. When earthquakes strike, bombs explode and tsunamis deluge cities, the human predisposition to help those in need reinvigorates community if only for a time. Such moments are suggestive of a utopian capacity to transcend social divisions but are of political relevance only when imagined in advance, so that measures can be taken to prevent or mitigate the sort of outcomes currently forewarned of by ecological scientists. For Freud, our survival was a question of regulating the primal instinct for pleasure through an apparatus internalised in the human psyche. Eros, the foundation of culture, is sacrificed to socially useful pursuits that guard against unpleasure while expanding, through a delayed gratification, its very possibility. The more 'advanced' and differentiated societies become, the more abstract is our relationship to others, and the greater is the need, according to Freud, to strengthen the repressive apparatus in the unconscious. Discontentment is the outcome that reality demands, and only by repressing and sublimating our desires is the survival of the species guaranteed. It is a strange kind of reality though – one that demands submission to a work regime that leeches the lifeblood of the worker and coagulates it in things whose value is determined by exchange rather than social benefit. It is more accurate to say that our survival is brought into question by this relationship, rather than supported by it. Submission to the reality principle of capitalism today guarantees hardship, uncertainty and alienation. In such circumstances, reality demands revolution. This was Herbert Marcuse's wager and it is as relevant today as it was in the 1950s when he wrote *Eros and Civilisation* (2006 [1955]).

Futures are foreclosed by finance industries to which even the unborn are indebted. The stench of an apocalypse pervades the senses, portending misery without the aroma of redemption and renewal. Apocalyptic prophecies today differ from those of the past in several key and interrelated respects. They are globalised, standardised, rationalised, atomised and commodified in physical reality, ideas and desires. Material life is overcoded by cinematic phantasmagoria and the explosion on sites such as YouTube of footage of terrorist attacks, tsunamis and executions in real time. End points are rationalised by scientists who establish the link between environmental devastation, industry and mass consumption, and by economists who describe the logic of capital as a natural and unstoppable juggernaut. The apocalypse is universal in scope, particular in cause, and isolated in the imagination of those who identify solutions in individual enterprise or see themselves as the narcissistic heirs of a post-apocalyptic scenario. Whatever the challenges we face as a species, the commodity, it would seem, is there to rescue us in the various market-based solutions to crises, be they economic, ecological or social. The harmonics of a collective imagination and enterprise is rent from history; self-aggrandisement becomes the modus operandi of choice in an uncontested reality. A culmination and convergence of three distinctive apocalyptic logics can loosely be mapped onto Jacques Lacan's three orders of subjectivity. First, the objective conditions upon which humanity depends have been universally shaped and undermined by processes of capitalist accumulation: a material (Real) logic. Second, visions of destruction – once the product of diverse localised myths and fantasies – have become homogenised and globalised: a symbolic logic. Third, this singular image of destruction is met, in the isolated thoughts of the individual, by no counter-hegemonic image of an alternative: an imaginary logic.

History, though, is never one-sided. It has a dual character, opposing tendencies charged positively and negatively, the twin poles of Eros and Thanatos, creation and destruction, life and death. The future is a void yet to be determined, a territory yet to be inhabited and an energy yet to be marshalled. It is a void of contestation where a collective force may either become a catalyst for emancipation or congeal in additional commodities put into circulation. The force of human desire is the basis of life and, through self-conscious and collective activity, the stuff out of which complex societies are formed. Marx named this force labour power, Freud libidinal energy, Lacan *jouissance*, Deleuze and Guattari desiring intensities. Herbert Marcuse, the first to develop a detailed theoretical synthesis of Marx and Freud, saw in the productive forces the historically unprecedented means to liberate the world from want and necessity. This would entail the desublimation or externalisation from the psyche of the repressive apparatus of the reality principle, namely the institutions of capital to which Eros, or the pleasure principle, had yielded. Taking as a starting point the idea of human subjectivity as an irrepressible force, connections can be established between theorists as diverse as Marx, Marcuse, Deleuze and Žižek. This is the foundation of a pragmatic and synthetic theoretical approach – embracing the positivity of desire, an excessive force, and the dialectics of antagonism, a self-negating force – to the issues and themes of this book. When theory centres on questions of ontology and epistemology, when standpoints are hardened according to differences that from an explanatory perspective are sometimes trivial, critique is itself deprived of its emancipatory value. Theory, rather than explaining abstractions, becomes merely abstract, decorative and obscure, empowering masters to decipher the text for enthusiastic disciples to follow: reality is made to fit their scholarly investment in theory. A genuinely critical theory is in permanent motion, it offers explanations of abstract processes and, through engagement, aims to liberate thought from stupidity, chauvinism, obscurantism, cynicism and fear. Material life, the languages through which sense is made of that life, and the force of human desire that puts our world in motion – in short, materialism, language and desire – are the DNA of critical theory, and the stuff that connects a diversity of theorists who at first blush appear to have little in common. Rather than propound a theory divorced from empirical reality that suits a politics without demands, this book, by utilising theory as a tool, a weapon even, will propose ways in which the energies described above can be wrestled away from their destructive encounter with capital.

Chapter Content

Totalled differs from my first book, *Capitalism's New Clothes*, in a number of important respects, but there are symmetries that justify calling this a follow-up. In that first book I outlined what I see as three overlapping and mutually reinforcing ideological injunctions of capitalism today: to be enterprising (exemplified by work); to be ethical (exemplified by common concerns about inequality and climate change); and to enjoy (exemplified by consumerism). That understanding is implicit in this current work, and is explicated at times through associated concepts such as 'reflexive exploitation' and 'guilt fetishism'. The first refers back to the argument that 'employability' is the overriding ideological injunction that demands from each of us an ever increasing amount of energy to fire the machine of capitalist abstraction, namely for profit. The second refers back to the way the effects of capitalism on people and planet are rendered intelligible by a perverse logic that places the individuated individual as both cause and market-friendly solution. These are the central points from *Capitalism's New Clothes* to which the present book returns, specifically in Chapters 4 and 5, though contextualised within the over-arching and in key respects different aims of *Totalled*.

Of central importance here are the ways in which human desires are tied to the capitalist economy, specifically in the relational capitalistic logics of work, communication and consumption, and more tentatively, how they might be untied, in a negative act of subtraction or, from the perspective of a more positive ontology, exceeded to the point that they are rendered inoperative. Taking its cue from Fredric Jameson's contention that 'a Marxist negative hermeneutic, a Marxist practice of ideological analysis proper, must in the practical work of reading and interpretation be exercised *simultaneously* with a Marxist positive hermeneutic, or decipherment...' (2002 [1981]: 286), the book oscillates between the negative and positive. In its *totality*, the situation, to be clear, is dire, and the prospects for the left appear at the time of writing far from excellent. It is not the purpose of this book to make syrup nor by the same token to wallow in misery or draw comfort from the cheap cloth of cynicism. The purpose is to derive from the analysis some clarity in regard to the obstacles to universal justice and emancipation and the possibilities under current material, ideological and libidinal circumstances of overcoming them. The book does not bombard the reader with statistics on poverty, inequality or environmental degradation; where not stated for argumentative purposes these are taken as read.

Chapter 1, 'Materially Determined Apocalypse', situates current apocalyptic thinking in the context of today's crises, struggles and ideological perspectives. Rather than make the banal and meaningless point that apocalyptic fantasies are common to all human societies, it seeks instead to identify a materiality to what is claimed to be an apocalyptic age. It separates biblical apocalypses, in which redemption from oppression was envisaged, from a capitalist apocalypse, in which the only outcome is destitution and despair. While a desire for an end point may signal a utopian wish for an end to class divisions and the suffering caused through them, apocalyptic fantasies today signal feelings of powerlessness and are, it will be claimed, for the most part reactive, not least to the increasingly apparent effects of global warming and the apparent inability to tame market forces.

Chapter 2, 'The Three Orders of Apocalypse', maps the Lacanian categories of the Real, the Symbolic and the Imaginary onto material processes, ideologies and subjective identifications, first centring on what can be seen as already occurring apocalypses through to their political neutralisation in popular culture. The apocalypse is mediatised and rendered a spectacle while at the same time generating a visceral affect not least because of how close to home – the centres of cultural production – the more egregious symptoms of capital now are.

Chapter 3, 'The Double Helix of Dissatisfaction', begins by expanding the definition of alienation sketched by Marx in the *Economic and Philosophical Manuscripts* in order to account for the different ways we are now subjected to capital. The subject is locked into two mutually reinforcing spirals of dissatisfaction, one that relates to work and the other that relates to consumption. This is expanded on in the following two chapters. The main purpose here is to provide a general account of the capitalist mode of production and some of its impacts and ideological mystifications in regard to which the fundamental relations are hidden. Central to this is the ideology of austerity and related conditions of scarcity redolent in images of economic and ecological crises.

Chapter 4, 'Production Spiral', approaches work and consumption as relational logics that cannot be separated, no matter how often critics of production or consumption attempt to do so. This chapter revisits arguments from *Capitalism's New Clothes* on how the work ethic is transposed onto an ethic of employability and the inescapable injunction to become employable irrespective of whether we already have a job or the condition of the labour market. This is crucial for identifying the common purpose and bind in which our position as a class economically if not ideologically antagonistic to capital is defined.

Chapter 5, 'Consumption Spiral', centres on the consumerist component of this class relation, the moment when value is taken out of circulation and destroyed. The alienating condition of labour intensifies the need for consumer products both as repositories of labour and as objects of desire. The capitalist form of consumption is not only a compensation for alienated labour, it is claimed here to be a cause of a relational (to work) alienation. The chapter 'updates' the culture industry thesis of Adorno and Horkheimer, last revisited by Adorno in the 1960s, in view of the rise of social media and products that are individualised by their consumers. Whereas for Marcuse the 'happy consciousness' found comfort in products whose properties were 'fixed', today the happy consciousness is derived from investments in a variety of apps, tools and so forth which are downloaded onto new machines that invite seemingly endless possibilities for creation.

The 'salvage' project begins in earnest with Chapter 6, 'Banquets of Worlds', which shifts the register by examining the utopian impulses pregnant in our drive to overcome material scarcities and feelings of dissatisfaction. Drawing on a number of perspectives, it is argued that utopia is an important political category that enables us to think about alternatives and challenge the proposition that capitalism is the 'only game in town'. Utopia is considered, with respect to utopian thinkers, as an impulse, idea and practice, of political value when attuned to possibilities within the current horizon and underlined by an aim to qualitatively extend that horizon.

Chapter 7, 'Clash of Axioms', considers the current strengths and weaknesses of movements opposed to capital and the obstacles to more generalised and politically effective forms of resistance. It approaches this in terms of the historical weaknesses of the left and the subject socialised through the neoliberal period, one that a genuine movement for emancipation has to work with rather than refuse. This is framed by way of a description of the antagonism between the 'axiom' of capital, namely surplus value, and the 'axiom' of communism, namely global emancipation from the commodity form and the realisation of a society based on common ownership of and determination over the means of production. Theories of state power, particularly that of Nicos Poulantzas (2000 [1978]), are deployed with respect to anti-statist, anti-centralist 'anarchist' tendencies on both the right and the left. The revolutionary proclamations of the 'multitude' are rejected as shrill and counter-productive, as too are the 'politics without demands' of recent movements such as Occupy Wall Street. We are not in a revolutionary moment and – barring some unforeseen 'event' that anyhow would be vulnerable to appropriation, as the so-called Arab Spring testifies – preliminary initially reformist steps, expanding the possibility for revolution, are what is required. If the compact of capitalism and desire has produced a car crash of sorts, the conclusion is that in amongst this wreckage there are empirical possibilities for salvaging the future from what at times appears to be a hopeless case.

The chapters are organised as a relay between the material realities that each of us in our different capacities encounter; the ideas through which those realities are interpreted, brought into question and challenged; and the practices adequate to those challenges. Each chapter addresses separate but interrelated issues and together they provide the depth of analysis required to make concrete propositions in the final chapter on how the excessive force of subjectivity can become divorced from the destructive excess of capital.

Totalled is about a subjectivity of a particular time and space, a westernised – colonised – time and space; it is about a subject whose impulses, beliefs and actions bring about changes in the material environment. We are subject to changes that are more or less rapid, more or less pronounced, more or less sudden. In this dialectic of history lies the possibility of another world, not the kind sported on the banners of an amorphous anti-globalisation multitude, but one of open possibility, an ongoing project in the *realisation* of a more just, equitable, liberated and joyous world. It is a dream to nourish, an idea to enact, a possibility to concretise.

1

Materially Determined Apocalypse

An excess of nature, the iridescent feathers of the peacock displayed to attract mates also, by their cumbersome weight, make their owners easy prey for hungry predators. Our human excesses are by contrast discerned in the objects created first in the mind before being fashioned by the body, stone made architectural wonder, iron made blade, civilisation a document of barbarism as Walter Benjamin once said. History does not end with the cutting of a ribbon to unveil a new monument, rather it continues in our every wandering motion. In contrast to the feathers of the peacock that are a chance mutation, the excesses of human civilisation are the result of self-conscious and collective activity. Not in a million years but in a matter of decades can we discern massive changes to our social environment that have brought about discernable changes in the character of the individual that in turn give rise to possibilities hitherto beyond the scope of a more archaic imagination.

Capitalism is not the result of natural mutation or developed from a singular design. For Max Weber it is an unintended consequence of a Calvinist belief in predestination. The chosen could not be known in advance of an ascent to heaven but clues could be discerned on earth by one's industry. Protestantism thereby entered into a pact with the work ethic as a gateway to heaven, enterprise became a new religion divorced from its godly provenance. For Marx, capitalism was born from the alienation of labour from immediate production, through forced dispossession and the force of necessity. As Marx wrote,

> The discovery of gold and silver in America, the extirpation, enslavement and entombment in mines of the indigenous population of that continent, the beginnings of the conquest and plunder of India, and

the conversion of Africa into a preserve for the commercial hunting of blackskins, are all things which characterise the dawn of the era of capitalist production. These idyllic proceedings are the chief moments of primitive accumulation. (2001 [1867]: 915)

A recurring theme of history, dispossession continues apace, with financial elites leaching off the productive economy as their politically entrenched allies open new possibilities for the expropriation of common property. An asymmetrical warfare is being fought on the provisions of life. Governments scythe daisy-cutter style through regulatory frameworks that once held the commodity at bay, as labour is caught between the rock of a low-wage economy and the hard place of mass unemployment. In this war, whose victims are nameless, dead eyes in the mirror reflect a utopian desire to become a privileged object of exchange. It is an unending struggle to become more exploitable than others, paid for by mortgaging future labour to an education in becoming fit for exploitation. Here artistic creation is recycled from a cloth industry torn from our backs and sold as objects said to increase satisfaction but actually small recompense for a class that lost the world. The victor's banner is everywhere a commodity: the land, the biosphere, genetic code, social infrastructure, public services, prisons and military apparatuses; mind, body and spirit. Neoliberalism is our legacy that stretches into the future, an everyday encounter in the commercial thoroughfares of now standardised town centres, in schools that educate us in the art of the statistical average and in hospitals where key services are parcelled out to private contractors. To breathe this air today is to inhale the stench of a billion living deaths.

Unlike the Protestant belief in predestination, the more secularised end-of-the-world prophecies today offer no redemption, spur no industry, provoke no revolution. By bringing Freud's theories of the human drives together with Marx's materialist analysis of history, we can examine the forces, both libidinal and capitalistic, that have set us on a path towards an apocalypse of a kind, but one in which there remains, however dystopian our situation, a faint possibility of redemption. Not by the hand of God or the market will this happen, not by chance mutation, but rather by the collective action of angry, disenfranchised and indebted masses. This chapter expands on some basic concepts from Freud, relaying them through more contemporary Marxist critical theory, to establish a foundation for later analysis and argumentation. Adopting this materialist approach, the chapter aims to distinguish the apocalypticism of our own age from that of the past.

Unstoppable Forces

Like steam in a boiling kettle, our capacity to adjust our surroundings through social activity, a vital activity described by Freud as libidinal, requires an outlet. In psychoanalytic theory, society acts like a spout to direct that force either coercively or, in more open systems, towards its dissipation in a broad range of socially useful activities: art, cultural production, work and so forth. For Bataille, this force or energy is an 'accursed share' that can be expended 'gloriously' in open systems or 'catastrophically' in closed ones (1999 [1946–49]). Gendered assumptions notwithstanding, the fatal flaw in Freud's dynamic theories of the human personality is their lack of critique of society – the society to which Freud claimed our libidinal energies must be sacrificed. Without such a critique, psychoanalysis, as Adorno pointed out, accommodates 'the ruling social norm' (2007 [1966]: 274). By bringing Freud and Marx together, critical theory addresses this lacuna: Marcuse by way of synthesis, Deleuze and Guattari by postulating Oedipus as a symptom and psychoanalysis as an ally of capital.

Capitalism, say Deleuze and Guattari, is an axiomatic that thrives on 'decoded flows of desire'. It is a not a closed system at all, but rather a system of 'anti-production' for the capture of desire, which for them is simply a force without object that wants nothing and lacks nothing. Capitalism manufactures a permanent space for surplus value that a guilt-ridden subject aims to fill. Progression coincides with destruction, in a system of never-ending and expanding crises that deterritorialises or decodes in order to reterritorialise or recode, to produce 'lack amid overabundance, but stupidity in the midst of knowledge and science' (Deleuze and Guattari, 2003a [1972]: 236). Capital has learnt from social machines, from the dynamics, instabilities and antagonisms of different formations or assemblages that fuel the flames of history. These feed 'on the contradictions they give rise to, on the crises they provoke, on the anxieties they *engender*, and on the infernal operations they regenerate'. Capitalism will not end by attrition nor by contradiction because 'the more it breaks down, the more it schizophrenises, the better it works, the American way' (Deleuze and Guattari, 2003a [1972]: 151). The function of the Oedipal complex is to ensure that people freely submit to this operation. Daddy threatens punishment for crimes of the mind: through progressive stages of socialisation we learn that desire is fundamentally incestuous or destructive and so learn to want to divert libidinal energy into tasks deemed socially productive. There is a lack to perpetually fill, exemplified today, as Maurizio Lazzarato (2012) points out, in personal indebtedness, the fear of a creditor, and what they might do if we fail to keep up our payments. In this age of austerity, indebtedness is seen as a symptom of unrestrained desire.

Whereas for Deleuze and Guattari desire (fundamentally at least) has no object, for Freud the entire libidinal economy is predicated on the relationship between the subject of desire and the object that gives pleasure. Pleasure is the base motive of human desire, not need as such. This seems evident whenever we prolong hunger or thirst by refusing bread and water until there is a prepared meal or flavoured drink at hand. The object of love is culturally mediated. Eros, or the pleasure principle, goes through a series of detours in order to attain the object. It freely submits to the reality principle by recognising in society a higher law that both rewards and punishes. Reality is after all a matter of intemperate climates and contingent hurricanes, against which society, like a shelter or the mother's breast, provides comfort and security. Eros wants to avoid unpleasure, which it minimises by preserving its energy for socially necessary tasks. In this sense Eros is a self-conserving drive. As Freud explained,

> Under the influence of the ego's instincts of self-preservation, the pleasure principle is replaced by the reality principle. This latter principle does not abandon the intention of ultimately obtaining pleasure, but it nevertheless demands and carries into effect the postponement of satisfaction, the abandonment of a number of possibilities of gaining satisfaction and the temporary toleration of unpleasure as a step on the long indirect road to pleasure. (2010 [1920]: 3717)

In societies with a limited division of labour, our desires are given over to the basic necessities of survival. In societies with a complex division of labour, such as our own, the means of production are more developed and the link between sacrifice of erotic energies and survival is more tenuous, at least outside of the slums and dead zones of anti-production. By way of caricature, in societies described by anthropologists as primitive, hunger was sated from meat pulled by teeth from the bone, now, in optimal conditions, raw produce no longer harvested by the consumer is transformed into culinary delights to impress friends at dinner parties.

The sphere of pleasure thus expands as culture refines the object for a more intense satisfaction. For civilisation to progress, the tenuous link between subject and society is maintained by increased feelings of guilt and social responsibility. A progressively more repressive superego keeps the primal drives of the id in check via the mediating ego, further draining energy from Eros, giving rise to resentments that in turn make the subject more prone to destructive outbursts. These can manifest collectively in riots, rebellions and revolutions. By resulting in more sophisticated apparatuses of repression, perhaps due to the guilt felt by participants after the event, revolutions that ultimately fail can for Freud, in this respect at least, be positive. This image is redolent in the burden of guilt carried by generations of workers for daring and ultimately failing to seize control of production and generalise prosperity in the name of communism.

The initial position of the Father as punishing authority and ideal ego/ role model is supplanted and multiplied in various institutions that we recognise today as schools, prisons, media industries and so forth. It is the reality principle, concretised in the education system, the workplace and shopping mall, an 'empirical hard core ... system of institutions, which are the established and frozen relationships among men' (Marcuse, 2002 [1964]: 195). As Marcuse bitterly observed, 'The individual pays by sacrificing his time, his consciousness, his dreams; civilisation pays by sacrificing its own promise of liberty, justice and peace for all' (2006 [1955]: 100).

A greater portion of erotic energies is drained into the accumulation process along detours to a vanishing point in which the return becomes proportionately smaller. As Marcuse wrote, 'The irreconcilable conflict is not between work (reality principle) and Eros (pleasure principle), but between *alienated* labour (performance principle) and Eros' (2006 [1955]: 47). Alienated labour weakens the creative power of Eros and in turn makes the subject more vulnerable to violent outbursts. Eros gives way to Thanatos, a drive towards achieving a former state of constant gratification blocked by the reality principle and manifesting in repetitive behaviour, extracting pleasure from the painful experience of being deprived happiness. The death drive aims for Nirvana, not to bring about the end to life but rather an end to pain and suffering. Alienated labour exacerbates this tendency, hence, according to Marcuse, by ending it lived experience would be closer to the oceanic love the subject craves. Through 'the quantitative reduction in labour time', Eros would absorb Thanatos leading 'to a qualitative change in the human existence ... The expanding realm of freedom becomes truly a realm of play – of the free play of individual faculties' (2006 [1955]: 222). Given the obvious connotations of the more individuated pleasures associated today with mass consumption, this does not in any way imply that liberation is simply the equivalent of self-expression. As Marcuse wrote in response to the new individualism that arose during the 1960s: 'no revolution without individual liberation, but also no individual liberation without the liberation of society' (1972: 48). This was, however, already made clear in 1956 when *Eros and Civilisation* was published, in which Marcuse stressed that the release of libido is destructive if it is not sublimated self-consciously and collectively. The Nirvana Principle of a life without tension is the utopian core of apocalyptic fantasies that dominate the westernised imaginary today.

The condition of scarcity is for Freud the reality principle that necessitates discontentment in the form of libidinal sacrifice. Yet, as has become clear, the more Eros services Capital, the greater is the concentration of wealth and power in the hands of the few and the poorer and more disenfranchised the majority of people become. Eros, as previously noted and as Lacan stresses, is a self-conserving drive. It does not want revolution but rather stability. The obvious rejoinder is that self-conservation under conditions of instability, insecurity and deprivation would rationally at least demand revolution. Lacan reserves this for the unquenchable and derailing death drive, which he associates with the concept of *jouissance*, a drive that, unlike desire which strives for something tangible, derives pleasure in the aim. Drive circulates around a non-existent thing, in Lacanian parlance the '*objet petit a*' or 'object cause' of desire. Real *jouissance* is that brief moment of ecstasy, a little death, typically identified in orgasm. Symbolic *jouissance* is the fantasy of the Other's enjoyment, in popular media the glamour of celebrity and 'how the other half live'. Imaginary *jouissance* is an ersatz enjoyment of an object, the kind of partial enjoyment we sometimes derive from consumer goods, an enjoyment that can from the perspective of symbolic *jouissance* often feel like an obligation: the injunction to enjoy, to have fun, to live life to the full as others appear to and in the manner that only commodities permit. There is no object that can satisfy drive, the thing is never 'it'. As Kesel writes, 'at the *imaginary* and *symbolic* levels, the desiring subject can have this impression, namely in the experience of *jouissance*. At the level of the *real* however, the drive does not reach its "thing"' (2009: 170). *Jouissance* can, in each of these respects, operate both materially and ideologically to aid in the realisation of profit from our investments in the production of surplus value.

Different ontologies that draw on, and sometimes challenge, the same theoretical propositions, have in common an understanding of the relationship between human drives or desires and the development of capitalism. For Marx, this is the species-defining capacity or vital force that we deploy to transform our surroundings and therein our own nature. For Marcuse the name for this force is Eros. For Lacan it is the reverse side of Eros, the destructive Thanatos that he identifies with the unquenchable surplus *jouissance*. Deleuze and Guattari suggest that everything emanates from a singular plane of immanence, and that differences are manifestations of varying intensities that assemble and disassemble in a constant state of becoming. These forces and assemblages fire up the abstract machine of capital, just as, for Marx, labour power is the source of surplus value. There are different purposes for which each of these theoretical contributions can help explain and unravel the predicament that this book identifies the whole of human society to be in. The value of this approach can be ascertained according to what it achieves, namely that it does indeed help us to understand, explain and develop a persuasive critique of current subjective and thereby social conditions as well as make propositions for transforming them.

The relevance of Freud today lies in the power of his theory to explain social conformity, in particular how ideology can absorb revolutionary aggression by positing an other (the Jew in Nazi Germany, the lazy welfare recipient in Conservative Britain, the Maori in Aotearoa/New Zealand) as the primary cause of social disharmony and individual dissatisfaction. It can also, as Adorno and Horkheimer and Marcuse have shown, explain the power of advertising, the power to create false needs for supplements to egos shown to be bare – more on this in Chapter 5 on consumption. Psychoanalytic theory underlines how irrational feelings rather than intellect can shape politics and, from the perspective of the left, shows that knowledge about the roots of our social malaise is not in itself enough to stir a revolutionary consciousness. For all of Freud's conservatism, libido remains a key concept for a diverse range of thinkers in explaining abstract phenomena. Marx himself often stressed that human needs are not reducible to survival but reflect the society and the sensual pleasures afforded at a particular historical juncture. As he wrote:

> when the limited bourgeois form is stripped away, what is wealth other than the universality of individual needs, capacities, pleasures, productive forces, etc., created through universal exchange? The full development of human mastery over the forces of nature, those of so-called nature as well as of humanity's own nature? The absolute working-out of his creative potentialities, with no presupposition other than the previous historic development, which makes this totality of development, i.e. the development of all human powers as such the end in itself, not as measured on a *predetermined yardstick*? Where he does not reproduce himself in one specificity, but produces his totality? Strives not to remain something he has become, but is in the absolute movement of becoming? (1973 [1858]: 488)

'Needs, capacities, pleasures and productive forces', an 'absolute movement of becoming' – this is not a sterile vision of the future but a joyous and endlessly liberating one that echoes in the work of Marcuse and also in Deleuze and Guattari, the Situationists and autonomous Marxists such as Hardt and Negri.

While Eros takes detours that separate us from nature and the exigencies of survival, we arrive at the point when the sacrifice of libido hastens rather than abates death. Eros begets Apocalypse. The conclusion to be drawn from this is that the current arrangements must themselves be changed if the pathologies inherent to them and which are displaced onto the individual are to be overcome. It is a conclusion that is all the more emphatic the more that the power of labour transfers over to capital in increasingly devastating quantities. They are quantities that compact and combust in warfare and ecologically unsustainable development, and which generalise a condition of scarcity thereby creating the real possibility of a twenty-first-century apocalypticism, to which we now turn.

57 Varieties of Apocalypse

> Whether it is the arms race or orders given to start a war that is itself dominated by that economy of speed throughout all the zones of its technology, a gap of a few seconds may decide, irreversibly, the fate of what is still now and then called humanity – plus the fate of a few other species.
>
> Jacques Derrida (1984: 22–31)

Humanity is well accustomed to massive, cruel, often tragic, loss. Countless genocides, unspeakable horrors and savagery, but always a trace, a document or relic, a vernacular passed on through surviving generations and now accessible in seconds on Wikipedia. The atomic bomb ushered in the age of absolute loss, the possibility that even language may not survive were there to be a global exchange of nuclear firepower. This is what Dixon refers to as a genuine apocalypse, 'What makes this appealing is the thought that if none shall survive, then, at last, all class, social, and racial boundaries will have been erased' (2003: 3). It is only in our own time that we can anticipate with scientific precision this kind of possibility, an ultimate destruction of all symbolic substance, of memory, of the capacity to bear witness or learn from mistakes. As technologies become more complex and our entire infrastructure depends on them, systems are more prone to meltdown. In 2000, Concorde was finally grounded after Air France flight 5490 burst into flames when a metallic strip left on the runway cut one of the wheels. In 2003, a blackout affecting 56 million Italians was caused by a storm that felled two trees onto a power cable in Switzerland (cf. Matthewman, 2015). Examples such as these underline how vulnerable we are to minor contingencies; these are nothing, though, compared to the contingent effects of global warming. As Susan George (2010: 175) notes, 47 per cent of humanity depends for its water on ten major rivers with their source in glaciers located in the plateau of Tibet. As a study sponsored by NASA recently confirmed, there is a high prospect that global industrial civilisation will collapse in the coming decades if inequalities and consumption, ostensibly of the elites, are not significantly reduced. As the authors put it, 'Collapse can be avoided and population can reach equilibrium if the per capita rate of depletion of nature is reduced to a sustainable level, and if resources are distributed in a reasonably equitable fashion.'[1]

Megarisks, megadisasters, megacatastrophes: according to some futurologists there is only a 10 per cent chance that the human species will survive this century (cf. Matthewman, 2015). Reform is not enough. Sooner or later the very rationale of capitalism, that of profit, must be brought to a close. It is not the Anthropocene, ecological catastrophe caused by humans, that we need to stress, but rather the Capitocene, ecological catastrophe caused by Capitalism (see Cremin, 2012).

Mark Fisher (2009) describes our age as one of Capitalist Realism, an ideology that posits no alternatives to current arrangements because, like all previous experiments in ending market domination, they would simply end in failure. As Marcuse put it, real possibilities have been relegated 'to the no-man's land of utopia' (2006 [1955]: 150). This is 'an essential element of the ideology of the performance principle', the principle of instrumental reason and exchange specific to capitalism, of endless sacrifice to alienating labour and debilitating mass consumption. There is a collective amnesia as regards the possibility of ending utopia, to bring an end, that is, to the idea that alternatives to capitalism are utopian in the sense that they are impossible, a point that will be elucidated in Chapter 6, 'Banquets of Worlds'.

When the energy for formulating alternative propositions appears spent what remains is a collective Thanatos, the fantasy of an end to suffering, an end to indebtedness, an end that more positively cannot be linguistically deconstructed, an end in the vein of apocalypse. But what kind of apocalypse is envisaged today?

An apocalypse, writes Evan Calder Williams (2011), is distinct from a crisis or catastrophe. Apocalypses are revelatory and redemptive, whereas crises are circular and imply an eventual return to normality. Catastrophes, Williams claims, are simply end points with no possibility of redemption. A capitalist apocalypse 'lifts the veil' to reveal the concrete realities beneath the abstract totality of exchange relations. Revolution is the missing category from Williams' list, catastrophic from the point of view of capital but triggered neither by the hand of God nor the Market. Revolutions result from self-conscious and collective action; an apocalypse is not something that people trigger or can have determination over. A capitalist apocalypse is therefore a contingent event, and the 'truth' it exposes is unlikely, beyond the immediate aftermath, to give rise to a common egalitarian purpose. It is a dream that requires no agent, just economic contradiction, and as Benjamin pointed out, and which by now ought to be clear, capitalism is unlikely to die a natural death. There was hope at least in the immediate aftermath of 2008, but those who dream of such endings are too quick to forget that capital sometimes thrives on crises, or at least certain elements of the capitalist class do. As Silver and Arrighi put it,

> a long and deep period of systemic chaos – analogous *but not identical* to the systemic chaos of the first half of the twentieth century – remains a serious historical possibility. While the end of the long twentieth century is inevitable, there is nothing inevitable about it coming to a catastrophic ending. Avoiding the latter is our urgent collective task. (in Calhoun and Derluguian eds., 2011: 68)

Such moments present us with opportunities to bring about change. But unless they are seized upon and, perhaps more fundamentally, unless there is a significant countervailing political force to enact change, catastrophe is the likely outcome. Benjamin Noys (2012: 13) claims that to recover the idea and possibility of human agency, philosophies that merely affirm the force of will must be eschewed for a negative thinking in which the destructive tendencies of capitalist abstraction are underlined in order for the subject to enact its own destruction. But if crises are 'revelatory of the ontology of capital' (Noys, 2012: 13) they do not in themselves give rise to political agency. They tend instead to force upon us a practical need for survival and investment in an economy whose return to growth appears concomitant with job creation.

Crises and apocalypses are not mutually exclusive. As David Noel Freedman puts it, 'Apocalypse was born of crisis' (quoted in Boyer, 1992: 23). An established part of folklore, anticipated in biblical texts and imagined throughout history, apocalypses today are simulated 3D spectacles on wraparound movie screens, ranging from *The Matrix* to *The Day After Tomorrow*, the one unmasking abstract processes and the other revelling in them. The themes of such films reflect on current fears and anxieties. They refract reality and, by normalising the unthinkable, have real material consequences. Reality precedes prophecy but prophecy itself serves as the fantasy frame within which endings are imagined and sometimes realised – the 9/11 event meaningless without a pop culture to create a déjà vu effect, a reality 'just like the movies'.

Apocalyptic times are born of crises, and, more precisely, they are born out of moments when people are confronted by a force that overwhelms them. In biblical times, the persecuted had God to avenge them. Our avenging Gods are Nature and the Market, but unlike the Gods of the Jews facing the Babylonian invaders, our Gods are indiscriminate. They are unable to discern the persecutor from the persecuted, the exploiter from the exploited. Nature punishes us for our 'excessive' consumption and the Market for our failure to adapt to economic 'realities'. To the Aztecs, the Conquistadors were the prophesied avenging Gods riding fantastical creatures and bearing weapons that emitted deadly rays (see Galeano, 2009 [1971]). The avenging God of Capital rides upon a fantastical economy bearing weapons of mass destruction, accompanied by the horsemen of the apocalypse that Žižek (2010) identifies in climate change, digitisation, biological manipulation and slums. These are empirically observable processes now so far advanced it is possible with a degree of certainty to deduce an outcome on par with cinematic spectacle. There is no common redemption in CGI-enhanced apocalypses. The collective body may be the victim but rarely the hero. In biblical prophecies, collective history is redeemed once the oppressor is defeated; there was no Ancient Realism in the vein of today's Capitalist Realism when 'great hailstones, fire and brimstone' pound on the Babylonian invaders holding siege to and sacking the city of Jerusalem (The Book of Ezekiel); or when plagues, sores, great whores and a blood-drenched moon await the Roman Imperial System in The Revelation of John, written during the reign of Emperor Domitian in 81–86 CE. The industrial proletariat of the nineteenth-century could at least turn to Marx and Engels' stirring polemic on capital, not a prophetic text at all (see Toscano, 2010), but rather one stressing the point that the end of tyranny and injustice is in the hands of the people not God, economic contradiction, or technologies that necessitate changes in social relations. After all, it was the prospect of a communist revolution alone that caused the ruling class to tremble. The class divisions still present are mystified in today's apocalypticism, where the end is indiscriminate and the outcome likely one-sided.

Drawing on Paul Virilio's work on the technologies of speed and annihilation, Deleuze and Guattari wrote that this blurring of real antagonism is a function of the capitalistic 'war machine', an assemblage of forces that elide state power but which can be appropriated into the repressive machinery of accumulation:

> This war machine is terrifying not as a function of a possible war that it promises us, as by blackmail, but, on the contrary, as a function of the real, very special kind of peace it promotes and has already installed; ... this war machine no longer needs a qualified enemy but, in conformity with the requirements of an axiomatic, operates against the 'unspecified enemy', domestic or foreign (an individual, group, class, people, event, world); ... there arose from this a new conception of security as materialised war, as organised insecurity or molecularised, distributed, programmed catastrophe. (2003b [1980]: 467)

A techno-warfare overwhelming the senses is taking place and fast approaching the event horizon. In the midst of this apocalypse is the dematerialising effect of what Virilio (2005 [1998]) calls the 'information bomb': virtual communication fallout that renders truth and fiction indiscernible leading to political paralysis. There is no exit here, hope is in slowdown, in a theory that circles rather than engages the materialist dialectic.

Hardt and Negri note a tendency among the academic left to regard states as fascistic and the loss of sovereign power as total. For such a mindset 'There are no forces of liberation inherent in such a power that, though now frustrated and blocked, could be set free. There is no hope of transforming such a power on a democratic course. It needs to be opposed, destroyed, and that is all' (Hardt and Negri, 2009: 5). Left apocalypticism relies on a divine violence that erupts as if from nowhere, the 'inexistent' perhaps that Alain Badiou identifies as the bearer of a revolutionary truth-event; or rather it relies on those without voice or determination who become subjects because of their fidelity to an open-ended 'truth-procedure'. One can only wonder what this means for the infidels who fail to recognise themselves as belonging to this procedure.

Fear and paranoia replace reason as conspiracy theories abound. As tempting as it is to identify the hallmarks of fascism in recent attacks on civil liberties, rendition and drone warfare, the United States, while perhaps on a 'proto-fascist' trajectory, does not yet embody fascism. Whatever the truth of the matter, the stockpiling of ammunition by Americans fearful that the state is itself preparing for total war on the gun-toting population suggests that such identification encourages a reactive fascist-paranoia.[2]

The *Daily Mail* reports that 'up to THREE MILLION "Preppers"' are arming themselves for the end of the world. The paper notes that one couple have constructed their own 'fortress' of guns and 25,000 rounds of ammunition. In another example, a man filled his swimming pool with a thousand fish so as to have plenty to eat when the apocalypse dawns.[3] *The Wall Street Journal* reports the booming trade in 'survival gear, freeze-dried food and underground bunkers'. Conservatives worried about Obama's re-election in 2012 spent nearly US$400,000 on pre-packaged meals; the equivalent of eight truckloads was bought from one website.[4] Referring to opinion polls, Catherine Keller points out that a quarter of the American population 'believe the Second Coming will occur within their own generation, along with the rapture and other premillennialist trappings' (2004: 8). Fear is sometimes rational. This kind of fear though is more akin to Zygmunt Bauman's description of it as being

> at its most fearsome when it is diffuse, scattered, unclear, unattached, unanchored, free floating, with no clear address or cause; when it haunts us with no visible rhyme or reason, when the menace we should be afraid of can be glimpsed everywhere but is nowhere to be seen. 'Fear' is the name we give to our *uncertainty*: to our *ignorance* of the threat of what is to be *done* – what can and what can't be – to stop it in its tracks – or to fight it back if stopping it is beyond our power. (2007: 2)

Capitalism generates crises and these are sometimes significant enough to generate demands for change. But crises, to qualify Evan Calder Williams' point, are never circular. Every crisis is resolved only partially and briefly through adjustments in behaviours that are more or less guided by reforms initiated by state and capital. Capital is defined by its motion, circular in that it begins with the production of value through labour and ends with its consumption before motioning back through the production process. Crises disrupt circulation such as when value is no longer realised in exchange because wages have failed to keep up with production. They set in train a spiralling motion of expanding and decreasing cycles of accumulation that in turn impact society, job prospects and so forth. Each adjustment creates a new set of conditions that give rise to further contradictions. As David

Harvey writes, nature mutates in a co-evolving dynamic totality of 'ideas, social relations, forms of daily life, etc', not a 'Hegelian totality in which each moment tightly internalises all the others':

> It is more like an ecological totality, what Lefebvre refers to as an 'ensemble' or Deleuze an 'assemblage', of moments coevolving in an open dialectical manner. Uneven development between and among the elements produces contingency in human evolution (in much the same way that unpredictable mutations produce contingency in Darwinian theory). (2010a: 196)

For 'second' or 'reflexive' modernity theorists, capitalistic and territorial logics no longer reflect the class relation, either in terms of the character of the state or the international division of labour. Current trajectories of state and capital are dehistoricised and merged into a more general non-dialectical framework of globalised flows and diverse non-class interests.[5] For Beck, in particular, the question is not simply about the 'production of risk', how it is produced and unevenly distributed, but rather the so-called 'boomerang' effects that everyone will sooner or later perish by. Risks such as global warming, for example, are the unintended outcomes of industrialisation that variously impact different parts of the world but which cause feedback loops of increasing intensity and devastation. There is no class dialectic, no prospect of a class struggle for determination of production, because class for Beck is a 'zombie category' of no empirical relevance. While questions are raised about the achievements of techno-economic progress, the class dynamics of risk – those within each territory where the poorest are the most vulnerable and are in no position to make calculations and adjust their behaviour accordingly – are not for him the central issue. Those in the flood zones of Bangladesh or living in the squalor of Mumbai have no risks to contend with, no calculation of odds, just a dull certainty requiring no reflection that life as encountered is non-negotiable. Our future, according to Beck, not adverse to the occasional apocalypticism, depends on 'non-state' actors such as NGOs and international organisations. They will 'manage global risks', or rather, we should say, they will fight phantoms because, as with 'terror' or 'global warming', you cannot organise a political struggle against 'risk'. Yet, for Beck, in this flattened dehistoricised 'risk society', the past loses the power to determine the present. Its place is taken by the future, thus, something non-existent, invented, fictive as the 'cause' of current experience and action. We become active today in order to prevent, alleviate or take precautions against the problems and crises of tomorrow and the day after tomorrow – or not to do so. (2012 [1986]: 34)

In slums and war zones capitalism does impact unevenly on people and indeed combines in the different histories and legacies of colonisation and imperialism. The fact of dispossession is the already-past and always-present capitalist apocalypse that some in the west, perhaps indulging in everyday calculations of risk, imagine as a utopian clean slate.

Regardless of how they were conceived, pre-industrial apocalypses were geographically bounded. Natural disasters, plagues and warfare could result in the total collapse of a particular civilisation, whereas now nuclear war, global warming and, perhaps less totalising, economic and even communication network crashes, have global consequences. Unlike in pre-modern societies they can be empirically anticipated. However there are similarities: as noted, biblical apocalyptic prophecies have their provenance in actual historical events with redemptive narratives favouring the oppressed. These are comparable to fundamentalist ideologies and millennialism today. The civilisation apocalyptic myths of the kind that paralysed the Aztecs are echoed in a contemporary fatalism as regards capitalism and nature. Retroactive apocalypticism, such as the attribution of the fourteenth-century bubonic plague to an act of God,[6] has contemporary parallels in the way famines, floods and tsunamis, or even events such as 9/11, are seen as a kind of 'blowback' for past environmental or foreign policy crimes. Mythology and modernity are the internal contradictions of an ideologically veiled totality that tolerates everything and admits nothing; fascistic-paranoiac misanthropy beside communistic-utopian humanism. This culminates today in postmodern apocalypticism and the uncanny relationship between cinematic spectacle and real-life footage of destruction. Spectacle, as Guy Debord pointed out, is an extension of the commodity to the visual plane, depoliticising on the one hand and affording an imperialist tool to instil fear and terror on the other, the shock and awe tactics of the US in their bombing of Baghdad being one example. The ephemera of visual media enter the dialogic sphere of internet communication, where Virilio's point that the overwhelming quantity of information is akin to the fallout from a nuclear bomb has resonance. Dissent is domesticated by a disconnect of critique and the capitalist laws of motion, evident in the writings of prominent sociologists, where at best there is only a fuzzy allusion to the source of crises. Consequently the end point is emptied of any utopian content.

Signs that, in the words of the Russian linguist V.N. Volosinov, are 'withdrawn from the pressures of the social struggle ... inevitably lose ... force, degenerating into allegory and becoming the object not of live social intelligibility but of philological comprehension' (1986 [192?]: 23). The intelligibility of language, Volosinov claims, lies in the 'clash of live social accents', when words and the meanings behind them are open to ideological contestation. Language is heteroglossic when antagonistic, monoglossic when refracted through the prism of a dominant group or ideology. In this secular omniscient age of cynicism, words such as 'apocalypse', 'crisis' and 'catastrophe' are commonly rendered impotent by the banal statement that these simply recur through human history. This misses the point emphasised by Volosinov – a member of the 'Bakhtin Circle' (including also M.M. Bakhtin and P.N. Medvedev) – that language is material through and through, historical and relational. The dead language of the apocalypse, or indeed of crisis, is politicised in the clash of live social accents, at protest camps, and in the polemic of the Manifesto when historically occurring processes within the dialectical totality of our age are rendered intelligible.

The material provenance of the apocalypse refracted in our time in the aforementioned ways, and framed by a post-political subjective fantasy originating in the symptoms of capitalist accumulation and expansion, crystallises in resignation to the force of nature and the market. This is elaborated in the next chapter, where we take the apocalypse through Lacan's three orders of subjectivity: the Real, the Symbolic and the Imaginary.

2

The Three Orders
of Apocalypse

Someone once said that it is easier to imagine the end of the world than the end of capitalism. We can now revise that and witness the attempt to imagine capitalism by way of imagining the end of the world.

Fredric Jameson (2003: 76)

Words brush against truths and sometimes those truths speak to a generation. Relayed by Fredric Jameson, the above observation of an unknown author succinctly nailed the ideological deadlock that condemns us to overwhelming destruction. Jameson wrote this now much-cited passage in 2003, four years before the US housing market crash in 2007 that precipitated the global financial crisis of 2008, when 'the end of the world' and 'the end of capitalism' became, for a time at least, tautologous. Now, as we have learned, the world kept turning and optimism is shredded. The end of the world is the dark side of capitalist realism, the recognition that none of the symptoms it gives rise to can be resolved by any system including this one. As Jameson later puts it, 'This particular incapacity to integrate a future of time into our own analysis of current society accounts for the tendency of bourgeois thought to alternate between images of regression or dystopian collapse, and conceptions of progress which amount to little more than the perfecting of what is there already' (2011: 105). In the 2008 crisis, 'Capitalism' became a global 'problem' for which no solution was forthcoming. In this chapter we take stock of what can be called the apocalyptic condition today, loosely framed using Lacan's three orders of subjectivity: the Real, the Symbolic and the Imaginary.

The Real can be thought of as the black hole at the centre of our galaxy. It is an empty void around which the visible galaxy, the Symbolic order of language, swirls. The Imaginary is also constituted from this symbolic star-stuff. It is an idea of the self as imagined from the place of another, earth as it were from the eyes of an imagined extra-terrestrial. Star-stuff are the words defining society and like the words defining identity they are only symbolic representations of a thing that can never fully be accounted for. Language is the means by which life acquires meaning and prevents us from getting sucked into an abject void.

The pattern of the stars is disturbed by activities at the centre of the galaxy in much the same way our symbolic universe of ideology and language is disturbed by changes in political economy. The visible galaxy today is different from the ideology prior to 2008, because the repressed material foundation around which the fictitious economy swirled and pulsated created a disturbance in the comforting idea that neoliberalism was a divine order that begot endless growth. This was a 'game changing' event encountered first as trauma, when for a brief period Keynesian economics became fashionable again, and then normalised as a crisis of state through a re-articulation of neoliberal ideology. Reality pulsates through ideology, in class antagonisms and in the processes that bring about changes in thought and sometimes action, in a dialectic that, as Marcuse put it,

> cannot be formal because it is determined by the real, which is concrete … It is the rationality of contradiction, of the opposition of forces, tendencies, elements, which constitutes the movement of the real and, if comprehended, the concept of the real. (2002 [1964]: 144)

The symbolic fiction that the people were responsible for the crisis by taking on more debt than their diminishing spending capacity could afford is one of many devices for re-establishing the legitimacy of state-led economic liberalism in the eyes of those who imagine themselves the victims of other people's 'excessive' spending. The Real will refer here to the materiality of the apocalypse in everyday life; the Symbolic to the ideological framing of reality; and the Imaginary to the idea of the self or what we might call the apocalyptic subjectivity. Given that these terms only make sense relationally, there is no strict delineation between the three parts that overlap in description, analysis and critique.

The Real Order of Apocalypse

The financial crisis in 2008 brought in its wake rational fears of people losing their jobs and their heavily mortgaged homes. In Britain, over 46,000 homes were repossessed in 2008 alone. The number of mortgages in arrears was by then at 377,000, up 64 per cent on the previous year.[1] In 2010, Tim Robson, aged 49, was one of many people added to the statistics of the unemployed. He had been a senior manager at a local council where he earned over £70,000 a year. By 2012, with his job seeker's allowance about to run out and on the verge of losing his home, he was being offered jobs that paid only £16,000 a year.[2] The fate of Mark Wood, 44, who starved to death in 2014 after his £40 per week disability allowance was cancelled, underlines the vulnerability of people on the margins in one of the most affluent countries in the world.[3]

A YouGov-Cambridge survey in 2013 claimed that '57% of Britons, 64% of Americans and 54% of Germans had been personally affected by the economic problems of their countries during the last five years to a "great" or "fair" extent. The French ... are gloomier – 80% of them claim to be feeling the pinch personally.'[4] In 2013, the charity Shelter reported that one in 35 homes in the UK were at risk of repossession[5] as 11 million homes throughout Europe are reported empty.[6] In the United States, where house values have dropped by 6.3 trillion dollars since the peak of the housing boom in 2005,[7] homelessness has reached chronic levels. By 2012, 640,000 Americans were without shelter.[8] Cities, according to one report, are rapidly becoming 'cesspools of filth, decay and wretchedness', words that would be not out of place in a Dickens' novel and are reminiscent of descriptions of slums in developing countries. In the bankrupted city of Detroit, 40 per cent of the streetlights are reported broken leaving large areas of the city shrouded in darkness. Without the funds to repair them, city officials planned to cut public services to encourage people to leave.[9] The solution across many US cities is to criminalise sleeping, eating, even sitting, in public places. The *San Francisco Public Press* reports that between 2007 and 2011 nearly 40,000 tickets were issued to homeless people for offences such as sleeping in parks, obstructing sidewalks and trespassing.[10] Suicide is an understandable response. *The Lancet* noted that the rise in unemployment is a major factor in accounting for the 35 per cent increase in official suicide rates in Europe since 2007. Between 2007 and 2009, the suicide rate among men in Greece rose more than 24 per cent and in Ireland more than 16 per cent. [11] In 2010, an average of two Italians per day took their own lives, including 362 who were unemployed and, among the class category neoliberals once championed, 336 entrepreneurs.[12] In 2011 a record 11,615 businesses in Italy filed for bankruptcy. [13] Figures such as these recall Friedrich Engels' words:

> When one individual inflicts bodily injury upon another, such injury that death results, we call the deed manslaughter; when the assailant knew in advance that the injury would be fatal, we call his deed murder. But when society places hundreds of proletarians in such a position that they inevitably meet a too early and an unnatural death, one which is quite as much a death by violence as that by the sword or the bullet; when it deprives thousands of the necessaries of life, places them under conditions in which they *cannot* live – forces them, through the strong arm of the law, to remain in such conditions until that death ensues which is the inevitable consequence – knows that these thousands of victims must perish, and yet permits these conditions to remain, its deed is murder just as surely as the deed of the single individual; disguised, malicious, murder, murder against which none can defend himself, which does not seem what it is, because no man sees the murderer, because the death of the victim seems a natural one, since the offence is more one of omission than of commission. But murder it remains. (2009 [1845]: 106)

The fear of being in the zone of death disciplines workers to discover in themselves a use for capital – the theme of Chapter 4 on the spiral of Production. The Real order of the apocalypse lies not in a speculative civilisational collapse. Rather it occurs at the everyday level, sharply felt by those on the economic periphery in the dead zones of the developing world and at home where life, if it has not already taken a turn for the worse, is in acute danger of doing so.

The Symbolic Order of Apocalypse

In 2010, Aotearoa's[14] conservative coalition government forced a change in the labour laws to persuade Warner Brothers to film *The Hobbit* there.[15]

The country is called 'Middle Earth' in tourist advertising campaigns and a highlight is Hobbiton located in the North Island.[16] In February 2011, Christchurch experienced a magnitude 6.3 earthquake killing 185 people and causing significant damage to the city, especially in the centre where the iconic cathedral was partially destroyed. Several tour operators set up guided tours of the city including on buses, Segways and even helicopter trips that flew over the cordoned-off area. Eighty cruise ships were scheduled to dock at the nearby port over the course of the following summer with some 20,000 or more passengers expected to make a pilgrimage there.[17]

Aotearoa, along with many other 'global' locations, courts cinema and catastrophe. It provides a backdrop for big budget movies that showcase the country's natural assets. *Lord of the Rings* put Aotearoa on the map, a map that replaces its territory, a hyper-real, as Baudrillard explained, in which there is no longer any distinction between image and reality. It is the world seen through American eyes, the country that pioneered industrial cultural production and continues to dominate in entertainment media.

The apocalypse is a stock in trade of media industries refracting a very peculiar US paranoia that, in being American, envelops the world and operates as a fantasy frame that operationalises desire on a global scale. It is a film genre that provides a framework to help the audience navigate through the twists and turns in rapture to the oncoming calamity. Benjamin Noys writes:

> Contemporary cultural history and cultural studies can only project out the 'destructive element' onto the usual historical signs of catastrophe and disaster. They fail to recognise the possibility of destructive processes that would deliberately rupture the imposed continuity of the accumulation of history, and so miss the opportunity to perform some necessary destruction of their own. (2012: 3)

When real-life events play in the register of a movie they break the fictional spell and the phantasmal distance from the thing is shattered: we momentarily get the impossible object of *jouissance* and experience our own little death before the phantasmal coordinates are rewritten. An episode of the *X-Files* spin-off *The Lone Gunmen*, aired in early 2001, centred on a plot in which the US government colluded with terrorists to pilot a commercial jet into the World Trade Center. It exemplifies Žižek's point that fantasy precedes or enables us to makes sense of reality, although such literal mappings are not required to produce an uncanny effect akin to a sudden encounter with a person whom you momentarily mistook for your dead mother. As suggested earlier, without a pop culture framing, 9/11 would not have acquired the symbolic status it did, and so it is not entirely facetious to claim that popular culture caused 9/11.

These specific events are the sublime objects that condense and symbolically register the subterranean feeling or forebodings that haunt the imagination. They stand in for the 'impossible *jouissance*' often read as signalling the end of an era and the beginning of a more uncertain one. This is how Žižek explains the cultural fascination with the sinking of the Titanic, which was taken to confirm a belief widespread at the beginning of the twentieth century that the age of peaceful progress was coming to an end – 'the time was waiting for it': even before it actually happened, there was already a place opened, reserved for it in fantasy-space. It had such a terrific impact on the 'social imaginary' by virtue of the fact that it was expected (Žižek, 1989: 74). And so today, as we view images of the wreck of the Titanic, 'we gain an insight into the forbidden domain, into a space that should be left unseen: visible fragments are a kind of coagulated remnant of the liquid flux of *jouissance*, a kind of petrified forest of enjoyment' (Žižek, 1989: 76).

Real life traumas appear to confirm what popular culture prefigures in its scientifically referenced scenarios. Fiction and reality appear to be in competition; the frequency and pace of each 'blockbuster', whether a film or an ecological catastrophe, leave one not so much gasping for breath as becoming blasé.

In the past, new technology enabled cultural producers to create effects that dramatically exceeded what had gone before. *Star Wars* was a revelation for a generation brought up on unconvincing attempts at sci-fi verisimilitude. For my generation brought up on video games, the first properly rendered 3D environments of games such as *Super Mario 64* seemed otherworldly. Such generational leaps are now much harder to discern. It takes a keen eye, for example, to notice much difference in fidelity between standard DVD and Blu-Ray. This is a problem currently encountered in the video game industry with new generations of consoles harder to justify because the graphics they enable relative to the previous generation no longer dazzle. This loss of an ability to excite is shared by this age of catastrophe, with the shock of the latest tsunami washing over the previous one. If there is a sublime object, it is one of acceleration: the condensation of all such events into a singular image of duration that denotes an apocalyptic *age*. In this nascent century there have already been many such signifiers in everyday reality, in headline reports and popular culture: the banking crisis, political unrest, dispossession by austerity, 9/11, the Boxing Day tsunami, Hurricane Katrina, Fukushima, the national surveillance scandal and, merchandising anxiety and fear, *The Day After Tomorrow*, *World War Z* and *The Walking Dead*. For every event, whether a pop concert or a terrorist attack, there is an army of spectators with mobile phones in hand taking pictures, draining them of what remained of their poignancy. In their parts and as a totality such events neatly reference the accelerating and increasingly catastrophic force of capital.

The Imaginary Order of Apocalypse

Roland Barthes once said that every photograph signals a catastrophe and captures an end point. Catastrophes in the past can today be witnessed at a safe distance through documentary reconstructions and fictional dramas: those of our accelerated present blur the line between fiction and reality. With the proliferation of cheap devices for capturing, uploading and instantly disseminating moving images of actual destruction, we exit the hyper-real and enter, for want of a better term, the zone of the hyper-imaginary. The disaster is brought home by its appearance on the virtual screen located in the actual war zone. In other words, the spectacle once enjoyed at a distance by a subject cushioned from a third world plundered for the security of the first punches through the screen and hits us in the face.

The camera, Benjamin wrote, reveals the unconscious optics of human life, drawing the viewer into an encounter with reality. Bourgeois culture, by contrast, is a phantasmagoria, projecting a fantasy of reality that obscures class relations. Reality itself becomes a phantasmagoria when framed for passive enjoyment or when it ceases to have any political significance, as for example in the images of famine victims used by charities. There is nothing new about this. What is new is the 'democratisation' of visual-capture technologies and the means to disseminate the images created with them. To illustrate this shift it is worth recalling the earlier period of experimental cinema, in particular the work of Soviet documentary filmmaker Dziga Vertov. A composite of sequences or a montage filmed from multiple viewpoints can reveal, Vertov claimed, the hidden parts of society within an organic totality. By socialising the means of production, essentially the camera, authorship shifts from the individual eye to a collective one, the world in montage seen through the eyes of millions. The purpose of *Kino-eye*, a manifesto for grassroots filmmaking, was to

create an army of cine-observers and cine-correspondents with the aim of moving away from the authorship of a single person to mass authorship, with the aim of organising a montage vision – not an accidental but a necessary and sufficient overview of the world every few hours. (Milne et al., 2012: 105)

As Deleuze explains:

What montage does, according to Vertov, is to carry perception into things, to put perception into matter, so that any point whatsoever in space perceives all the points on which it acts, or which act on it, however far these actions and reactions extend. This is the definition of objectivity, 'to see without boundaries or distances'. Thus in this respect all procedures are legitimate, they are no longer trick shots. (1986 [1983]: 83)

Authorship has today transferred over to millions of cine-observers and correspondents as raw images are presented on YouTube in montage form through every hyperlink clicked. The composition is not random because the images are filtered by complex algorithms that organise them by key words and the number of views. Any sequence whatsoever can be composed, edited and personalised by anyone using such sites, creating a montage of anything and everything: families enjoying the afternoon sun, candid shots of celebrities in compromising acts, police brutality, executions, advertising and porn. Images of disasters taken by those in the throes of them are overlaid on YouTube with text and sentimental or dramatic music, re-establishing distance through these cheap industry standards. As Baudrillard said of the 9/11 attacks,

The role of images is highly ambiguous. For they capture the event (take it as hostage) at the same time as they glorify it. They can be infinitely multiplied, and at the same time act as a diversion and a neutralization (as happened for the events of May '68). One always forgets that when one speaks of the 'danger' of the media. The image consumes the event, that is, it absorbs the latter and gives it back as consumer goods. Certainly the image gives to the event an unprecedented impact, but as an image-event. (2003: 27)

The hyper-image exits the screen like the cartoon doppelganger who jumps out from a frame that the protagonist thought a mirror image of himself. In the famous scene from the Marx Brothers' *Duck Soup*, the mirror breaks and the doppelganger attempts to mimic within the empty frame the increasingly eccentric movements of Groucho Marx, who is unsure whether the mirror has in fact shattered and what he is now witness to is indeed reality. This shattering of the imaginary distance is achieved in the real proximity in time and space between the cine-correspondent of a disaster, catastrophe and so forth, and the cine-observer. The event once enjoyed at a safe distance now threatens to fully consume the spectator, to produce real changes in their life up to and including actual bodily harm and death. 'It hits home', as the rather uninspired slogan for season two of the US series *Homeland* put it. Someone in lower Manhattan learning about the World Trade Center attacks from the television rather than through their window would be an obvious example. Events such as these, though, extend spatially beyond the blast zone and radiate throughout the world in ripples or aftershocks, the original televised event operating like an early warning system for an approaching tsunami.

War correspondents have of course traditionally acted as the eye, and sometimes the conscience, of the world. Their reports were and largely still are produced for, broadcast through, and framed by major news providers. Like the kino-eye, those who construct the hyper-image are not professionals. They are amateurs on the scene by chance. If the footage that the camera contains survives the event, traditional forms of media filtering can then be bypassed as the image is posted on uncurated websites. The eye survives the body to reveal the hidden optics of an apocalyptic (collective) unconscious. It is an eye that bears witness to reality, a reality already framed by a culture industry internalised in the human psyche (see Chapter 5). In other words, the apocalypse is framed for and by the other, a big (media) Other. The cine-observer's eye is held in the mind of the cine-correspondent as the authenticator of a really occurring apocalypse. Authorship of the end times thereby transfers over to a million kino-eyes.

Real life is authenticated in the shaky images taken by amateurs using handheld cameras. It is a verisimilitude adopted and made popular in films such as *The Blair Witch Project*. A claustrophobic fear is rendered palpable by the use of camcorders that actors hold to create a first-person perspective. More recent high budget end-of-the-world disaster movies such as *Cloverfield* use the same technique. The Real is affected first in cinema and then actualised by really occurring disasters captured by eyewitnesses, in a redoubling effect of affective intensity. Baudrillard declared that reality appears just like the movies. The movie is reality. Adorno and Horkheimer had already anticipated this, their warning that cinematic realism would eventually collapse any distinction between fiction and reality has been realised in simulated 3D and video games celebrated for their 'immersive' qualities. 'The more intensely and flawlessly his [the producer's] techniques duplicate empirical objects,' they explain, 'the easier it is today for the illusion to prevail that the outside world is the straightforward continuation of that presented on the screen' (1997 [1947]: 126).

Unlike 9/11 or ecological catastrophe, the visceral power of the global financial crisis can only be filmed as allegory. As Alain Badiou writes:

> The way the global financial crisis is described to us makes it look like one of those big bad films that are concocted by the ready-made hit machine that we now call the 'cinema'. It is all there: the gradual spectacle of the disaster, the crude manipulation of suspense, the exoticism of the identical – the Jakarta stock exchange in the same spectacular boat as New York, the link between Moscow and Sao Paulo, the same banks going up in the same flames – the terrifying repercussions: ouch, ouch, and the best laid 'plans' could not prevent Black Friday, everything is going to collapse … But there is hope: the little squad of the powerful has taken centre stage. They are as haggard and as intent on what they are doing as characters in a disaster movie. (2010: 91)

Whereas the 'spectacle' of economic meltdown in countries such as Argentina in 2002 could be 'enjoyed' at a safe distance in the dominant spaces of hyper-real production, here the spectacle engulfs the homeland through its direct impact, but as allegory lacks a defining image that testifies to the suffering caused.

Reality itself is framed by the cine-correspondents as if it were a genre film they bear witness to. It represents an object for the big Other to enjoy, a composite of future cine-observers peering into a frame that reveals the present as catastrophic past. By viewing an unfolding catastrophe through a camera lens, those on the scene gain an illusory spatial and temporal distance from it as if they too are passive observers watching from the comfort of their own homes. In doing so the eye posited as the eye of society includes itself out, when in reality it is as if the only way to authenticate and gain distance from it is through a mediated hyper-real that an unconscious optic aims to reproduce. The amateur caught at the scene with camera in hand and CGI in the psyche is a poet, artist and musician: Stephen Spielberg, George Lucas and Michael Bay. The distance is illusionary: the image overspills from the frame into reality. The image is super-sensory: sight, sound, touch, taste and smell.

Susan Buck-Morss' interpretation of the hyper-real as an *inverse* simulacrum bears comparison to the hyper-image. She writes:

> If there *is* a simulation produced by television, it lies on the other side of the apparatus. It is the simulated 'whole world' that watches, the virtual collective assembled in cyberspace, of which viewers, sharing the same televisual experience, imagine themselves to be a part. (2002: 254)

The chant of protestors that 'the whole world is watching' is constructed according to this wager. Jodi Dean (2009) would claim in criticism that no other is required for such chants to achieve their symbolic efficacy. The participants are the world and therefore everyone is included. The symbolic efficacy of the hyper-image is dependent on a presumed audience concretised in the body of the original observer-cum-correspondent who in that moment is the world. The image or clip is made for everyone by everyone. As Deleuze writes, 'from the point of view of the human eye, montage is undoubtedly a construction, from the point of view of another eye, it ceases to be one; it is pure vision of a non-human eye, of an eye which would be in things' (1986 [1983]: 83).

In documentary filmmaking there is a limit, as Žižek (2006) notes, to what is filmable. An intrusion upon a couple's loving encounter would undermine the intimacy the image wants to evoke, which is why fiction is a much better vehicle for conveying human emotions. The kino-eye films the love scene they are part of as if looking into a mirror for pornographic effect: that is, of being in the scene of a pornographic film. Returning to Buck-Morss:

> Whether camera image or easel painting, whether filmic montage or architectural design, what matters is that the image provide a sensual, cognitive experience that is capable of resisting abusive power's self-justification. Visual 'art' becomes political in this way. It makes apparent what the phantasmagorias of power cover up. Such an aesthetics differs in meaning from aesthetics within modern bourgeois culture – and at the same time revives the oldest meaning of the term. (2002: 101)

Whether in the bedroom or in front of a raging tsunami, the camera maintains a distance between the eye and the body, the image and the action, into which the phantasmagoria is inscribed. The phantasmagoria is authenticated as an empirical phenomenon and lent authenticity through the technology and the medium in which it is delivered. They are images that 'shock the world', condense feelings of impending doom and stand as poignant examples of social, economic, political, cultural and ecological disintegration and decay – in short, civilisational collapse. They are affective images. One such image is the widely circulated photograph of an Australian family chest-deep in water as they cling to a wooden jetty for their lives while flames consume everything around them. Dante's Inferno is evoked by the menacing orange hue of the billowing smoke and the family's faces full of anguish and terror.[18] Present through its absence as the logical taker of the shot, the photographer is an empty placeholder for the viewer's ego that completes the familial circle from which nobody not even the viewer can escape.

A more controversial collection of images was taken of Muammar Gaddafi in the throes of death. Mark Lawson writing in the *Guardian* suggested that

> the pictures of the terrified, wounded and then possibly dead Muammar Gaddafi used on TV bulletins and the print and online editions of

newspapers in the last 24 hours seemed to me to be, by some distance, the most graphic and distressing representations we have ever seen of a recognisable individual during his final moments.[19]

I leave to one side the moral implications of circulating such images, the main focus of Lawson's piece, and refer to another point he makes about the cultural shift represented by the images. He continues:

> The most significant (and probably irresistible) change, however, is that the dissemination of contentious images has now largely left the desks of editors and regulators. Symbolically and crucially, the footage of Gaddafi's capture and assault was shot not by a crew but by a crowd on cellphones. TV or newspaper editors who ethically decide to bin the most distressing images know, unlike their predecessors, that the views will be generally available elsewhere and that curiosity will draw a large part of the audience there.

Whether enjoyed as 'death porn' or not, drama escapes the screen and the audience becomes culpable in their enjoyment of the images and montage footage they are the authors of. It is not the image that disturbs us but rather our enjoyment of it. This is the hidden message of warnings before news reports that the viewer may find the images disturbing. The photographs of Gaddafi's murder would for the westernised viewer perhaps register a barbarism akin to that of the Middle Ages. But it is not something that happens 'on the other side of the world' to 'other people' or indeed in another time, because the real power and poignancy of the images lie in the fact of their dissemination for the enjoyment of the apparently civilised westerner included in the form.

Absolute death is the end of all symbolic substance, a future without trace. This 'second death', according to Žižek, 'liberates nature from its own laws and opens the way for the creation of new forms of life *ex nihilo*' (1989: 149). By depriving the subject of all symbolic substance, a new order can emerge. The zombie is between these two deaths, on the border zone plaguing the world it is unable to fully leave behind. Žižek (1992: 23) explains with reference to Lacan that the living dead were not properly buried, they return because society owes them a symbolic debt. Some of the most chilling images are those of people facing imminent and inescapable death. Executions are one example but perhaps more affective are those of the unknown citizen who becomes a symbolic placeholder in which the viewer can imagine himself to be: the 'falling man' seemingly accepting his fate, his body motionless in the famous still image dropping head first from high up the World Trade Center. Not so well known but also poignant is that of the man who knelt in the sand with his back to the oncoming Boxing Day tsunami of 2004. Neither dead nor alive, unknown and voiceless, such images and clips, viewed frequently on Google Images and YouTube, signify the dead zone between two worlds that our society appears to be in, experienced as it were by alienated labour and those struggling to find a socio-economic foothold.

The hyper-image acquires different levels of intensity according to the degree that it registers a common fear, paranoia, death wish or recognition of a genuine threat to westernised societies, such as global warming, economic collapse or authoritarian violence. They are made common by the circulation of information, media sensation and pop culture spectacle. Their power is also determined according to how close the audience is to the event in space and time or the extent to which the image operates as an early warning of a certain catastrophe. The most intense and perhaps most fascinating of images are those produced by correspondents in the midst of imminent threat to life.

In 2013 a diver filmed a shark attack on himself.[20] He lived to tell the tale and posted the footage on YouTube. With their dead eyes, permanent motion and random, often fatal attacks, sharks symbolise a contingent threat to a tourist's enjoyment. The hyper-image is always contingent even though the thought of valorising it may not be. Always with a camera at hand, the hope in so many of us that we will be there when something significant happens authenticates life as unmediated experience.[21]

The most affective hyper-images are those filmed by people running from approaching tsunamis,[22] imploding buildings or earthquakes. These are typically accompanied with sounds of the filmmaker's screams, protestations and gasps of disbelief. *102 Minutes that Changed America* is a documentary pieced together in real time from amateur footage of the 9/11 event. A contemporary spin on *Man with a Movie Camera*, the images shift between the impact, people's bewildered expressions, panicked reactions and verbal responses. If Vertov envisaged the camera as the means 'to see without boundaries or distances', what such images concretise or empirically reveal is unmediated catastrophe, terror and violence. As with the sinking of the Costa-Concordia pleasure liner, filmed by crew members seemingly indifferent to the plight of the passengers, over 30 of whom were about to drown,[23] reality reaches what Yolanda Gampel calls an 'indeterminable uncanniness', a point when 'a mass franchised sensibility' usurps an unreal reality that people have witnessed (cf. Davis, 2002: 6). More poignant still are the clips that South Korean students took of themselves moments before the Sewol ferry capsized and the water consumed them, faces of death and petrified enjoyment.[24]

Life is framed for remembrance, a keepsake, proof of participation, but also as a spectacle for popular entertainment. Whatever the image meant for the person who filmed it, the montage effect produced from the many angles of those on the scene is no longer the work of a single author. It passes into the collective psyche as a common image made by an unnamed collective. The cultural commentator and satirist, Charlie Brooker, noting the similarity in how Hollywood blockbusters and news are presented, raises a question as to whether the collapse of any distinction between fiction and reality is as hypnotic as it seems.[25] He reports that when shown previews of Peter Jackson's *The Hobbit*, shot in twice as many frames per second as standard films, audiences complained that the images were too smooth and so gave the appearance of raw news footage. It will become more difficult in time, says Brooker, to tell the two apart. The hyper-image oscillates with hyper-reality, between what is really happening in the world and to us, and what only happens to others.

The symbolic order of the apocalypse overcodes and draws its substance from the real order of the apocalypse, the apocalyptic imaginary caught between the phantasmagoria and the reality it is part of. This imaginary is sustained by the way events open to the clash of live accents are relayed through the monoglossia of mass media framing. In them we discover the unconscious optics of the human psyche. A world turned upside down. The spell conjured in this carnivalistic space is broken when opened up to dialogue, more precisely by bringing the hyper-image back to life through the intelligibility that Marxist analysis and critique affords. We can speculate on how the viewer interprets the image. No speculation is required as to the effect of capitalism on life or the extent to which as subjects, however conscious we are, we are bound to its circuit of destruction. This is the topic of the next three chapters.

3

The Double Helix of Dissatisfaction

> There is one thing that is worse than being exploited by capital, and that is not being exploited by capital.
>
> Rosa Luxemburg (quoted in Calhoun and Derluguian, 2011: 182)

There is an inescapable logic in these words even some 100 or so years after Rosa Luxemburg wrote them. It is rational for individuals to think of themselves as commodities that can be marketed to capital. The better we are at doing this, the more completely we map ourselves onto commodities, the greater the chance of earning a wage and being socially valued. The greater the chance that, flush with cash, we can raise our heads high and pronounce to our friends when out for a drink: 'I think it's my round.'

'Spiral' is the operative word for this process, and the next two chapters trace the interlocking spirals of work and consumption, a double helix of dissatisfaction, of peaks and troughs on which our passions rise and fall in an opposing and co-evolving motion. Production, distribution, exchange and consumption are relational moments of a totality. Marx is often criticised for his 'productivist' leanings, but in fact he encourages us to think about these 'moments' in a holistic way:

> The conclusion we reach is not that production, distribution, exchange and consumption are identical, but that they all form the members of a totality, distinctions within a unity. Production predominates not only over itself, in the antithetical definition of production, but over the other moments as well. The process always returns to production to begin anew. That exchange and consumption cannot be predominant is self-evident. Likewise, distribution as distribution of products; while as distribution of the agents of production it is itself a moment of production. A definite

production thus determines a definite consumption, distribution and exchange as well as definite relations between these different moments. (1973 [1858]: 99)

Like a cake that has to be baked before it can be eaten, production is of foremost importance. Any attempt to play down its significance – as theories on consumerism often do, perhaps by equating it with industrial labour – is to engage in the sort of mystifications Marx warns against. Distribution is also an important factor, relating to the social distribution of labour as well as the flow of (other) commodities: mass migrations to cities and so forth, and the spaces both concrete and virtual, common and commodified, in which we socialise and 'network'.

Labour power is assembled into value-producing machines. It spins commodities. The faster they pass from one moment to the next, the better for capital, the sooner it can realise profits without borrowing so heavily that economic crashes ensue. For this machine to function, desire must be made to want to produce social use values (things that many others want) for the purposes of exchange and also to consume them. And so Deleuze asks during an interview with Michel Foucault, 'how is it that people whose interests are not being served can strictly support the existing power structure by demanding a piece of the action?' This is because of *investments*, he claims, 'investments of desire that function in a more profound and diffuse manner than our interests dictate'. But, crucially, 'we never desire against our interests, because interest always follows and finds itself where desire has placed it' (in Foucault, 1977: 214). We are not deceived, Deleuze tells us. That we are invested in this abstract machine should not come as a surprise given how dependent our livelihoods are on it. When the economy does badly it is often the poor that suffer, when it does well there would be cheers all round except by now it is clear that economic growth is no indication the poorest among us will in fact benefit. To reiterate, without the collective strength and determination to force a different social compact, there is no alternative to exploitation, and *under these conditions* being exploited is preferable to not being exploited at all, even for workers at Foxconn. The point that Deleuze wants to make is that we are not simply resigned to this fact; rather, we enthusiastically embrace it as if we are freely choosing to be exploited which, in a sense, we are. 'Exploitation', though, is a slippery word, so before getting into our stride let us add a few qualifying words.

Exploitation first and foremost corresponds, as Marx stressed, to the surplus value that capital expropriates from labour, the source of value. It is what is taken from us without remuneration. In this respect alone can exploitation be spoke of as material through and through. All other exploitations described below are conditioned by the logic of surplus value but do not directly contribute in its production. They are potentially useful to capital and have potential exchange value. So, second, and further to Marx, exploitation denotes the investment of subjective energy by those with nothing to sell except their labour power in social reproduction through childcare, home maintenance, emotional support and so forth, the work typically, but not exclusively, of women in patriarchal society. We can include in this category unpaid labour of any kind that is not directly employed by capital, for example, the consumer scanning items at a supermarket (see Chapter 5), social media and urban space where information is produced that capital can harvest. No individual capitalist can exist without the employment of labour; many can exist without recourse to any of these examples of indirect exploitation; but the capitalist class, that is to say capitalism as a whole, could not exist without at least some of these factors in operation, what might be called 'exploitation of the social fabric' by capital as such. Third, and the central theme of the next chapter, exploitation is also a reflexive process of thinking about and being active in making oneself useful for capital. It includes those developing new skills beyond labour time – whether in paid work, full-time study or unemployed – to enhance the value of their labour to improve their job prospects and mitigate the possibility of redundancy. In Foucauldian terms, reflexive exploitation can be described as the production of subjective use values. The stress on the word 'exploitation' here highlights that these processes are inseparable from the labour relation and are exploitative in so far as the subject consciously reflects on its worth to the production of value for capital. As Hardt and Negri (2000) note, the knowledge, affects and connections the subject produces can also serve non-capitalistic uses. To qualify, this time with reference to Weber, reflexive exploitation operates within an iron cage and is embarked on instrumentally to improve job security and prospects but, in the final analysis, it also equips the subject with skills, attributes and abilities that can serve a counter-hegemonic purpose. We could add a fourth, Lacanian-inflected category of exploitation, namely the sublimation of our passions or libidinal energies into the object of consumption. Inasmuch as the ability to consume depends on our willingness to labour, often tied to the credit we take out, this sublimation stands as a class relation. Finally, though not necessarily exhaustively, the worker is exploited by creditors to whom they are indebted; unlike capital, the worker can only pay that debt through future labour. The debt is symbolic in the first instance and becomes material as soon as interest is paid on it.

These interrelated forms of exploitation are characteristic of the class antagonism today, with implications for how we live, think and act. The theme connecting all of them is that the subject in question has nothing to sell except their labour power. Householders, shareowners and so on are also in this category unless they can make a living by exchanging physical and virtual objects without recourse to labour or welfare. Those who persist in the so-called informal economy, slum dwellers and so forth who have no apparent use for capital, are still largely exploited and likely 'want' to be, typically by 'entrepreneurs' who do not pay taxes, by consuming things produced in the formal economy and so in respect of this in the indirect ways described above.

Capital draws its energy from the senses as much as it aims to seduce them. It alienates us from sensuous life while also compensating for this loss through products advertised for their sensuous qualities, a concept to which we now turn.

The Alienated Condition

Labour is, in the first place, a process in which both man and Nature participate, and in which man of his own accord starts, regulates, and controls the material reactions between himself and Nature. He opposes himself to Nature as one of her own forces, setting in motion arms and legs, head and hands, the natural forces of his body, in order to appropriate Nature's productions in a form adapted to his own wants.

Karl Marx (2001 [1867]: 257)

Nature builds no machines, no locomotives, railways, electric telegraphs, self-acting mules, etc. These are the products of human industry: natural material transformed into organs of the human will over nature... They are *organs of the human brain, created by the human hand*; the power of knowledge, objectified.

Karl Marx (1973 [1858]: 706)

'A child seeing the tightrope-walkers singing, the pipers playing, the girls fetching water, the coachmen driving, thinks all this is happening for the joy of doing so; he can't imagine that these people also have to eat and drink, go to bed and get up again. We, however, know what is at stake.'

Theodor Adorno quoting Hebbel (2000 [1951]: 227)

A bird with a long beak designed for grubbing beneath the sand may well look on with envy at the duck that swiftly dives under the water for fish that are plentiful. Humans by contrast can observe both creatures and learn from them. They can design tools with which to grub and fish. The hand connects with a hammer to nail a coffin that briskly travels along the production line. It connects with a keyboard to write the obituary in an open-plan office under the supervision of team leaders. It clenches in a fist to signal readiness to revolt before grasping for whatever instrument can advance the cause. Mind, body and soul connect with various and more massive tools and weapons, machinic assemblages, producing affects or forces that can either enslave or liberate. Our capacity to adapt nature in an image held in the mind is the source of material wealth, the means by which great cities arise and our needs and desires change. It is the species-specific capacity that has become an object opposed to us.

Chapter 1 began with a quote from Marx about the emergence of capitalism through primitive accumulation. Without access to soil or control over the basic means to nurture and produce the goods that survival depends on, people have been progressively forced to identify themselves as commodities. The subject dispossessed of the collective means of production becomes a subject without substance, an empty shell that acquires a substance-like quality when representing what capital wants and is willing to pay for. Alienation describes a condition, bestowed upon people in the birth pangs of capitalism, that persists today in a more pronounced way than Marx could have anticipated.

One of the few sources in which Marx describes alienation or estranged labour is a draft never intended for publication, the *Economic and Philosophical Manuscripts*. The first point Marx makes is that under capitalist relations of production the object of labour is no longer something that affirms sensuous life but, by being in the possession of another, opposes it. Alienated from the act of production through a division of labour that reduces many of us to cogs in a machine, we become disengaged, passive and listless. Labour is a vital realm of freedom, self-expression and pleasure but, given over to capital, all that remains to 'man' are his animal functions, with pleasure experienced only in the narrow spheres of 'eating, drinking, and procreating, at most also in his dwelling and dress' (Marx, in McLellan, ed., 1990: 81). Marx qualifies this point elsewhere by stressing that capitalism expands the sphere of pleasure in the realm of consumption, thereby expanding our aesthetic needs against which the reproductive value of labour is judged. In *Wages, Price and Profit*, for example, he writes:

> Rapid growth of productive capital calls forth just as rapid a growth of wealth, of luxury, of social needs and social pleasures. Therefore, although the pleasures of the labourer have increased, the social gratification which they afford has fallen in comparison with the increased pleasures of the capitalist ... Our wants and pleasures have their origin in society; we therefore measure them in relation to society; we do not measure them in relation to the objects which serve for their gratification. Since they are of a social nature, they are of a relative nature. (Quoted in Harvey, 1984: 48)

In other words, our needs, wants and desires change in accordance with the development of capitalism and in particular the expanding market for consumer goods. The 'reproductive' value of labour is reflected in our accustomed standard of living and is the yardstick against which the value of our contribution to the labour process is judged. Dispossession and exploitation at its most extreme resembles the abjection Marx describes in the *Manuscripts*. Nevertheless, as wages fail to keep up with rising living costs in the more privileged spaces of accumulation, there is perhaps a general tendency towards this point envisaged in the dystopian scenarios of the apocalyptic imaginary.

The argument that has caused the most controversy is, to my mind at least, self-evident: that humans are possessed with the capacity to reflect on the world and adapt the natural environment, and in turn their own nature, through self-conscious and collective action. Marx calls this our species-specific capacity, which is not the same as saying that human 'nature' is any way fixed. It is a point Marx returns to throughout his writings, notably in *Capital*, where he writes, 'what distinguishes the worst architect from the best of bees is that the architect builds the [honeycomb] cell in his mind before he constructs it in wax' (2001 [1867]: 284). Capital expunges this vital quality of labour in order to advance, and the more it does so, the emptier we are.

An immense power residing in us all, the force or vitality of the species sparks fires to fuel engines that have in time enabled us to span the globe and today produce great monuments to international finance. Changes in the labour process have brought about a greater differentiation of tasks, some of which require specialised knowledge and so-called interpersonal skills. Capital wants a 'well-rounded' subject, one that can deal with customers, get along with others in the work team, and be sensitive to the employer's needs when carrying out tasks. It is not simply our hands we are alienated from. It is also our minds and the socially cultivated personality. Forced to compete for access to jobs, we become, as Marx suggests, opposed to one another. 'Man' is estranged from 'man'. We become competitors rather than comrades, vulnerable to ideologies claiming that immigrants threaten our jobs and welfare recipients threaten our surplus wages because of the taxation required to 'support' them. Where a premium is placed on 'networking', the instrumentalisation of personal relationships is simply an intensification of this kind of estrangement.

Marx's description of commodity fetishism also encapsulates these different aspects of alienation. Labour is embodied as dead or past labour in the commodities that are sold on the market where our relationship to them is fetishised by exchange. The commodity embodies the concrete sensuous life exhausted from labour, mystified by the value we place on it in the realm of abstract exchange. The fetishised commodity is a phantasmal object, writes Žižek (2004: 94), appearing to the subject as something real: we know that commodities embody social relations but still value them as if there is no other relationship to them apart from, perhaps, one of direct unmediated exchange. The relationships we form are not with workers, such as those at Foxconn in China where safety nets are erected to prevent suicides. Whatever our knowledge of the conditions under which others labour, concretely our relationship is with the product. This much is evident when even the most enlightened among us express rage, typically at the sales clerk, because the item is faulty, fails to perform as promised or, *even worse*, was available cheaper elsewhere. We lose sleep anticipating what Santa might bring or even what he might deny us, though rarely, if ever at all, over social issues that by day we read about. Even environmentalists dream about electronic goods, not the waste they produce.

The ultimate fetishised commodity is of course money: capital in motion when used as a form of investment, and the 'universal equivalent' object of exchange or measure by which the value of all other commodities are defined. Money has a magic-like power of materialising goods as if they come from nowhere. It is a God-like commodity, as Georg Simmel noted:

> It may appear as an irony of history that, as the moment when the satisfying and ultimate purposes of life become atrophied, precisely that value that is exclusively a means and nothing else takes the place of such purposes and clothes itself in their form. In reality, money in its psychological form, as the absolute means and thus as the unifying point of innumerable sequences of purposes, possesses a significant relationship to the notion of God – a relationship that only psychology, which has the privilege of being unable to commit blasphemy, may disclose. (2004 [1900]: 237)

The commodity, in short, is fetishised, and the processes and relations involved in its creation mystified, as money with the power to materialise practically anything whatsoever becomes the object of desire. As Simmel further elaborates:

> money, unlike a precious metal used for jewellery, does not need to balance the unlimited desire for it by a growing distance from direct needs, because it has become the correlate of the most basic needs of life as well. This remarkable dual character of money with reference to desire for it is presented in a detached form by avarice and extravagance, since in both instances money has dissolved into pure desire for it. Both exhibit the negative side of what we have also observed as a positive side to money, namely that money enlarges the diameter of the circle in which our antagonistic psychic drives flourish. What avarice exhibits, as it were, in material paralysis, extravagance reveals in the form of fluidity and expansion. (2004 [1900]: 252)

The high point of capitalistic excess, noted in the prodigious monuments to international finance that obstruct the city skyline, is also the point when resources – be they jobs, housing, pensions, healthcare, the raw materials of nature and so on – are scarce, unaffordable or fast becoming exhausted. With rentiers and financiers leeching off productive labour, the ability to consume is undermined and impacts the 'real' economy, indebting future generations to the accumulative logic. As Maurizio Lazzarato explains:

> What matters is finance's goal of reducing what will be to what is, that is, reducing the future and its possibilities to current power relations. From this perspective, all financial innovations have but one sole purpose: possessing the future in advance by objectivising it. (2012: 46)

Capitalism embodies Eros, taking more quantities from the subject than it gives back in wages or consumer products.

While alienation persists in much the way Marx describes it, there are changes in both intensity and extension evident in the effects of deregulated and service-oriented labour markets on the nature of work today. Alienation has expanded to parts of the world where residues of non-capitalistic modes of production prevailed even recently: a prodigious and rapid expulsion of peasant populations from the land and migration to the industrial workhouses of the city has taken place throughout the so-called developing world and in China in particular. In economies typically identified as 'consumerist', where many of the products from these burgeoning enterprise zones end up, an increasing portion of labour is expended – in the workplace, at home and in activities without remuneration – in order to enhance employability. Consequently, the time and space in which the subject is able to 'recharge', to socialise and enjoy some leisure time, is shortened, narrowed, enclosed by commerce and instrumentalised.

The artist who conducts their work in non-alienated time has to think increasingly of the marketability of their creations while being pressured to divert energies to the task of getting a job or remaining in one. Teachers, academics and intellectuals increasingly work to managerial priorities, spending more time on the expanded category of service work. Urban spaces in which working people, artists and political activists could afford to live quickly become gentrified zones where the 'chic' that artists lend them is capitalised upon. It is a well-established process that such inhabitants are increasingly mindful of but, despite brave attempts to keep property developers out, are largely unable to oppose. Alienation increases qualitatively as our species capacities are mined more deeply and quantitatively by absorbing more of our time in value creation and exchange. With families under increasing strain, the commitment, particularly to childcare that women have traditionally made and continue to make in the home (a commitment now also made by some men), becomes, to put it in colloquial terms, a mug's game. The person who commits their energies to the family cannot risk refusing the call to develop their employment credentials lest personal relationships that are under increasing strain should collapse. The many blows to self-esteem that those earning a wage suffer resurface in the home where emotions are strained to breaking point and the burden of alienated labour is felt by all. For children, education becomes a self-reflective process of anticipating what their qualifications will achieve on the job market, and – as governments increasingly see education as a private rather than a public good, and fund it accordingly – they request compensations from the increasingly shallow pockets of parents. In the digital age, friendships are rationalised into byte-sized manageable fragments or 'dividuals' as Deleuze calls them, appearing in virtual form on retina-quality visual displays. Capital, as Marx pointed out in the unpublished 'sixth' chapter of *Capital*, has penetrated every aspect of human existence.

Circuits of Capture

The conception of capital is admittedly a totalising or systemic concept: no one has ever seen or met the thing itself, it is either the result of scientific reduction (and it should be obvious that scientific thinking always reduces the multiplicity of the real to a small scale model) or the mark of an imaginary and ideological vision. But let us be serious: anyone who believes that the profit motive and the logic of capital accumulation are not the fundamental laws of this world, who believes that these do not set absolute barriers and limits to social changes and transformations undertaken in it, such a person is living in an alternative universe; or, to put it more politely, in this universe such a person, assuming he or she is progressive, is doomed to social democracy, with its now abundantly-documented treadmill of failures and capitulations.

Fredric Jameson (1988: 354)

Advertisers famously deployed psychoanalytic techniques in order to sell products. The same techniques are implicit in the labour process. Let us now loosen our ties with Marx and gather breath by bringing psychoanalysis and its critics fully to bear on the question of surplus value. Lacan is a good place to start.

'It begins with a tickle and ends in a blaze of petrol. That's always what *jouissance* is' (Lacan, 2007 [1969]: 72). Signifiers dance in the gap between the bodily itch and its satisfaction, coordinated within a movement called subjectivity. *Jouissance* confirms and reveals itself through entropy, a dance of dissatisfaction in which each movement opens up a space for the next. This 'spoliation' of *jouissance*, Lacan argues, is what Marx condemned in surplus value: 'surplus value is surplus *jouissance*' (2007 [1969]: 108). Thus capital and subjectivity are set in motion by a constitutive gap, a gap for making profit/signification, the closure of which brings about crises. And here, like pauses in the beat, crises anticipate new rhythms that as they kick in revitalise the dance and guarantee our hopelessly entwined future.[1]

According to Lacan, 'Once a higher level has been passed, surplus *jouissance* is no longer surplus *jouissance* but is inscribed simply as a value to be inscribed in or deducted from the totality of whatever it is that is accumulating' (2007 [1969]: 80). Surplus *jouissance* tied to the commodity form creates value in the act of labour, realises it in the act of exchange and destroys it in the act of consumption. Beginning with a tickle, ending with bombs, it is the fuel that enables capital to circulate, expand and ultimately destroy everything that human life depends on.

Libidinal energy is expended or, as Lacan puts it, is 'despoiled' in a circular motion, beginning with production through to consumption in an endless return, expressed by Marx not in libidinal terms but in the formula M-C-M'. Money (M) is invested in means of production (MP) and labour power (LP) to produce commodities (C), be they goods or services, that consumers have a use for, and, if affordable to them, exchange for money (M) at a price that exceeds the original investment by capital in order that surplus value (') is realised. In an inverse movement, the more our labour power is invested in surplus value, the more wealth is accumulated at the top and further utilised in an ever-expanding operation of accumulation; the more that labour power is invested in the circuit the more disproportionate relative to capital is the return. The subjective drive for the missing though never existent thing underscores the knotting of desire to moments in the circuit relating to these surpluses. As Žižek explains:

> it is not a surplus which simply attaches itself to some 'normal', fundamental enjoyment, because *enjoyment as such emerges only in this surplus*, because it is constitutively an 'excess'. If we subtract the surplus we lose enjoyment itself, just as capitalism, which can survive only by incessantly revolutionizing its own material conditions, ceases to exist if it 'stays the same', if it achieves an internal balance. This, then, is the homology between surplus-value – the 'cause' which sets in motion the capitalist process of production – and surplus-enjoyment, the object-cause of desire. (1989: 54)

Exploitation for Lacan, however, becomes a strictly internal affair. The non-existent 'object', to which the drive attaches itself, is what exploits us, proletarian and bourgeois alike, the latter repeatedly investing surplus profits to expand the operation. While Lacan's coupling of surplus-value and surplus-*jouissance* mystifies as much as it reveals, it does provide useful tools for conceptualising how labour is put to work, as shown in the next chapter.

As Marcuse had with Freud, Žižek helped radicalise Lacan by underlining the potential symmetries between psychoanalysis and Marx. Referring to Hegel's 'self-relating absolute negativity', Žižek aims to show that the death drive carries out the task of 'emptying the place' of symbolic substance in order that the process of creation can occur (cf. Vighi, 2012: 5). While the logic by which Žižek arrives at this point differs, it parallels Deleuze and Guattari's aforementioned claim that capitalism produces lack. For Žižek, though, the emptying of the place is an invariable of the libidinal subject not strictly correlative to a system of 'anti-production'. In the context of capitalism, however, there is little to distinguish the conclusions of both perspectives that we endlessly seek to fill a place that reveals itself to be empty because the object, whether a job or a consumer product, can never satisfy. Whereas for Deleuze and Guattari emancipation occurs through certain assemblages of desire that exceed 'state science' (the apparatus of capture and so on), for Žižek the subject must first be emptied of its phantasmal identification with the regulatory authority of a (non-existent) big Other of Capital before embarking on a positive process of revolutionary transformation. In the final analysis, the lost object always returns to exploit us: according to Lacanian theory, we are never liberated. It is a problem that Žižek recently appears to recognise when he says 'Lacan unveiled the illusions on which capitalist reality as well as its false transgressions are based, but his final result is that we are condemned to domination' (2012: 18). Because there is no fundamental relationship to lack with Deleuze and Guattari, the point is not that the fantasy must be 'traversed' and a new symbolic order predicated on lack established, but rather that the positive force of desire already immanent to life must be liberated or subtracted from the negativity of capital.

The empirical fact of lack, conceived as 'scarcity', is the basis of the libidinal economy of the subject in capitalism, and does not so much justify repression as necessitate it. The double helix of dissatisfaction can be thought then as the production of two opposing, co-evolving and, depending on how its origination is conceived, manufactured lacks, that the subject in a process of self-overcoming is active in sparking, and that fuel contingent machines of various and increasingly massive kinds. Beginning with alienation as Marx describes it, the lacks in question concern the availability or absence of life-enhancing labour and non-commodified forms of consumption. The fact that the only way to overcome these corresponding lacks is on terms that are largely not of our choosing forces the libidinal subject into a spiralling pact with capital, a spiral towards apocalypse. The ideology of austerity aims to depoliticise the effect this sacrifice might otherwise have; it discourages any questioning of the purpose and cause of the sacrifice.

The Oedipalised Economy of Austerity

However superficially our desires are satisfied, capitalism does, even in these straitened times, appear to be the only system to permit pleasure at least for those born into fortune, who are lucky, industrious or talented. As wages stagnate while the cost of living rises, labour is spent on the unending task of getting onto the proverbial ladder. The 'happy consciousness', Marcuse said, must be satisfied that, despite everything, the system delivers.

Such beliefs, if they persist, are under increasing strain. Ours is the age of diminished prospects, of the mantra that there is no alternative to the hardships daily endured and justified in the name of austerity. Regardless of whether we believe the system can 'deliver', what matters, Žižek wants to stress, is that we still act as if it does. The 'fetishistic illusion' is not overcome through our knowledge of inequality, injustice and exploitation, the ironic distance we maintain from the things we do enables us to go on living with this knowledge. As 'crisis' becomes absorbed into a language of austerity, responsibility shifts from builder, to banker, to policy maker and finally, because the circuit begins and ends there, to the individual. Crisis, as such, is publicly owned by the state then parcelled out and privatised to the individual.

'Scarcity, which has justified institutionalised repression since its inception,' Marcuse wrote, 'weakens as man's knowledge and control over nature enhances the means for fulfilling human needs with a minimum of toil' (2006 [1955]: 92). To recall: according to Freud, the condition of scarcity is the natural condition that demands a continual sacrifice of libidinal energy in a collective process of self-overcoming. Scarcity is the condition of life for many in economies of material abundance where inequalities are becoming more extreme. A scarcity of jobs, surplus wages and now cheap credit imposes austerity, defined as forced or extreme economy, on many. It is a material fact engineered and exacerbated in systems of anti-production depoliticised by the total mobilisation of institutions of ideological persuasion. The ideology of austerity operates in a feedback loop: the greater the scarcities the more persuasive to common sense is the claim there are not enough resources to go around. Scarcity is posited as the result of corruption in economies said to be underdeveloped or seen to be hostile to capitalist penetration. Or it is the result of the excessive consumption of low-paid workers. The more effective the ideology is in persuading us that scarcity is a natural condition (rather than augmented and to an extent invented by capital), the sweeter is the pill, and the more we have a political left that regards individual excesses to be the cause of global warming and embraces a joyless asceticism if only to admonish those with very little in life for their wastefulness. The Oedipalised economy of austerity most obvious in the current rhetoric of government is neither unique to the present nor is it simply an ideology of government and its official parliamentary opposition – it is internalised and promulgated by people at every level of society and with different political affinities.

At any given moment, people really do believe that austerity is necessary, that 'consumers' must rein in their spending, that poverty can be overcome through hard work and that the global population, irrespective of the mode of production, has exceeded the planet's carrying capacity – we 'consume' the equivalent of 1.5 planets per year according to the Global Footprint Network.[2] We can be fooled by the economic logic some of the time but many on the left, it seems, are fooled by the ecological logic all of the time. These logics are of a piece, one feeding and reinforcing the other, the latter persuasive only if this is forgotten.

Between 1980 and 2005, Calgar Keyder notes (in Calhoun and Derluguian, eds., 2011: 164), the productivity of the US workforce increased by 70 per cent and over the same period hourly wages rose by only 4.4 per cent. Productivity does not, as Marx said of 'vulgar' economists, magically create demand, and this is certainly the case today. The loss of the capacity of workers to absorb surpluses through their wages can temporarily be offset by the availability of cheap credit, on condition that interest on debts is paid or, if wages stagnate or diminish, there is a reduction in the cost of living – the opposite being the case in recent years. The gamble on future wealth taken by the financial industries proved, at least from a broader economic perspective, to be a reckless one, with few prospects that the shortfall can be made up in the 'real' economy. Manufacturing industry has increasingly turned to financial investments to address shortfalls in profit ratios. For example, between the early 1980s and the early 2000s the total profits generated by US businesses from financial products rose from 10 per cent to 40 per cent. General Electric, a key manufacturer of industrial machinery in the US, now generates more than half its profits from financial investments (see Daniel Chirot in Calhoun and Derluguian, eds., 2011: 117–8). 'A synoptic view of the current crisis', Harvey explains, would suggest that 'while the epicentre lies in the technologies and organisational forms of the credit system and the state-finance nexus, the underlying problem is excessive capitalist empowerment vis-à-vis labour and consequent wage repression' (2010b: 118).

To keep up with competitors, the individual capitalist has to keep investing surplus profits in new technologies that shift the balance in the 'organic composition' of capital from the worker, whose capacities can 'variably' adjust to meet new demands, in favour of machinery or an invariable 'constant' capital. A worker, for example, can enhance their knowledge in order to produce more efficiently whereas a machine's value atrophies until it has to be replaced – it cannot self-generate improved specifications. Replacing labour with machinery and making those still employed work harder for their money can benefit capital in the short term but in the long term, irrespective of whether it provokes workplace militancy, can be disastrous. There are limits after all in how much 'capacity' can be squeezed from labour – locally or globally – and how much those on reduced incomes relative to the cost of living can borrow to spend on commodities. There is a limit to how much credit capital can borrow in order to reinvest before surplus value is realised in exchange. While temporarily arresting falling rates of profit, neoliberalism has created a structural deficit, resulting in crisis, by reducing labour costs through redundancies and increasing levels of exploitation at home and abroad. By such lights, the bourgeois 'victory' over the working class is a pyrrhic one.

Austerity is the reality principle of post-2008 capitalism; it is institutionalised by regressive policies designed to cut spending, rationalise work according to managerial diktat, parcel out services to private contractors and, in the case of students, privatise the costs of education. If the way out of recession is to stimulate spending, then austerity as a policy measure makes no sense at all. Moreover it appears, as with Barack Obama's calls for sacrifice and Cameron's calls to tighten the proverbial belt, that austerity contradicts the consumerist injunction to enjoy. As Clarke and Newman put it:

Austerity in the context of British political culture … evokes two sorts of political sensibility: the promise of hardship and the memory of post-war collective solidarities. The two are combined, although not very stably. The promise of hardship sits uncomfortably alongside the glittering culture of consumption elaborated during the last three decades. Is austerity a punishment for excess? Has over-consumption – won at the cost of increasing public and private indebtedness – turned on us? Is there a (puritanical) penalty to be paid for those dubious pleasures? Did we, indeed, suspect that 'having it so good' was too good to be true? Austerity thus produces an odd politics of affect in a society dominated by the promises of growth and ever-expanding consumption. (2012: 307)

The ideology of austerity not only shifts responsibility onto the individual, it covers up a fundamental contradiction at the heart of the European monetary system and the single currency in particular. Mark Blyth explains the bind that European states are currently in: it is not that banks are too big to fail but that banks are 'too big to bail'. The 'combined asset footprint' of the top three French banks, for example, is 316 per cent of France's GDP, vastly outweighing US exposure to their banking system. As Blyth points out, 'No sovereign, even with its own printing press, can bail out a bank with exposures of this magnitude' (2013: 82). And so…

> If states cannot inflate their way out of trouble (no printing press) or devalue to do the same (no sovereign currency), they can only default (which will blow up the banking system, so it's not an option), which leaves only internal deflation through prices and wages – austerity. This is the real reason we all have to be austere. Once again, it's all about saving the banks. (Blyth, 2013: 87)

With those peddling it unable to come clean about this, austerity functions both economically and ideologically to preserve the banking system in the hope of maintaining the single currency that Germany has staked Europe's future on. The policy may founder economically but it can achieve its ideological aim of quelling dissent and, in the meantime, provide new opportunities for capital to repress wages and penetrate areas of the economy previously under state control. Countries affected by different legacies of class struggle are lumped together, even though, through nationalisations, labour reforms, welfare and such like, they have addressed internal contradictions in different ways. Greece will be forced to sell more of its assets and Spain will be unable to pursue measures that reduce unemployment. From a European perspective, the scarcity of available credit and jobs, and the loss of sovereign power, have to be framed as a consequence of excessive spending by states and consumers because there is no other solution except a fundamental re-write of the policies on which the monetary union was formed.

Suzanne Moore, writing in the *Guardian*, points to anecdotal evidence of how persuasive the claim that individuals are to blame for their predicament remains:

The idea that ultimately the poor must help themselves as social mobility grinds to a halt is illogical; it is based on a faith for which there is scant evidence. Yet it is the one thing that has genuinely 'trickled down' from the wealthy, so that many people without much themselves continue to despise those who are on a lower rung.[3]

Clearer evidence comes from a report by the Joseph Rowntree Foundation in a study of the British Attitudes Survey. It claims there is a 'general trend' towards blaming the individual for poverty, rather than society, with just 27 per cent of Labour voters citing social injustice as the main cause in 2010, down from 41 per cent in 1986 when the Thatcher government's attack on welfare recipients was in full swing.[4] In 2011, 31 per cent of Labour supporters claimed that those on welfare were 'undeserving', compared to 21 per cent in 1987.[5] It is a well-documented phenomenon, but all the more startling in the context of the 2008 crisis, when social justice moments had such a powerful voice in the media. Guilt is both internalised and dispersed; to an extent, economic woes are presumed not to be the responsibility of the state or even financial institutions, but of ourselves or somebody else.

Regardless of how persuasive it is to voters, the economic justification is widely contested beyond parliamentary circles. This is not so much the case for the ecological justification. Population growth is the most persistent of the various justifications for austerity, here in the name of planet Earth. This much is easy to contest when, for example, between 1980 and 2005 the population of Sub-Saharan Africa increased by 18.5 per cent and carbon emissions there by only 2.4 per cent. In the same period the population of North America increased by 4 per cent while the continent's carbon emissions rose by 14 per cent.[6] As Joel Cohen writes:

A numerical estimate of how many people the Earth can support may be a useful index of present human activities and of present understanding of how to live on the Earth; it cannot predict the constraints or possibilities that lie in the future...

At any given time, a *current* but changing human carrying capacity is defined by the *current* states of technology; of the physical, chemical, and biological environment; of social, political, and economic institutions;

of levels and styles of living; and of values, preferences, and moral judgements. (Quoted in Angus and Butler, 2011: 60)

The ecological justification for austerity rests on the assumption of an uninterrupted circulation and expansion of capital and takes little account of the more complex dynamics and relations that affect this movement and growth. It is not that the global population has exceeded the carrying capacity of the planet but rather that the capitalist mode of production has. Nevertheless, across the political spectrum, the putative causes of and solutions to global warming largely centre on the individual, on individual corporations or simply and more frequently on the individual.

The real problem is not industry as such or even that the wealthiest are the main culprits because of the amount they consume,[7] but rather the logic of capitalism itself. The headline figure made popular by the Occupy Wall Street movement, of the wealth disparity between the 1 per cent and the 99 per cent, is not reflected in the campaigns to reduce carbon emissions, if the emphasis on everyday consumption is anything to go by. An article in the *Guardian* published after the Deepwater oil disaster in the Gulf of Mexico, cited by Angus and Butler (2011), contained the headline 'We're all to blame for the oil spill' and claimed:

Moreover, and perhaps most important, we should not only consider responsibility for oil production but also for oil consumption. Business and finance are not isolated from our own choices. Companies such as BP can only do what they do because we want what they sell. We're all too happy with cheap oil...

Happy – or compelled to use it? The roads, out-of-town supermarkets and so forth, that sustain and rationalise car use, undermine claims that individual users are responsible or can achieve much by making 'informed' choices about how they negotiate the city. As David Harvey writes, urban life is suburbanised by the 'mobilisation of effective demand through the total restructuring of space so as to make the consumption of products of the auto, oil, rubber, and construction industries a necessity rather than a luxury' (1989: 39). It is not the end user that burns the most carbon. With motorcars, only a third of carbon emissions come from usage. Another third is from production and another third from waste (cf. Kay, 1998). Capital does not conspire in the attempts by ecologists to institutionalise limits to retail consumer carbon emissions but does benefit in so far as attention shifts to the consumer, whose only recourse is to consume the different kinds of products that business makes available – if they can afford them. We are told we cannot afford to continue using oil, but we know we cannot afford not to; both our use and our rejection of oil are restricted, putting us in an impossible position and setting us up to fail. Meanwhile, capital's use of oil continues to dwarf even the most stubborn retail consumer's.

In 1991 Larry Summers, now economic advisor to Barack Obama, said:

> There are no limits to the carrying capacity of the earth that are likely to bind any time in the foreseeable future ... The idea that we should put limits on [economic] growth, because of some natural limit, is a profound error and one that, were it ever to prove influential, would have staggering social costs. (Quoted in George, 2010: 169)

The economy would certainly suffer if restrictions were placed on individual consumption given, as Harvey (2010b: 107) points out, as much as 70 per cent of US economic activity relies on it. As the ideology shifts from one of denial to reluctant acceptance that global warming is largely 'anthropogenic', divisions emerge within the capitalist class. The hirsute popular entrepreneur Richard Branson is not untypical in making an impassioned plea to do business differently. In a manifesto for capital with inflections of Marx and Engels, *Screw Business as Usual*, Branson writes:

> Capitalism as we know it, which essentially started around the time of the Industrial Revolution, has certainly created economic growth in the world and brought many wonderful benefits to people, but all this has come at a cost that is not reflected on the balance sheet. The focus on profit being king has caused significant negative, unintended consequences ... For over a century and a half cheap labour, damaged lives, a destroyed planet and polluted seas were all irrelevant when set against the need for profit. (2011: 20–1)

Probably to maintain his popularity among those who naively think him to be of and for the people, Branson argues for a 'different' way of doing business, identifying capitalism as both cause and solution. Others such as Derrick Jensen (2006) reason that it is not capitalism per se that is the problem but rather human civilisation itself. His argument can be summarised as follows:

1. Civilisation is destructive and unsustainable
2. Humans are destructive and incapable of containing global warming
3. Global warming effects an equilibrium by returning human society to a pre-industrial state which is a positive outcome
4. Civilisation will inevitably come to an end, we should precipitate its downfall

Judging by the popularity of Jensen's books and others within the genre, by their sympathetic reviews in mainstream media and representations in popular culture,[8] this position, while extreme, is far from isolated, and indeed is a subtext of Gareth Edwards's 2014 reimagined *Godzilla*. In the original, Godzilla was of course a metaphor for the dangers of nuclear war. In the 2014 version nuclear weapons play their part but the subtext has shifted to global warming, with the improbable monster now guardian of mother nature. It rises from the ocean to fight two radiation-feeding parasites that like a tsunami plough their way through cities destroying everything in their wake. With the help of one plucky individual, Ford Brody, played by Aaron Taylor-Johnson, who does his best to mitigate the negative impacts of the military's attempts to contain the danger, Godzilla restores a metabolic balance. The unreality of *Godzilla* is not the monster itself but rather the fact that in the incredible scenes of destruction the fleeing crowds are not capturing it on their mobile phones. Whereas the original warned humanity against military adventurism, the message of the most recent version is that neither science nor technology, and least of all the collective body, can stop nature from destroying civilisation and, if anything, with humanity as the parasites, we ought to be giving it a helping hand. This ideology is a refraction of the misuses and abuses of nature, echoing in a popular vernacular that has authored passivity in the face of what appears to be an inevitable catastrophe rendering the future of humanity null and void. The popularity of the ideology has prompted Alain Badiou to write:

> Let's start by saying that after 'the rights of man', the rise of the 'the rights of Nature' is a contemporary form of the opium of the people. It is an only slightly camouflaged religion: the millenarian terror, concern for everything save the properly political destiny of peoples, new instruments

for control of everyday life, the obsession with hygiene, the fear of death and catastrophes ... It is a gigantic operation in the depoliticisation of subjects. (In Feltham ed., 2005: 139)

A full-spectrum ideology is in operation from Branson through to Jensen, from the green advertising of major corporations through to the lifestyles promoted by environmental campaigners and adopted by the self-righteous. Eco-politics is Oedipalised as an internal guilt complex, to be gotten rid of by ecological practices such as eco-consumption, recycling, restraint and, ultimately, by recognising our limits and welcoming civilisational collapse.

The mystifications that austerity promotes, whether in regard to the economy or relatedly to ecology, are enduring ones. As Rosa Luxemburg put it, 'Force, fraud, oppression, looting are openly displayed without any attempt at concealment, and it requires an effort to discover within this tangle of political violence and contests of power the stern laws of the economic process' (2003 [1913]: 432).

In the next two chapters we take a closer look at how the subject is wedded to its material condition, has an ideological affinity to and is libidinally invested at the principal sites where relational and co-evolving scarcities are produced, beginning with production in Chapter 4, and ending with consumption in Chapter 5.

4

Production Spiral

The much reported looting of stores during the urban riots that swept across England in 2011 exemplifies the extent to which commerce has exercised upon the libido a heightened desire for goods, a desire that can no longer be legitimately attained. It also testifies to something more fundamental: that there is no correspondence between the object of desire and a normative moral law. Now, more than at any period in late capitalism, the individual has become divorced in its libidinal orientation from an obligation towards a societal big Other. This is one example of the individualism of our era, in which the call for a return to 'moral values' sounds shrill, especially given that such a call stands in stark contrast to what commerce demands. As a relationship to an extimate or non-existent cause, *jouissance* does not obey a moral authority in the traditional sense of the word. Pleasure lies in the little transgressions by which the subject affirms their independence and disconnection from society. In place of a morally certain and self-righteous big Other, we have a more ambiguous big Other that invites us to make an ersatz choice to do as we please in a society in which choices are circumscribed by material conditions. The superego injunction is an indirect one, as Žižek claims: instead of saying 'you must', it says that you *may*. The rioters in 2011 took the injunction too literally by failing to recognise the underlying meaning of the law, the hidden kernel of every ideological junction: submission to the law of surplus value. One has the choice to consume as one pleases only by acknowledging, consciously or not, that pleasure comes at the price of this primary sacrifice, in concrete terms, to employers and creditors. In other words, in order to consume we must first have a job or demonstrate, when taking out a loan, a capacity and willingness to return the debt through our labours or perhaps by selling heavily mortgaged homes that miraculously increase in value.

However much we identify our pleasures with objects for sale and, as many cultural theorists have suggested, recognise our identities in them, the primary or underlying identification is with work. The majority of our time and energy is invested in the labour process, whether on the job or in an endless preparation for it. The sacrifices to work require many detours through dense forests of uncertainty in which hang the occasional fruits – accolades, promotions, lines on the CV, getting one over on the boss – to sweeten the journey. Fleeting moments of *jouissance* enable us to circle the blackness and gain a sense of purpose and belonging. The conditions under which we labour are made more tolerable because in our imaginations the actual job we do or strive for is not primary to our sense of self. In our non-class identities, our likes, dislikes and loves, nightly revelries, happy days and holidays, the underlying relations that structure life direct us in our choosing. Work is the foundation of all societies, integral to a sense of self, a sense of belonging, dignity and respect. In a society such as ours, it is difficult to imagine work to be anything other than a burden when for so many it is routine, dispiriting and demoralising.

The rigid hierarchies and stultifying conformities that protestors in the 1960s rallied against were, once the struggles culminating in France in May 1968 were defeated, internalised in more discreet systems of control. Bureaucracies were superficially flattened, industrial labour outsourced, and egos courted with overtures to their unique personality traits, values, talents and achievements. According to Boltanski and Chiapello (2007), management seized on the aesthetic demands of the protestors by establishing new organisational principles that spoke directly to them and which became in time a measure according to which candidates were selected. The industrial labourer required skills, physical dexterity, strength and stamina; the post-industrial worker, flexibility, networks and smiles.

The rise of zero-hour contracts enabling employers to hire staff without any legal requirement to guarantee even a minimum number of hours exemplifies the shift towards insecure and intermittent labour. According to the Office of National Statistics, in 2013 there were nearly 583,000 zero-contract labourers in Britain.[1] To describe these workers at the lower end of a multilayered class stratification, Guy Standing (2011) has helped popularise the term 'precariat', a term that superficially highlights the nature of work for so many but on closer inspection is a further mystification of the class relation. The extremely rich are the 'elite', the 'salariat', those in corporations and administration with job security, holiday pay, pensions and so forth. There are highly skilled and highly paid 'proficians' or 'self-selling entrepreneurs, living opportunistically on their wits and contacts'.[2] Then there is the residue of the 'old' unionised working class. The 'precariat', on the other hand, float between temporary contracts and periods of unemployment. Without pensions, statutory paid holidays, job security or identification with a specific profession, they are, Standing enthusiastically claims, unencumbered by the nostalgia affecting the old working class and so have the capacity, unlike unionised workers, to embrace new thinking on how to regulate capital in view of changes in the labour market. 'Social misfits', the 'dregs' of society, are the new lumpenproletariat.

For Standing, the precariat is not simply a neat term signifying the insecure and intermittent nature of labour. Despite the description being compatible with Marx's analysis of the proletariat as those without property whose conditions of labour increasingly deteriorate, Standing's precariat is not a proletariat. It is not simply a name for describing a circumstance of labour. It is a name for a new economic relation. Standing distinguishes a 'bad precariat' – angry and bitter at governments bailing out the banks and, as he suggests, problematically nostalgic for a golden age of full employment, even seduced by 'neo-fascist' ideologies – and a 'good precariat', 'unburdened' by a yearning for a return to full employment. This 'new' class, as Jan Breman writes in her review, coincidently wants Standing's 'politics of paradise': 'universal basic income, lifelong education, residency rights for migrants, cooperatives and the revalorization of work, as steps towards "more equal access" to five key assets – economic security, time, space, knowledge and finance capital' (2013: 133). For a global class, the prescription is remarkably localised to fit the current policy preferences of a liberal intelligentsia.

Standing wants to reinvent the wheel and does so by designing a square. He is by no means alone. Over the past 30 or more years, one figure after another has lined up in a tag-team in which each takes it in turn to pronounce that the fundamentals have changed, offering neat phrases with which to establish their career until eventually they are knocked from the ring by the force of contradiction.

This chapter now begins in earnest, where the circuit of capital ends: at the moment of consumption. More tangible than work, brighter and more colourful, in the act of consumption the commodity is fetishised and through relations of exchange we are defined as consumers. The consumer society must first be demystified before we proceed to examine the labour relation that conditions every other aspect of life including our identities as consumers.

The Consumer Society Does Not Exist

With the emphasis on production in this chapter it may appear counter-intuitive to begin with a discussion on consumption. But the necessary first step in establishing the primacy of the former is to qualify the idea that we live in a 'consumer society', speaking of course about the principal sites where many consumer goods, manufactured increasingly though by no means exclusively in low-wage economies, are bought. 'Production' is taken here to refer to all labour that produces value, not simply industrial labour as is often presumed by the term. This includes the production of value prior to employment, such as when a person self-consciously develops skills or life experiences in the hope of getting a job, holding on to one, or being promoted. These can be termed 'potential use values', in which the intention is to make them available to capital for the purposes of exchange.

From devouring a meal to donning an item of clothing, consumption from the cave to the condo is an ineluctable aspect of human existence. It is only when consumption overwhelmingly shapes how people think, socialise and desire, or rather determines what it means to be human, that it becomes an ideology and thus appropriately referred to as 'consumer-ism' – a point that Zygmunt Bauman (2005) elucidates in Work, Consumerism and the New Poor. But if 'consumerism' is indeed the opiate of the masses it does not follow that people have become 'consumers' in the sense of conforming to an identity that defines us as a species. As Raymond Williams said, the word 'is now habitually used by people to whom it ought, logically, to be repugnant' (2005: 187). Moreover, the uneven nature of consumption both within consumer-oriented societies and between nations – as attested to by the numerous statistics on income inequalities, levels of household debt, rates of unemployment and consumer spending[3] – gives us pause to reflect on precisely who it is we are talking about and what consumption means and entails for different people. In an unqualified way, the word 'consumer' reduces human existence to a relationship with the checkout; it raises the commodity to a brand ironed onto every individual – including students, hospital patients, even the dead whose commodified funeral rituals are organised in their name.[4] As Marcuse wrote, 'the so-called consumer economy and the politics of corporate capitalism have created a second nature of man which ties him libidinally and aggressively to the commodity form' (1969: 11).

Whatever might be said about the shift to 'post-Fordism' and the significant role that mass, diversified consumption has in shaping identity and atomising the subject, the notion that even in the heartlands of consumerism 'we' live in a consumer society is misleading. Work, in that it enables consumption and as a relation of capital determines the form of consumption, is still of central importance to most people given how much of life is organised through it whether they 'identify' with their labours or not.

Rather than describe how work and consumption relate to one another, Bauman offers a linear narrative in which a consumerist aesthetic has replaced the work ethic. Not only do people identify themselves as living in a consumerist society, he says, but also the 'way present-day society shapes up its members is dictated first and foremost by the need to play the role of the consumer, and the norm our society holds up to its members is that of the ability and willingness to play it' (2005: 24). The role of work in orienting the subject, defining their achievements and being a source of satisfaction (which Bauman regards as central in the era of mass production, now apparently over) has, accordingly, been supplanted by consumption as the principal site from which the subject derives a sense of identity and belonging. The narrative is summarised as follows:

> The passage from producer to consumer society has entailed many profound changes; arguably the most decisive among them is, however, the fashion in which people are groomed and trained to meet the demands of their social identities (that is, the fashion in which men and women are 'integrated' into the social order and given a place in it). (Bauman, 2005: 24)

Bauman claims that while there was certain logic to naming the era of industrial capitalism a 'producer' society, this should be qualified by the fact that people in all societies from the beginning to the end produce. Baffling, then, that he deems it appropriate to call capitalism in our own time a 'consumer' society when from beginning to end people in all societies consume, but also in different ways, for different purposes and with different consequences today. The main objection to Bauman's description of how identities are shaped and oriented through consumption is the way he separates this out from production, which he seems to equate simply with the production of material objects. However insightful he is on consumer behaviours, Bauman's sweeping claim that ours is a consumer society obscures the role that work continues to play in our lives and indeed the ineluctable fact that mass production is still the material basis of consumption. Work not only determines our capacity to consume but also how, with regard to employers, we orient our own identities, attitudes and experiences. As with consumer behaviour, such activities, while originating in society, are fetishised as belonging to an atomised sovereign individual expending considerable libidinal energy on the task of labour, paid or otherwise, with consumption as the reward wherever work is unable to satisfy. For Bauman, subjective anxieties centre on consumption – whether, for example, the right purchase choice has been made – but the anxiety that work engenders is more profound and of greater material significance. Nonetheless, Bauman writes,

> The roads to self-identity, to a place in society, to life lived in a form recognizable as that of meaningful living, all require daily visits to the market place. In the industrial phase of modernity one fact was beyond all questioning: that everyone must be a producer first, before being anything else. In 'modernity mark two', the consumers' modernity, the brute unquestionable fact is that one needs to be consumer first, before one can think of becoming anything in particular. (2005: 26)

In Bauman's work the subject has a snake-like tendency to perpetually shed its skin, discarding identities in much the way it discards the products it identifies itself with. It is as if the subject is permanently embarked on a catastrophic line of flight that sucks it, to employ Deleuze and Guattari's apt metaphor, into recurring black holes of identity crisis. The subject adapts to its surroundings but the latter, to be sure, are never as fleeting or contingent as the pleasures of consumption. Bauman describes identity in plural terms, but little thought is given though to the continuities or, putting it in Deleuzian terms, the molar formations that ground the subject while change happens, by and large, on a more nuanced molecular level.

Furthermore, according to Bauman, 'Consumption is a thoroughly individual, solitary and, in the end, lonely activity' (2005: 30). This may be true up to a point, but, particularly given the importance of brands, identities are always relational and governed by the perspectives of others, with consumption more often than not a social experience. By consuming we enter into association with others and earn our place at the dinner table, the pub or the cinema with friends. It is the mapping of the commodity on to social life that makes consumption all the more compelling, and by such lights, and in qualified agreement with Bauman, makes the commodity that comes to embody social life important to identity formation.

In *Consuming Life*, Bauman claims that one cannot be 'a subject without first turning into a commodity, and no one can keep his or her subjectness secure without perpetually resuscitating, resurrecting and replenishing the capacities expected and required of a sellable commodity' (2007: 12). The description fits the labour process where the unending aim is to become a sellable commodity. Whereas concrete labour is abstracted to produce surplus value, consumption is a concrete activity that unlike labour is not abstracted from the individual who consumes the thing.

With his emphasis on production, Michel Foucault's account of subjectivity is more persuasive. His work does not challenge Marx; rather, it adds nuances to Marx's account by examining how subjectivities are produced for capital. Foucault identifies how, at a micro level of everyday life, the subject is active in producing a 'docile' body for capital. As Thomas Lemke explains:

Foucault showed that labour power must first be constituted before it can be exploited: that is, that life time must be synthesized into labour time, individuals must be subjugated to the production circle, habits must be formed, and time and space must be organized according to a scheme. Thus economic exploitation required a prior 'political investment of the body'. By this theoretical reorientation Foucault hoped to complement and enlarge Marx's critique of political economy with a 'critique of political anatomy'. (2002: 58)

Foucault's work is highly complex. A detailed account of the dynamics of power and knowledge traced through a discursive genealogy is beyond the scope of this book.[5] For the sake of brevity, it is useful to borrow the account of the production of subjectivity in an organisational context from Peter Fleming's review of biopower. Biopower, Fleming writes,

indexes … [the subject's] everyday qualities or 'life itself' to the needs of economic regulation, governing modern western societies from a distance and making it, ironically, all the more irresistible for doing so. In other words, it captures what the subject of power already is, rather than composing or reconstructing him or her into a desired image. (2014: 2)

As Fleming elaborates, management ideology has from the 1970s through to today drawn increasingly on the 'whole person' and, as Boltanski and Chiapello claim, the more discreet qualities of people and their ability to nurture relationships become a condition for their inclusion in a firm. In their essay *Dead Man Working*, Cederstrom and Fleming describe the extent to which the labour market is absorbed into every pore of our being:

In an eccentric and extreme society like ours, working has assumed a universal presence – a 'worker society' in the worst sense of the term – where even the unemployed and children find themselves obsessed with it. This viral-like logic of the corporation has even spread into our most intimate pastimes, precipitating a novel and inescapable cultural malaise, writ-large by a complete, irreversible and ominous *dead end*. (2012: 2)

Recalling the 'scientific and technical worker' described by Andre Gorz, Deleuze and Guattari write, 'Although he has mastered a flow of knowledge, information, and training, he is so absorbed in capital that the reflux of organised, atomised stupidity coincides with him, so that, when he goes home in the evening, he rediscovers his little desiring-machines by tinkering with a television set' (2003a [1972]: 236) Cederstrom and Fleming's interpretation of the current conjuncture suggests that even such minor releases are plagued by anxieties about work to the extent that every waking *and* sleeping hour is taken up by thoughts about it. Like Gregor Samsa of Kafka's *The Metamorphosis*, we have all awoken from a night of uneasy dreams only to find ourselves transformed as it were into large but helpless insects. This metaphor of alienation fits their argument that the dividing line is no longer between capital and labour but rather between *'capital and life'* (2012: 7). The problem with this is that by defining the division in such terms, the more crucial contradiction between capital and *labour* may be lost. The class division, as Fleming (2014) elsewhere reminds us, underscores the subject's own self-governance; what, in view of the general strengths and weaknesses of a particular class and its ideological predilections, a person is prepared to do. To qualify Lemke, one might say that the subject must exploit its own capacities to the degree that the life chances and circumstances to which they are habituated depend on employment in order to be exploitable as a worker.

Foucault offers a detailed method for analysing the processes and procedures by which the subject produces for itself a body fit for labour. It is a process prior to the abstraction of labour power by capital in which the class relation is embodied and through which the value of our activities are increasingly determined. We are always in a process of objectifying ourselves. As Marx, in one of the rare examples where he describes this phenomenon, writes:

> The communal substance of all commodities, i.e. their substance not as material stuff, as physical character, but their communal substance as commodities and hence exchange values, is this, that they are *objectified labour*. The only thing distinct from *objectified* labour is *non-objectified* labour, labour which is still objectifying itself, *labour* as subjectivity. Or, *objectified* labour, i.e. labour which is *present in space*, can also be opposed, as *past labour*, to labour which is *present in time*. If it is to be present in time, alive, then it can be present only as the *living subject*, in which it exists as capacity, as possibility; hence as *worker*. (1973 [1858]: 272)

The *Grundrisse* from which this comes is a touchstone for Hardt and Negri, whose books on the theme of immaterial labour also draw extensively on Foucault and Deleuze and Guattari. Deleuze's influential 'Societies of Control' essay is widely cited by autonomist theorists and offers a useful corrective to Foucault's own interpretation of power within a more 'striated' disciplinary context.

The more institutionalised disciplinary regimes that Foucault famously compared to the all-seeing prison panopticon are supplemented, replaced even, according to Deleuze, by societies of control. The flows of people and capital intensify and exceed spatial boundaries through a 'worldwide' axiomatic wherein high industry develops on the periphery and 'internal

Third Worlds' manifest in centres reserved for 'so-called postindustrial activities' (Deleuze and Guattari, 2003b [1980]: 469). Institutions are no longer compartmentalised by their specific disciplinary modes to which people adjust but co-evolve and scramble into one another. Consider, for example, the way that business values, practices and accounting procedures have penetrated the public sector; or, from the perspective of the individual, how work is no longer delimited by or enclosed within the workplace, and identity is no longer anchored to a particular firm or mass worker. Or recall the earlier example of manufacturing industry deriving profits from financial investments. Rather than a contradictory binary of individual/ mass, individuals have become '*dividuals*', and masses have become samples, data, markets, or '*banks*' (Deleuze, 1992: 5). Think, for example, of the way that desire is now framed in terms of what the amorphous 'market', 'consumer' or 'voter' wants, and how recipients of disability benefits are judged for eligibility according to coded sets of criteria. Whereas 'disciplinary man' produced energy in compartmentalised sequences, at work, when consuming and so forth, 'the man of control is undulatory, in orbit, in a continuous network' (Deleuze, 1992: 6) akin to surfing, says Deleuze, rather than, we could add, more enclosed sports such as tennis and football with their strict rules and specific disciplinary procedures.

The ambiguous relationship to control heightens anxieties, has reduced the subject in its capacity to define itself according to shared ethical standards, and has forced upon it a mode of reasoning that further maps it as 'dividual' to the commodity form. Like the commodity, the individual, for it to have value or capitalise on its knowledge or 'data', must be in perpetual motion and endlessly chase the coveted position of employee of choice in a society where no job holds the place - or rather secures the position - of the subject. For Hardt and Negri, as suggested, this is typified by the shift towards an 'immaterial' labour of affects and networks of association. The influence of selected passages of the *Grundrisse* and Deleuze's short essay are apparent in Hardt and Negri's first collaboration *Labour of Dionysus*, this passage being one of the more persuasive:

> Living labour produces life and constitutes society in a time that cuts across the division posed by the workday, inside and outside the prisons of capitalist work and its wage relation, in both the realm of work and that of nonwork. It is a seed that lies waiting under the snow, or more

accurately, the life force always already active in the dynamic networks of cooperation, in the production and reproduction of society, that courses in and out of the time posed by capital. (1994: xiii)

More profoundly, no longer bound to the factory, the worker produces capital independent of the bourgeois class and rents this out to them. Contractual labour can be thought of as an instance of this. Much as they would rent a computer, the capitalist 'rents' the labourer's skills, dispositions and so forth for a temporary period.

Hardt and Negri perform a similar jump to Bauman by developing from partial observations a totalising schema of how capitalism now operates. Their work – a classic example of dialectical thinking when it comes to conceiving the potential of a 'biopolitical' (neoliberalised) production of subjectivity, one that through self-conscious adaptation can also be a weapon against capital – misses the very real contradictions that underlie and enable the reproduction of capital. (Foucault misses them too.) By making different identity formations, such as those based on gender, race or ethnicity, of equal significance to class they see revolutionary potential in each. Their stress on the importance of such divisions is to be welcomed; however, basing their work on an erroneous reading of history and capital, they reject the fundamental point about class, namely that, unlike with those other divisions, it is the one antagonism that cannot be overcome without arresting the capacity of capitalism to generate surplus value (as Žižek notes). Hardt and Negri's misreading is informed by their misconception (apparently shared by Žižek) that the labour theory of value rests on the idea that Marx was describing an 'embodied' industrial labour, whose value could be calculated simply by the hours that the worker 'clocks' into the firm. Alternatively – as this book is attempting to do – Marx's insights on the value form, if supplemented rather than substituted, can be enriched through psychoanalytic theories of object relations.

By Hardt and Negri's reckoning labour is now in large part a machine-like 'constant' capital, no longer employed for its flexibility to adapt and produce additional surplus value over time but rather, as with the 'precariat', renting itself out and increasing capacities between contracts. Hardt and Negri's capitalism is flat and free-flowing, made up of deterritorialised networks in which there is no strict dividing line between classes. Deleuze and Guattari's critique of the capitalist axiomatic is more nuanced in its description of surplus value, stressing the contradictions recognised by Marx between smooth flows of people and capital and various 'striations', be they nations, classes, organisations and laws. They differentiate between a plane of 'consistency' from which 'singularities' flow and a plane of organisation where value is generated by capturing the force of desire through different 'abstract machines'. The money form is a concrete use value in exchange that becomes 'immaterial' or abstract in financial flows in much the same way that concrete labour is rendered immaterial when abstracted for surplus value. Moreover, all labour, as Sean Sayers (2007: 448) suggests, is biopolitical in that it produces new forms of association and gives a character to commodities that evoke emotional responses; in short it affects social life in many complex ways.

The University Dilemma

> You are the product of the university, and you prove that you are the surplus value, even if only in this respect – which you not only consent to, but which you also applaud – and I see no reason to object – which is that you leave here, yourselves equivalent to more or fewer credit points. You come here to gain credit points for yourselves. You leave here stamped, 'credit points.'
>
> Jacques Lacan (2007 [1969]: 201)

Lacan's goading of students during an extraordinary exchange at Vincennes in 1969 underlines the point, not that students are hypocrites as he seemed to suggest, but rather that, whatever we might desire politically, material realities will sooner or later come back to haunt us. However noble an artist's dedication to form, unless they are making a living from their art, sooner or later they will have to apply for jobs or deal with the threat of having their benefits suspended because they are not 'actively' seeking employment. Ethics are tainted by an iron-cage instrumentality, all too apparent in my own role as a university lecturer. This involves teaching, among others, Marx, Marcuse, Deleuze and Guattari and Žižek, and I make my own political affinities to these thinkers clear to my students. At the same time I go to great lengths, partly but not entirely due to managerial pressures, to ensure that even those who fail to show up to lectures – a number which seems to increase each year – can write the kinds of essays that get them the grades they covet and instrumentalise their studies for.

My sense of what is at stake was sharpened by my own experience of being on the dole for five years before going to university and never receiving more in any one year than £8,000 (from a grant to study for a Masters degree) until I finally got a full-time permanent lecturing position at the age of 36. In the two years between completing a PhD and getting a full-time job, I worked for universities as a contract labourer, receiving at one elite 'Russell Group' institution £5,000 for a year teaching a course on globalisation. I remember how shocked the privileged but committed and conscientious students were when at the end of the year I told them how much I earned. This was in 2006. It is hard to imagine that such disclosures would generate much response today. In many ways I was 'lucky' in that my student loan at the end of my undergraduate degree was a manageable £4,000 and that I received grants for further study.

The university is today an enterprise that markets itself as businesses do, is structured like a business, and judges itself and its employees according to spurious 'metrics' and league tables. Auckland, for example, is a 'world ranking university' as we are constantly reminded, but this, as elsewhere, is a misleading claim when judged against the ratios of students to lecturers and the shoddy condition of the physical infrastructure in Arts and Social Science faculties. Under pressure to recruit students at both undergraduate and postgraduate levels, universities are now in the habit of marketing dreams. The lack of public sympathy to the changes in the sector are in part symptomatic of how much worse it often is for those working or trying to get a job in other occupations. The precarious intermittent nature of employment today is both sobering for the professional 'critical theorist' and provokes further determination to render visible those relations that are, here as elsewhere, mystified. If for no other reason than to open a space for critical thought and dialogue whatever this might achieve, the academic can, unlike in many professions, maintain a sense – however shallow it becomes – that their labours are not entirely alienated. As Simmel writes:

> For the practical content of the activity of the artist, the official, the preacher, the teacher and the scholar is measured against an objective ideal and gives subjective satisfaction to the performer according to these standards. But then there is also the economic success of these activities,

which as we know is not always a constant function of their objective and ideal success. Not only can the economic success of these activities be pushed by the lowest dispositions so much into the foreground that it relegates the objective ideals merely to a means; but also, for more sensitive and idealistic people, the material success of the performance may be a consolation, a substitute, a salvation for the insufficiency that is felt with regard to the primary goal. (2004 [1900]: 312)

The irony of a Marxist snatching his own piece of *jouissance* when students submit critical essays, or when he has his work favourably cited and adds publications to his CV, is not lost. It underlines a point, though, that work can, even while alienating, stimulate the libido and be a reason why we permanently strive for a 'better' job – and gain comfort in our burgeoning CVs – where it is hoped that the *jouissance* lost in the production of surplus value may be taken back in increasing quantities the higher up the ladder we are. Given how much is 'spent' on education, it is reasonable to suppose that many people would happily forgo some of the pleasures they derive from consumption for a more spiritually rewarding job. Rather than deny, then, the deep-rooted identification of pleasure with work, or, as I shall later argue, with consumption, critical theory, as Hardt and Negri recognise, has to contend with the person as they really are, more precisely with their libidinal orientations determined by material circumstances, rather than project and judge people according to an ethos about how they ought to live. Arguing against the 'productivist' logic, Kathi Weeks writes:

The glorification of work as a prototypically human endeavour, as the key both to social belonging and individual achievement, constitutes the fundamental ideological foundation of contemporary capitalism: it was built on the basis of this ethic, which continues to serve the system's interests and rationalise its outcomes. (2011: 109)

While that may be the case, the correlation between work and satisfaction is not primarily capitalistic. I am more inclined to support Marx's original claim that labour is a species activity, and proceed from this point to criticise not work in itself but rather the material circumstances in which we work, the ideologies that justify the exploitative dimension of labour, and the libidinal energies that go into sustaining it. In short, the problem is not labour as such but rather alienated labour. As Engels put it:

As voluntary, productive activity is the highest enjoyment known to us, so is compulsory toil the most cruel, degrading punishment ... Why does he work? For love of work? From a natural impulse? Not at all! He works for money, for a thing, which has nothing whatsoever to do with the work itself; and he works so long, moreover, and in such unbroken monotony, that this alone must make his work a torture in the first weeks if he has the least human feeling left. (2009 [1845]: 129)

The wealth of the richest 1 per cent of the world's population is now 65 times greater than that of the poorest 50 per cent.[6] Such concentrations of wealth underline the extent to which neoliberalism has succeeded in confirming Marx's claim in the *Economic and Philosophical Manuscripts* that:

the more the worker produces, the less he has to consume, the more values he creates the more valueless and worthless he becomes, the more formed the product the more deformed the worker, the more civilised the product, the more barbaric the worker, the more powerful the work the more powerless becomes the worker, the more cultured the work the more philistine the worker becomes and more of a slave to nature. (McLellan, ed., 1990: 79)

Furthermore, the more the labour relation saps our energies the greater is the surplus labour that ceases to have value to capital. Youth unemployment in Europe now stands at 24.4 per cent and, if only to demonstrate the disparities between nations within the Eurozone, is at 57.4 per cent in Spain, 58 per cent in Greece and 'only' 7.8 per cent in Germany.[7] According to the International Labour Organisation, globally there were 202 million people without a job at the beginning of 2014.[8] This does not, of course, tell us about the conditions of labour for those slumming it in the informal economy or the kind of hardships and humiliations those in employment, or not, endure. Statistics do not speak for themselves, they do not inform us about the circumstances that produce them: they can obscure rather than enlighten and are often fetishised by a left stoking its own moral indignation about wealth disparities, but doing little else. Popular books on inequality, the environment, the food industry and so forth can become Trojan horses that politicise the terrain a dominant class had guarded with their ideological monoglossia. But many such horses arrive empty, lacking the analysis and critique to expose the structural factors the statistics frequently clothe. The left-liberal intelligentsia who write and consume such books love the statistics. They hate the lessons of Marx.

As with statistics on climate change, we need to get beneath them in order to understand the reasons for their persistence, something Marx has done for us with regard to inequality and unemployment. While the underlying factors are the same as in the 1800s, shifts have occurred in labour relations that have brought about significant changes in the subject and its relation to others. The alienation Marx describes, particularly concerning our relations to one another, is now acute.

While acknowledging the uneven nature of capitalist development, including, as noted above, within continental zones but also within nations and cities, generalisations can be made about the labour process and the impact of neoliberalism in the hegemonic centres of power. The legitimacy of these centres has rested on individualised notions of freedom and choice, which were historically (well, for 30 years or so) underpinned by relatively high and stable levels of employment and universal access to welfare. The narrative of how labour in these privileged sites of accumulation became precarious and intermittent, how unemployment grew to such levels, and how opposition to the dismantling of regulations favouring labour, welfare and industry failed, is now established. Harvey (2005) traces the neoliberal project to the Chicago School of economists influenced by the Austrian political philosopher Friedrich von Hayek and early experiments in Chile and New York before the model was fully rolled out in Britain and the United States, forced upon the south by the IMF and World Bank under the label of structural adjustment, and eventually globalised after the fall of the Soviet Union through 'shock therapy'. Various forms of dispossession accompany these changes, from the 1973 coup in Chile, the smashing of trade union power in Britain and the United States, engineered de-industrialisation and unemployment, through to large-scale privatisations, particularly in developing economies and the former Soviet bloc. As noted, changes in management structure were, according to Boltanski and Chiapello, influenced by movements in the late 1960s that justified a shift towards more flattened network forms of control predicated on the rhetoric of inclusivity, recognition and the valuing of personal differences, attributes and expressions. The combined effects of these changes, along with a postmodern cultural relativism and an end to the 'meta-narratives' of competing ideologies, Marxist and psychoanalytic theory especially, was to further fragment the workforce, lead to breakdown of communities, and engender a possessive individualism and narcissism more pronounced than perhaps at any time in human history.

Graduates are usually considered to possess society's greatest intellectual and emotional capital, and they are skilled in forging the connections now said to be crucial to business. Yet according to a European-wide survey of over 300,000 graduates, it takes five months on average before a job is secured. Business graduates, for example, will need to send out an average of 38 applications before getting a job.[9] The investment, both monetary and libidinal, in getting and securing a job under capitalism is vastly disproportionate to what the subject receives in return, the payback of salary, security and *jouissance*. The subject – defined by lack, on account of being without assets, without a job, without political militancy, indebted and without a future – is, in short, without property. The most abject have no value to capital, are in possession of nothing that capital wants, are without the capacity to secure meaningful employment or play a meaningful role in society as consumer; they are surplus labour, surplus to requirements: unemployable. If there is a way forward, it is only according to a logic that capital with the support of the state imposes, a symbolic big Other that presents itself in every call and compulsion to become employable. Refusal is not an option.

The Oedipalised Economy of Employability

The most succinct definition of the reversal constitutive of drive is the moment when, in our engagement in our purposeful activity (activity towards some goal), the way towards this goal, the gestures we make to achieve it, start to function as the goal in itself, as its own aim, as something that brings its own satisfaction.

Slavoj Žižek (2000: 304)

The shift from desire to drive was fully systemised in respect to labour at the moment that work became 'flexible' through the systematic dismantling of labour regulations, the passing of anti-trade-union legislation and so forth, combined with attacks on the industrial base and the privileging of finance capital via the ideology of neoliberalism and the entrepreneurial self. Surplus labour is a structural element of capitalism; what changed was that the emphasis shifted from simply competing for a job to improving employability regardless of whether there are jobs available or whether a person is actually employed.[10] Employability operates at the level of drive in that satisfaction lies in the aim (there is no object to attain) rather than the outcome (an actual job). We cannot get rid of it and we cannot get enough of it; there is no end to employability because there is no job that can end dissatisfaction or be materially secure in duration, and arguably no movement that can currently force a more stable compact between capital and labour. The lack in capital symbolised by the job vacancy can be filled; it is the void of surplus value (the Real) that operationalises the drive as an unending task to accumulate use values employers may or may not want.

Employability is sustained by up to three parties: the subject, the boss (if the subject is employed), and the phantasmal 'big Boss', the big Other, a symbolic refraction of capital and the State in the entirety of social relations. The process of becoming employable involves a gathering up of signifiers – accredited skills, traits and experiences – orbiting the master signifier of employability. 'It is language that uses us. Language employs us, and that is how it [the big Other] enjoys' (Lacan, 2007 [1969]: 66).

Question:
How can I keep busy while I'm unemployed?

Answer:
If you can demonstrate to employers that you have been doing everything you can to find work and to keep your skills and knowledge up to date, most will overlook the fact that you are currently unemployed.

Always remain positive – rejections are part of life. Each 'no' that you get moves you closer to that all-important 'yes'.[11]

Oedipus is very much 'alive': the more the subject responds to the injunction to develop new skills, gain 'relevant' experience and so on, the more obscene are the demands of capital and the further away is that all important yes.

Scarcity of jobs operationalises the performance principle that Marcuse spoke of. Capital relies here on the excess of knowledge to increase surplus value that it calculates as necessary for generating profit, the increase of which dovetails with the subject's own desire to exceed what it already knows by chasing the surplus valorised by the master signifier of employability. Idiosyncrasies, even resistance to 'corporate diktat', are calculated into the operation through the perverse superego injunction to enjoy, with the typical refrain that employers want 'humans' not robots, for staff to 'have a life outside of work' or not take work 'too seriously'. The greater the 'ironic' distance we maintain towards our labours, the more tolerable the job, the better for capital. It is a distance nonetheless to be qualified in reference to the kind of advice a labouring subject takes up. Consider this typical advice from a career site on what to say during an interview:

> It's really important that you pick something that's personal to you: something that you're really, really proud of. Because when you start telling a story like that you'll start reliving all of the emotion that you felt during that time. You'll probably get a big smile on your face. You'll probably sit up in your chair. Your energy levels will rise and you'll become more engaging with the interviewer. The way that you'll make the interviewer feel through body language ... is also just as important ... so long as you're really genuine and passionate about what you're talking about that should be great, a great answer. However, keep the benefit in mind ... make sure if you tell me maybe you've run a marathon, tell me the benefit to me [the employer]. So that's when you would come in and say well everything I put my mind to I achieve, I'm really self-motivated, I don't like failing and that's the benefit then to me.[12]

Psychometric testing, interviews and requests for personal statements and evidence of hobbies, interests and activities outside of work and in the 'non-profit' sector ensure that the employability injunction in all its ambiguity is understood. Becoming employable is an unending repetition of the failure to be the equivalent of what capital wants, underlined by the question *what does capital want from me?* At the vacant heart of both parties is the *objet a* – the perfect job in the case of the worker; self-reproducing surplus value for capital – that would end dissatisfaction. A communistic impulse for non-alienated labour – the end of employability – is the utopian object of an isolated individual that politically short-circuits a collective decision to bring an end to capitalism. The relation to the actual work that is done is decentred as the struggle shifts from striving for better working conditions to an individualistic enterprise of getting a (better) job or simply maintaining one. Never sure what our employers want from us, advice columns and career sites provide clues on how to become a use value for capital. LoveMoney.com is typical in its advice on how to 'survive' unemployment:

> If you feel yourself sinking into despair/apathy/complete inactivity, you need to drag yourself out of it as soon as possible. That could just mean getting out of the house, even if you don't feel like it...
>
> Or, to help motivate your job hunt, you could set yourself inexpensive rewards for getting things done. So three solid job applications = ice cream and a DVD – or something along those lines...
>
> Finally, try to keep yourself groomed and in reasonable physical shape. When you're out of work, it's all too easy to live in your pyjamas. Look good and you'll feel good.[13]

Unemployment = applications = ice cream; employability enters the metonymic daisy chain of desire powered by surplus *jouissance* anchored to the commodity form in an unending process of becoming employable regardless of whether we have a job. The commodity becomes the mirror double, here from the appropriately named Monster.com:

> When a company is determining how to advertise their products to consumers, they focus on its [*sic*] unique selling points – the things which make the product different from any other. It may be that it is smaller, lasts longer or tastes better than its competitors. The same principle applies to you when you are applying for a new job.[14]

In sum, employability decentres employment, shifting the signifier from the actual job to a phantom job that has no material location in the economy, does not exploit us in a Marxist sense nor demand anything from us. In and out of the accumulative circuit, the subject's libido is oriented to the creation of value that capital may or may not want. The phantom job stands in for the capitalist laws of motion: it is no longer a particular capitalist that exploits us, but rather the more abstract and ephemeral Capital. It is a phantom that the student imagines as he or she develops the CV and chooses courses according to whether they provide the skills employers can make use of. Capital overcodes the spatial and temporal totality of life: in the job, at the dole office, at home, in leisure, retroactively signifying the past, now and for the foreseeable future: the void in capital is writ large at the job centre, with 'transferable' skills acting as the generic suture of the imponderables in each vacancy. The striving for further employability of those already employed guarantees that, if for no other reason, public sector workers will do the additional tasks required to ensure that, despite the cutbacks, hospitals, schools, bureaucracies and so on still function. Refusing such work or simply 'working to rule' by performing tasks according to the stated aims of the bureaucracy – police catching criminals rather than simply fixing the 'stats' (see Žižek, 2012: 95) – has to be weighed against the demands of the big Boss/big Other which haunt us when there are job cuts or if we desire another job or promotion. In becoming employable, one is simultaneously becoming unemployable, recognising that however successful we are it is never 'it', we are never employable enough and so must continually strive to fill the void of capital in order to avoid redundancy. The crises upon which capital innovates are thereby homologous to the crises of subjective stagnation that require us, especially the unemployed, to get out of bed and become what the Other wants.

Jouissance, according to Lacan (2007 [1969]), is 'despoiled' in surplus value, we literally invest libido in 'it'. The consequence of this, as already noted, is unemployment, anxiety and the further need to expend whatever energy is left in the service of capital. This self-circulating, spiralling, amplifying condition puts the labourer more fully at the mercy of the employability injunction. The more that is invested the greater is the lack, the closer we are to an abject void that inspires a more intensified and desperate attempt to draw a circle around it. At touching distance from disappearance, an ideological suture becomes all the more important in sustaining the subject in its phantasmal attachments to capital. Consumption, for sure, is one symptom of this need, a way of compensating for the loss incurred. Another is the idea that there will eventually be a payoff for all our efforts when capital finally recognises our worth by awarding us a (good) job. If not this one, then the next or the next – one day the *jouissance* taken from us will be returned. This metonymic process is unending, each new job erecting new obstacles and providing new incentives to keep moving, keep investing, keep despoiling. The promise of a return redolent in the rhetoric of employment is never fulfilled; the diner, as Adorno and Horkheimer pithily wrote, must be satisfied with the menu. *Jouissance* is not so much despoiled in the act of labour as it is in the labour process, whether abstractly as exchange value or prior to a future employment as concrete use value that it is hoped can be realised through exchange.

Fantasy operates at two levels, first in the ideological orientation of the subject to a future boss and second in the orientation to the life seen to exist outside the labour relation where, to be sure, the subject's personal knowledge, connections and affects are developed and eventually mined. The CV retroactively instrumentalises activities that were not at the time interpreted as having any instrumental value. Careers guidance and the teaching of students from a young age about the value of their education and 'extra-curricular' activities, presenting the action, behaviours and attitudes of others as a measure of the competition we have to beat, engender an awareness hitherto absent from consciousness of what must be done.

A cage in which all of labour is trapped, the iron clad certainty that a failure to instrumentalise life will result in personal failure and social exclusion is shrouded by the veneer of self-determination over life chances and by the payoffs that come to those who 'make the most' of their opportunities, however limited they are. The trap becomes a freedom that Baudrillard nicely explains when he writes:

> The 'liberated' man becomes fully responsible for the objective conditions of his existence. This is, to say the least, an ambiguous destiny. In this way, the 'liberated' worker, for example, falls prey to the objective conditions of the labour market. (2001: 51)

But Weber already understood this when he said that 'The Puritan wanted to work in a calling; we are forced to do so' (2003 [1904–5]: 181). Contrary to Bauman's narrative, the 'work ethic', while disavowed by some, is sustained by our own apparent determinations to improve our CVs. We may not regard ourselves beholden to a work ethic but it is an ethic nonetheless that conditions our every waking and sleeping hour. The centrality of work to our lives is ideologically displaced in both time and space. Temporally, workers 'disidentify' from their labour through activities that (are seen to) enhance future employment; spatially they disidentify through an exaggerated sense of there being an outside to labour, the spaces of seemingly free association and pleasure. In this way, the actual labour abstracted as exchange value, however onerous, is displaced through an ideological orientation to, and investment in, future employment, through activities seen as enhancing the prospects of a better job and the 'life outside work'. The Puritan took comfort in the *Bible*, the industrial proletariat in the *Manifesto*, the individuated subject of our time in the *CV*. As Monster.com explains:

> Your CV is one of the most powerful weapons in your job-seeking armoury and is often the first point of contact with a potential boss, so it's vital to make this document as powerful as possible.
>
> ...the key to developing a knock-out CV lies in actively seeking opportunities to broaden your appeal and demonstrate why employers should consider you over other candidates. In a competitive job market it's those job seekers who invest the most in their personal development who will reap the rewards.[15]

The separation of identity from immediate labour, particularly the sense that the present condition (whatever that may be for the subject) can be overcome through individual enterprise, endeavour or even good fortune, undermines the investment the worker may otherwise have in the firm and thereby any desire to act collectively to improve conditions therein. The contrast to industrial labour at the height of trade union power is stark. At the risk of sounding nostalgic, attacks on working conditions were met head on by a labour force in battle as if everything depended on victory. The miners' strike of 1984–85 is exemplary of this. Today's student occupations, often short-lived and only partially supported, take place against a background that eventually quells dissent. Today we occupy public spaces, tomorrow we work on our CVs: a sobering reminder that refusal is only ever partial.

What then, in this crisis era, do employers want? Apart, that is, from low cost contract or 'zero-contract' labour? According to Leo Benedictus[16] – who provides statistical data from the 'search company' Adzuna and 'decodes' the meaning of words, both of which his *Guardian* readership is likely to be appreciative of – the 'Top 10 things employers are looking for' are: organisation; communication skills; motivation; qualifications; flexibility; a degree; commitment; passion; a verifiable track record; and innovation.

Without the resources of a business, I conducted a similar analysis some years ago of job advertisements in situation-vacant columns. As if to prove how pointless the research of lonely scholars has become, Adzuna is able to discern from a much larger sample of over 500,000 ads that 'organised', mentioned in 99,862 of them (average salary £ 34,479), is the most frequently cited term. Having translated the word, Benedictus suggests emphasising on your CV 'that you're used to working hard – and showing enthusiasm for it if you're called for interview'. Similarly to other sources of advice, the author is neither duped nor duping: he acts in good faith on the basis that such information will genuinely help someone secure a job. But this advice is given in a context in which job opportunities are becoming increasingly scarce and the quality of jobs is deteriorating. Such advice becomes more prevalent, detailed and, it can be inferred, reflective of the needs and anxieties of the labour force. Our interests may not be served by the atrophying of labour but our investments in the labour market intensify and, in this productive spiral of dissatisfaction, without the political means to do anything about it, it is in our interests to follow such advice as best we can.

Whether or not they are in paid employment, individuals reflect on their worth and dredge from a reservoir of images a body that can be exploited. The subject exploits an idea of a past self – a dead labour congealed in a narrative about its present capacities and future potentials – by anticipating the value of projects and activities for capital. In thinking of the process of becoming employable as one of reflexive exploitation rather than biopower/ political production, class returns to the centre of analysis as a collective body that must be exploited by capital and whose exploitability depends on it exploiting itself by mining its past for achievements in order to become exploitable in a strictly Marxist sense – in other words, and for those who have watched too much American TV, to become capital's 'bitch'.

Shifting the register to Deleuze and Guattari, here purified of the postmodern interpretations favoured by some, the already alienated subject identifies itself as an assemblage of discrete objects-cum-traits or singularities in proximity to and forming part of the abstract machine of capital. Whatever morsels can be taken are cannibalised in the vernacular of employability that, through assessment, evaluation and (numerical) translation, makes the subject dividual. Employability is a molecular journey entering different zones of proximity with organic and non-organic objects: with people and machines, networks and teams, the Twitter app and Apple Mac. Different affects, skills, abilities and attitudes of increasing and decreasing intensities, poise and passion are required: leader-machine, motivator-machine, enthusiast-machine – tick, tick, bang, the molecular changes are subtle and never so fluid that the molar identity and narrative becomes liquid. Lines of flight are dangerous. The novelties they engender give Apples their shine; but for every investment in novelty there are graveyards of investors – and their useless machines! Lines of flight take us on migratory and career-changing journeys into black holes of unemployment. By contrast, molarity is a stabilising force, a familial semblance of an image that reassures and authenticates the changes in subjectivity as being consistent with others, the big Boss. As number cruncher, Capital does not want a dividual as such, it wants a human that can be quantified and validated from job references. Watch for the micro-Fascist within, say Deleuze and Guattari: watch that the process of becoming employable and the crumbs that fall from the capitalist's plate are not enjoyed so much that you begin to imagine everything would be all right if only others had the same opportunities as you have.

Employability, then, is a master signifier that holds minor signifiers together, defining, in highly porous ways, what it means to employable. The command *be employable* is directed at everyone and interpreted according to the role in the division of labour the worker wants to occupy. It is enacted without exception by everyone who is invested in capital as labourer or potential labourer. To not be invested is to be excluded. Žižek's claim that ideology is operationalised in action rather than in thinking is relevant here. Whatever we think of the process or even the performance, still we do it or risk becoming unemployed and eventually unemployable. Reflexive exploitation is prior to, and in the time of, material exploitation, with the paid worker being exploited twice over: first in their desire to overcome alienation by being the equivalent of what capital lacks and, second, in the actuality of being exploited by capital.

Past efforts and adaptations are the dead flesh hanging from a not-yet-dead body, alive enough to motion towards an already dead future. Can the career be sacrificed? Can the injunction be refused? Is there any line of flight capable of escaping the bind without getting sucked into another black hole of unemployment? We return to these questions in Chapter 7, when considering the different parts and interlocking spirals explored in the book that constitute an abysmal and apocalyptic totality. On which note, it is time to journey on and down under, to examine the spiral in opposing motion: from the perspective of consumption.

5

Consumption Spiral

The city of Auckland is situated on a narrow isthmus between two harbours and on a volcanic field that has shaped its topography via 50 or so eruptions, the last of which was around 500–600 years ago. Ravaged by commerce, beautified by magma, vulnerable to international finance, volcanic eruptions and tsunamis, the stunning natural vistas cannot disguise the ugliness that has resulted from colonisation and Aotearoa's own virulent brand of neoliberalism. If Auckland were to symbolise the conquest of nature by humanity we would have to conclude that, as with the colonisation of humanity by humanity, the legacy is a tragic one, and perhaps, in view of this, we would welcome an eruption to level the Central Business District that dominates the skyline. At the bottom of the CBD slope is the quayside where, throughout the course of the long summer, cruise ships dock. From a distance one can see that they are greater in size and almost in height than even the tallest financial towers. They float alienated from the city on which they moor. They are monstrous reminders of what our desires have given birth to and now find refuge in. As passengers, today we travel between cities colonised by Westfield shopping malls and surf Amazon.com in an attempt to remedy the collective nausea that commerce has engineered. This chapter considers the spiralling dissatisfactions at the centre of our consumerist relation to capital.

For Walter Benjamin (2003 [1927–40]) the Parisian arcades of the nineteenth century were places of wonderment in which a wandering *flâneur* could find refuge from the rain. The tableaux artfully arranged in the shop windows displayed a wealth of human creation that, as Benjamin knew, came at the price of human misery. These utopias in miniature were at best a hint of the abundance that might one day be enjoyed by all. The conspicuous consumption by which the affluent classes defined themselves became in time a seductive force that pacified the masses. Two great wars and the scientific management techniques of Taylorism that improved the flow and efficiency of industrial production, famously adopted by Henry Ford and also the Soviets, paved the way for the so-called consumer society we know today and on which it appears we merrily sail.

During fits of nostalgia, I remember the fine arcade in the centre of Sutton, South London, that I visited as a child. I was not surprised to discover, when visiting the town some 20 years later, that in its place was a shopping mall as generic as the rest of Sutton had become. Shopping malls have replaced arcades in many towns and cities. Georg Ritzer (2005) calls them Cathedrals of Consumption where the commodity is the Cross to which the consumer is nailed. God is Capital. Extending the analogy further, the culture and entertainment industries, backed by the IMF and military force, are the missionaries preaching consumption, and their advertising, movies, pop music, celebrity gossip and news trivia are the religious pamphlets.

Consumer goods, said Adorno and Horkheimer (1997 [1947]: 154), are like mass-produced Yale locks, the difference between them 'measured in fractions of millimetres'. By identifying with these miniscule differences, people become pseudo-individuals divested of any substantive individuality. The analogy remains apt. The commodity exemplifies a kind of individualism, that of a disconnected, atomised, thing-like person who discovers in products their own sense of self and even their superiority to others. The fetishised commodity entices the senses. They are beacons that guide us through perilous journeys in identity formation, sirens that draw us onto the jagged rocks of dissatisfaction against which society is shipwrecked.

This chapter begins with an examination of the alienation of pleasure in consumption before redefining the culture industry in view of the expanded role of the consumer in adapting products using virtual tools.

Libidinal Sponges

In 2001 President George W. Bush said 'Get out there and shop. It's the American way.'[1] In 2011 Barack Obama called instead for a 'shared sacrifice',[2] here speaking to the rich but also by implication the rest of us. Australia's answer to the 2008 global depression resonates more closely with Bush's call up to the reserve army of shoppers. Kevin Rudd's Labour Party administration supplemented Bush's injunction with monetary aid by giving every citizen a one-off cash payment costing AUS$10 billion, or 1 per cent of annual GDP, the catch being that it had to be spent.[3] The capitalist consumes to accumulate, and the worker to satisfy needs and desires.

Commodities give meaning to life. They provide an anchor for subjectivity. They are objects around which people socialise. Commodities become us. Needs and desires were long ago scrambled. The conquistadors pursued their desire for gold to the point of bringing about a civilisation's end. But only in our time has desire, whether for bread or gold, become so universally bankrupting. This is not because we have desires in excess of need and have failed to regulate them according to means or ethics. There is nowhere else to go except the shopping mall where commodities are bought and eventually consumed, putting desire in an ineluctable relationship with universal abasement and destruction. Adorno nicely explained the finer points of consumption:

> In his purposeless activity the child, by a subterfuge, sides with use-value against exchange value. Just because he deprives the things with which he plays of their mediated usefulness, he seeks to rescue in them what is benign towards men and things. The little trucks travel nowhere and the tiny barrels on them are empty; yet they remain true to their destiny by not performing, not participating in the process of abstraction that levels down that destiny, but instead abides as allegories of what they are specifically for ... The unreality of games gives notice that reality is not yet real. (2000 [1951]: 228)

There is a dialectical tension between pleasure and consumption. On the one hand, consumption is joyous, playful, even celebratory of life; and on the other, it is a spiral of dissatisfaction, the liquidation of use value by fetishised relations of exchange, ending with apocalypse. Advertisers help us to recognise a use in things, things we become dependent on because they help alleviate feelings of anxiety and alienation. Pleasure is embodied in them. Consumer products can be thought of as libidinal sponges for whatever energy is remaining to us after the exhaustive labours of producing surplus value, tending to the home and baby, and ensuring the CV is up to scratch. We can never consume enough because we are never employable enough. Alienation does not cause consumption, it simply fetishises it, creating an allure even among the most marginalised. This was much in evidence during the 2011 English riots, as one report explained: 'there is an almost total absence of an alternative culture with anything like the same allure that might reanimate political being and recruit it to the cause of social justice' (Treadwell et al., 2013: 8). Bauman has a point when he claims that:

> The age of cultural hegemony seems to have passed: cultures are meant to be enjoyed, not fought for. In our type of society, economic and political domination may well do without hegemony; it found the way of reproducing itself under conditions of cultural variety. (2004 [1991]: 274)

Consumption is a substitute for the breast, the first object, according to Freud, that appears to exist 'outside' of us and that presents itself after a heartfelt cry. Something lost and recovered, the object of pleasure shifts from the breast to the commodity, playing out trauma with each subsequent loss and recovery. Without loss there is no anticipation or excitation at the prospect of the thing's re-emergence: no fantasy, no *jouissance*, no need for libidinal sponges. From Mickey Mouse to Super Mario, Calvin Klein to Ted Baker, Sony Walkman to Apple iPad, capitalists through the mediations of the culture industry – advertising, cinema, magazines and websites and so on – compete with one another to provide the universal alternative to the breast. Adorno and Horkheimer, and later Marcuse, described much of this as a false need. As seasons change, eyes are on the latest fashions. The expression of differences through style is integral to the thing we call culture, a basic source of pleasure and means by which to gain a sense of belonging. This differs from an ego that sheds clothes to keep up with rapidly changing fashions. Like homeopathic remedies clinically proven to have no health benefits whatsoever, their value is aligned to subjective feelings and in turn brute monetary exchange. But is there such a thing as a false need when through a lifetime of exposure to the culture industry even the most superficial of pleasures have deep associations? The urban dweller can no more do without a stylish coat than a cave dweller could do without the warmth of an animal skin. There is no false need that has not already become essential to a sense of who we are. Rather than deny or call for the repression of desire, the challenge is for desire to turn not against the capitalist form of consumption as such but rather against the underlying conditions that have made consumption what it is. As Raoul Vaneigem put it, 'There will be no proletarian emancipation unless we strike the shackles off pleasure' (1979: 11). This also means, I shall argue, removing the shackles of the 'average consumer's' guilty association with ecological degradation and global poverty.

> In the end, there will be little else for us to do but shop. The world in which we were trapped is in fact a shopping mall; the windless closure is the underground network of tunnels hollowed out for the display of images. The virus ascribed to junkspace is in fact the virus of shopping itself; which, like Disneyfication, gradually spreads like a toxic moss across the known universe. (Sze Tsung Leong quoted in Jameson, 2003: 77)

We need to be clear. What is understood by pleasure and encountered in late capitalism as pleasurable is no measure of the kind of sensations that a society liberated from the commodity form would enable. The pleasure from consumption is timeless: the pleasure from fetishised commodities mediated by exchange value is not. The inattentiveness of the average consumer, so quick to judgement and dismissive of anything not immediately satisfying or unusual to experience, and their 'personal opinion', predicated on whether something is 'entertaining' or not, all this results from, or at least is generalised under, current forms of cultural production.

Alienation as Consumer

> I have often noticed that we are inclined to endow our friends with the stability of type that literary characters acquire in the reader's mind. No matter how many times we reopen 'King Lear', never shall we find the good king banging his tankard in high revelry, all woes forgotten, at a jolly reunion with all three daughters and their lapdogs. Never will Emma rally, revived by the sympathetic salts in Flaubert's father's timely tear. Whatever evolution this or that popular character has gone through between the book covers, his fate is fixed in our minds, and, similarly, we expect our friends to follow this or that logical and conventional pattern we have fixed for them. Thus X will never compose the immortal music that would clash with the second rate symphonies he has accustomed us to. Y will never commit murder. Under no circumstances can Z ever betray us. We have it all arranged in our minds, and the less often we see

a particular person the more satisfying it is to check how obediently he conforms to our notion of him every time we hear of him. Any deviation in the fates we have ordained would strike us as not only anomalous but unethical. We would prefer not to have known at all our neighbour, the retired hot-dog stand operator, if it turns out he has just produced the greatest book of poetry his age has seen.

Vladimir Nabokov (2006 [1955]: 302)

The narcissist's regular postings of flattering selfies on Facebook are framed by locations that shout fun, each confirming that, despite evidence to the contrary, life as experienced is one of uninterrupted success and joy. Like the ectoplasm of a phantom, those that drift onto the friend list present variations on the theme. The uniqueness of their character likewise demonstrated by the self-same digitised snap-shots. They are so generic that the experience they represent could be exchanged without the slightest narrative impact on either individual. The principal advantage that digital media has over the physical unmediated encounter is that those who deviate from the norm can at least be exorcised by the click of a mouse button without there being social or legal consequences.

We want familiarity, predictability, with just enough of something 'new' to excite us. Capital trades on this, which is why brand names are so important to us. We want to feel secure about other people's desires, that we 'get them', and that, by valuing our choice of style, they get us. When new products come to market we seek assurance from review sites and friends before making an investment. The heteroglossia of different opinions, ideas and desires is stabilised by the monoglossia of a single accent of a marketable good to which production and the self are aligned. Commodities today have become more 'niche' oriented and by the same token more compelling ego substitutes. The subject itself, where not entirely average, becomes a niche equivalent of the vegetarian meat substitutes displayed in the freezer cabinet at Tesco.

From the beginning of time until the end, people will produce and consume, but whereas an end to work is often seen as liberating, an end to consumption is death. In other words, work is socially necessary at all times and consumption is individually necessary at all times. It is easier therefore to be persuaded of the timeless value of consumption than of work. The concept of commodity fetishism elucidates the dual relation between and inversion of work and consumption, sensuous activity stripped from us and emblazoned on the object. Dispossession originates in labour but consumption too originates its own distinctive and relational alienation.

First, the object of desire is an object opposed to us. While the possible sources of pleasure have multiplied under capitalism, the means and satisfactions they enable are highly circumscribed. The consumer is alienated from needs that are mediated by the broader social conditions – to be admired, to be understood – and which are impossible to satisfy with commodities. Desires are frustrated and cause frustration, dramatically during the 2011 English riots, and repeatedly in the (sometimes lethal) aggression of consumers at sales time.

Second, the high price of commodities alienates us from social activities that involve consumption. Participation itself is curtailed and the consumer is alienated from the society of others. When financial restrictions mean we have to see fewer friends than we would like – because we have to decide between a round at the pub, *or* the cinema tickets, *or* entertaining at home (more expensive than dining alone: not only does one have to provide more food, but it cannot just be one's usual baked beans, in order to save face and prove one's power of consumption) – then our lives as social beings are not fully realised.

Third, we are alienated from our political rights and social spaces by the colonisation of the urban environment by shopping malls and such like. Privately owned streets do not allow protests. 'Loitering' teenagers enjoying each other's company – but, transgression of transgressions, *not shopping* – are moved on from malls by security guards. Skateboarders are derailed by the joy-depriving spikes on concrete edges in sterilised urban spaces.

Fourth, we are alienated from consumption as a social activity. Consumption becomes instead an activity we engage in independent from others. Other consumers are time-wasting obstacles we have to avoid as we make our way around the store and decide which checkout to queue up at. Worse, other consumers could get to the last bargain item before us; the first circle of hell is a pre-Christmas mall. Shop assistants are no better than our 'fellow' consumers: pushy, or slow, they have an uncanny ability to 'disappear' at exactly the moment one wants directions to the appliances aisle. We no longer have a human relationship with our friendly grocer, who lives in the same street as we do – instead, we automate ourselves in order to form a transaction assemblage with supermarket self-service kiosks or with chain store servers, who are not people either, but underpaid, have-a-nice-day automatons. In this globalised world – where every high street looks the same, and where our sense of unique space disappears when leaving our front door – it is better to stay at home, and make our impulse purchases the way we buy our porn: privately, deniably, at once furtively and in the only space in which we are still recognised as persons. Even as we seek confirmation of our choices from friends and websites, our desires and the choices we make appear as our own rather than socially determined, begetting the individualism decried by cultural theorists.

Fifth, we are alienated from the idea of consumption as a species activity. Every living organism consumes but only humans take a moral stance towards consumption, learning to feel ashamed about their own desires and calling upon others to repress theirs. This is exemplified by religious asceticism, economic thrift and, specific to capitalism, markets for products said to be kind to people and nature. While it is important that we do reflect on the destructive impact of capitalist consumption and seek ways to transform our socially mediated needs and desires, this can only happen through a transformation of production. 'Green' choices and certificates of socially responsible supply chains only mask the symptoms, they do not deal to the cause, or even the destruction itself: they are simply another (unaffordable) option, not the blanket substitute. It is capitalism, as such, that generates a more universal feeling of shame for its own purposes and alienates the subject from desire as an object opposed to itself and humanity. When human desire appears to be the fundamental cause of environmental degradation, it is not the creative capacity of the 'species' as such that we are alienated from but rather the species itself.

Sixth, we are alienated from others who consume. The pleasures of others come to be resented or held up as an ideal on which to model our lives: rivals and role models, competitors and ideal-types, people to envy, undermine and cosy up to. Exemplars include celebrities at one end of the scale, resented and idealised, and immigrants and welfare recipients at the other – only resented.

Capitalism expands the realm of pleasure at the same time that it expands the realm of scarcity, denying the senses while also seducing them. Having deprived us of our activity, not without irony does consumption promise deliverance from the alienation of its own making.

If, then, what the consumer desires is 'excessive', it is only as a measure of what the reality principle imposes, in other words of what we can afford. Bataille was correct to observe that when desire has no effective outlet, the outcome is catastrophe. In today's capitalist society, work and consumption, for the reasons already made clear, are not 'effective' outlets.

A Crisis of Consumption

Here is a question: *Does a crisis of consumption mean there is a crisis of subjectivity?*

To recall, in the early part of the 1960s, Marcuse described what he called the 'happy consciousness': a person comforted by the availability of mass consumer goods, and satisfied with the system as it is and with their place in it. The pleasure principle, he said, is absorbed by the reality principle, though the outlook appeared to have changed by the early 1970s when he wrote, 'The rising standard of living ... enforced the constant creation of needs that could be satisfied on the market; it is now fostering *transcending* needs which cannot be satisfied without abolishing the capitalist mode of production' (1970: 16). Marcuse speculated that the consumer would become capitalism's gravedigger. What we now know is that in desperate times people are more likely to crave iProducts than organise for social revolution. In the 1960s expectations were on the rise and in more recent years they have been cultivated to fall. The superego law of diminishing expectations interpellates the subject to want more but expect less and disavow the shoddy consequences of material deprivation through wild fantasies and grandiose beliefs, a heady brew of apocalypse, narcissism and celebrity. A crisis of subjectivity can be delayed indefinitely as long as the real conditions of existence and their likely consequences are disavowed rather than confronted. As lifestyles to which people are accustomed become harder to maintain, dissatisfaction intensifies and in turn, the urge to overcome this dissatisfaction becomes irresistible, and we attempt to do so in the workplace and shopping mall in increasingly atomised ways.

As noted, the reproductive cost of labour relates to the amount of wages required to meet expectations and as a measure of what we are prepared to work for. For example, an immigrant without citizenship may contribute the same amount of value to the firm as a legal worker but, due to her status, she is prepared to do the job for a lot less money thereby producing more surplus value. The reproductive value of her labour, what it costs capital to employ her, is therefore lower and the surplus value higher. The immigrant gets what in market terms they are 'worth'.

Tracking surveys of changes in the price of commonly purchased goods provide some indication of where our money goes, how far it stretches and how, in time, our expectations are altered to match new realities. The 'shopping basket' of goods for one class is of course very different to that of another. Were it not for the trivial cost of such fripperies, the superrich would likely feel a little anxious after reading Forbes Cost of Living Extremely Well Index and learning that the price of Russian Sable Fur coats is skyrocketing, although likely relieved to learn that a strengthening dollar has made dinner at La Tour d'Argent in Paris more affordable.[4] Exchange value is not strictly correlative to price; a weak euro, for example, can mean that goods are cheaper in Paris than they would be at home for the sterling-carrying tourist. Fluctuating exchange rates can bring the cost of living down as wages stagnate and consumption rises. For many, the opposite has pertained, not least because of the rising cost of housing and rental fees to landlords. As the charity Shelter reports, the average family in Britain today spends 59 per cent of its income on rent.[5] As wages fail to keep up with living costs, people feel increasingly 'squeezed', a perception that in some cases reflects reality but in all cases underlines the shift in consumer consciousness towards a more diminished sense of expectation.

The remainder of this chapter examines how the ideology and practice of consumption has adapted with changes in technology and with knowledge of the effects it has on people and the natural environment.

Biopolitical Culture Industry

Like Marx himself, critical theorists who have synthesised and developed his ideas make claims about culture and society that are specific to a particular time and space and are not therefore assumed to be fixed and unchanging. The culture industry thesis is not rendered irrelevant because of new technology or diversified consumption and subjective savvy. Like all dialectically and empirically informed propositions, the thesis must periodically be adapted to reflect change and remain relevant. For this reason Adorno is not the final word on a phenomenon he helped coin.

The 'culture industry' denotes a mass-production style approach to cultural production in which the aesthetic sphere as an object of exchange becomes a commoditised lubricant to help smooth the flow of capital. Profits are maximised by standardising music, films, any cultural artefact whatsoever, to a specification that plays to the largest audiences whose anxieties are eased through purchases that because of their popularity others are likely to approve. The parts making up the cultural artefact become inconsequential to the whole. Like the experiences of those on the friend list, each element of a song or blockbuster movie is substitutable. No translation is required, and so the audience now familiar with the product does not have to think, requires no perspective or in-depth knowledge: pleasure is desublimated and shallow. Through advertising, movies and so on, associations are manufactured between commodities and a subject's personal feelings. A beauty product will smooth over blemishes masked by doctored images of stars, and IKEA furniture will turn homes into havens evoking the aesthetic of home improvement shows; in short, deficiencies we were hitherto unaware of are brought to light and remedied through the purchase of commodities that embody ideals, the secret of their success. The message of the culture industry is disseminated through global media expanding the market for goods that necessarily become more standardised thus engendering a more globally homogeneous subject and culture. A fun aesthetic comes to predominate. Fun enters the political sphere and becomes a social obligation. Through the ideology it promulgates, the culture industry negates the possibility of alternatives to the current system. The political universe is closed.

New communication technologies enable people to bypass cultural monopolies by disseminating their own messages online and fashioning commodities to their specific tastes. This is one of the principal changes since Adorno wrote *Culture Industry Reconsidered* in the 1960s and in regard to which the culture industry is described as *biopolitical*. This concept, introduced in the previous chapter, was coined by Foucault and adapted by Hardt and Negri, who suggest:

Our reading not only identifies biopolitics with the localised productive powers of life – that is, the production of affects and languages through social cooperation and the interaction of bodies and desires, the invention of new forms of the relation to the self and others, and so forth – but also affirms biopolitics as the creation of new subjectivities that are presented at once as resistance and de-subjectification. (2009: 58)

Under the auspices of neoliberal administration, the subject produces for him or herself a body, language and affects aligned to the demands of capital. It is a subject, as Deleuze and Guattari explain, whose affects are excessive to capital but that can also be captured in order that the machine functions. These affects translate into bodily (and extra-bodily) creations that, as Hardt and Negri note, can also be deployed to resist capital and even de-subjectivise what capital has made us. The subject, it will be claimed here, appropriates the techniques and ideologies utilised for and embodied in the culture industry aesthetic to produce what amounts to the same or even inferior. In other words, the subject produces for him or herself artefacts utilising the same culture industry standards that are in their form and substance more or less identical. The culture industry is internalised and reproduced by the subject, principally though not exclusively using digital media. As in the case of digital media and, it should be noted, most if not all other media forms, what the subject creates can also be utilised to negate (the ideology of) late capitalism. The claim that the culture industry is biopolitical will be demonstrated through examples.

We cannot be forced to desire something. No administration or culture industry is so totalising that agency is rendered impossible. As Foucault, quoted by Hardt and Negri, said, 'Power is exercised over free subjects, and only insofar as they are free … At the very heart of the power relationship, and constantly provoking it, are the recalcitrance of the will and the intransigence of freedom' (2009: 59). Foucault's point that power can only operate where it can be contested, or Gramsci's point that hegemonic powers rely for their legitimation on evidence that people can freely dissent, are essential to the success of cultural production in evoking choice, manipulating desire and disguising the power of media industries in shaping it. Without this there would be no tangible means by which the subject could assert its individuality or for the ideology of individualism to flourish. A passage in Adorno's *Culture Industry Reconsidered* essay is worth quoting at length:

The two-faced irony in the relationship of servile intellectuals to the culture industry is not restricted to them alone. It may also be supposed that the consciousness of the consumers themselves is split between the prescribed fun which is supplied to them by the culture industry and a not particularly well-hidden doubt about its blessings. The phrase 'the world wants to be deceived' has become truer than had ever been intended. People are not only, as the saying goes, falling for the swindle; if it guarantees them even the most fleeting gratification they desire a deception which is nonetheless transparent to them. They force their eyes shut and voice approval, in a kind of self-loathing, for what is meted out to them, knowing fully the purpose for which it is manufactured. Without admitting it they sense that their lives would be completely intolerable as soon as they no longer clung to satisfactions which are none at all. (2001 [1963]: 112)

The popularity of formulaic productions that millions line up for at corporate-owned multiplexes tells us nothing about what people think about them. If anything, patrons are likely to be in on the joke, by recognising the throwaway quality of the corny dialogue and predictable outcomes, though nevertheless enjoying the work as light harmless entertainment. Taxed enough by the travails of everyday life, most people do not want to be tested by the more challenging productions of cinematic auteurs. Even the most inattentive can recognise that what they are being entertained by is the product of a process that mimics the standardising techniques of industry. Without the alibi that the culture industry manufactures, an alibi confirming the punter's own canny awareness, the humour would be lost, the fun rendered obscene. Life, after all, is far too serious to be taken seriously. Rather than dismiss the culture industry thesis on the basis that our engagement with media has changed or that Adorno perhaps overstated its impact, it is more useful on the basis that it still has explanatory value in exploring how the culture industry has evolved, become more extensive and in certain respects more intense.

Telemorphosis and the Hyper-Image

As earlier pointed out, Adorno and Horkheimer (1997 [1947]) warned that with advances in technology the difference between cinema and reality would become increasingly hard to discern. The term telepresence has been used in video game analysis to denote the phenomenon of fictional worlds becoming so immersive that they feel real. This is not so much an imagined relationship to virtual worlds as, along Deleuzian lines, an affective one. The process can be defined as one of telemorphosis: a symbolic order of mediated signs to which the imaginary is oriented is felt to be real, and so the (conscious) separation of external representations from the inner psyche dissolves. An example already discussed is that of the hyper-image, the conflation of cine-correspondent and cine-observer. Telemorphosis is a more general term for the process by which mediated relationships to cultural artefacts increasingly appear unmediated and thereby authentic to self. It signifies a culture industry so embedded in contemporary life that it is no longer recognisable as an external or ideological phenomenon. Rather it is internalised. The procedures, forms and contents that for Adorno and Horkheimer defined the culture industry are re-animated in the subject's own seemingly independent creations and, we could add, pseudo-ironic detachments. Streeck writes,

> The vast variety of alternative possibilities of consumption in affluent post-Fordist markets provides a mechanism that allows people to conceive of an act of purchase – concluding, as it often does, a lengthy period of introspective exploration of one's very personal preferences – as an act of self-identification and self-presentation, one that sets the individual apart from some social groups while uniting him or her with others...
>
> Sociation by consumption, then, is monological rather than dialogical in nature, voluntary rather than obligatory, individual rather than collective. (2012: 35)

New technologies enable the subject to bring about changes in mass-produced artefacts, say by 'mashing up' and doctoring images or by assembling content into media forms such as Facebook or personalising products by downloading tunes and Apps. The techniques can be deployed without the need for specialist knowledge or training; using them is 'child's play' as any parent who marvels at their young prodigy's new media wizardry can testify. Has authorship transferred over to the masses? Are these new forms of cultural production suggestive of potentialities for non-alienated labour and identity formulations that are heteroglossic, thereby escaping the monoglossia or homogenising effects of culture monopolies? In short, has culture in late capitalism returned to the commons, have we gained authorship of the montage and is the subject thereby becoming substantial again – desubjectivising by refusing identity think – or has the culture industry entered a 'late', more sophisticated phase of mass deception?

Prosumers of the World, Unite!

The unity of an object is realized for us only by projecting our self into the object in order to shape it according to our image, so that the diversity of determinations grows into the unity of the 'ego'. In the same manner, the unity or lack of unity of the object that we create affects, in a psychological-practical sense, the corresponding formation of our personality. Whenever our energies do not produce something whole as a reflection of the total personality, then the proper relationship between subject and object is missing. The internal nature of our achievement is bound up with parts of achievements accomplished by others which are a necessary part of the totality, but it does not refer back to the producer. As a result, the inadequacy that develops between the worker's existential form and that of his product because of greater specialization easily serves to completely divorce the product from the labourer.

Georg Simmel (2004 [1900]: 459)

The culture industry is biopolitical. The subject produces for him or herself a commodity-like thing that is both a simulacrum (of a hegemonic representation) of an ideal-type, a neoliberal subject and culture industry artefact, and, by degrees, exceeds such representations, gifting commerce new opportunities to capture affects and congeal them in products to appeal to emergent tastes and dispositions. In short, the subject provides the fine-tuning to enable the production of culturally differentiated commodities that speak more directly to every conceivable personal nuance.

Advances in technology have given rise to media forms that enable *personal* refinements, hitherto the task of industry. Commodities now are often shells for adding substance. There is little substantial difference between a Samsung Galaxy and an iPhone or one iteration of an iPad and another; the difference lies in what is done with them, the apps downloaded, the photographs inserted and so forth. The consumer does the job of pseudo-individualisation. Like IKEA furniture, culture is bought unassembled and put together – administered – to plan, the process itself is an isolated one. Commerce provides the full package. It provides the tools and instructions for manipulating the object in order that it better bears the ego. It is a culture industry transposed into the home in which, as with pop culture facsimile, the tools for creation require little in the way of skill, knowledge or dedication to understand and utilise them. These pick up and play mechanics ensure that everyone, in the midst of societies of control, with means to purchase the utility, can become re-animated by their sense of autonomy over the creative process. Whereas the subject was deceived by the culture industry into believing that complex art could be appreciated without any prior knowledge or effort, the subject here is deceived into believing that art can be produced without expertise, or else, and this also holds for the 'educated', that what is created, whether an image, movie clip, pop jingo or blog, is intrinsically of the same value as, and for the narcissist better than, anything else.

The typical refrain today is that, due in large part to technology, we are no longer consumers but rather 'prosumers' – individuals whose actions *produce* surplus value for the capitalists we buy from, as we *consume*. But, as with many terms coined by cultural theorists, both the term and the theory it represents require interrogation. Consumption has always involved activity; things are rarely simply used up. Onions, courgettes, tomatoes and garlic are not idly taken from the cupboard and eaten. The labour that women typically add creates meals deemed useful or desirable to a hungry family. Lego bricks are not bought to scatter on the carpet. Their enduring appeal is in what Josh and Carla can do with them. Through productive activity, the consumer adds form and substance, the consumer consumes by creating. If this was all that being a 'prosumer' entailed then by such a definition humans from the beginning of time have been prosumers.

Consumption is not simply passive, but is often an act of creation, or, ineluctably attuned to capital, co-creation, with the work ethic transposed onto what appears to have no instrumental purpose or relation to the economy. What theories of prosumption misguidedly claim is that our unpaid creations are now leached by capital for the production of surplus value. This, to qualify, is not simply in the sense that creations can be turned into products, but also that acts of creation bypass the wage relation altogether and, seemingly without a labour force to turn them into commodities, directly produce surplus value. Imagining he found his feet and did the footwork himself, it would be the equivalent of a capitalist knocking on Josh's door to collect the little Lego bridges, cars and houses he has made in order to sell them for profit. Something purchased from capital is made use of. Regardless though of how that use indirectly enables business to develop new products, the activity is not one of exploitation as it would be for a paid employee whose labour is abstracted and thereby alienated from them. If, for example, packing our own shopping bags at the supermarket were to constitute alienated labour then the term would be so broad as to have no explanatory value. Moreover, if such activities 'produce' surplus value, then it would have to be claimed that all 'labour' irrespective of any paid relation is abstracted in Marx's sense. It is worth recalling here a criticism Marx once made of economists:

> Labour as mere performance of services for the satisfaction of immediate needs has nothing whatever to do with capital, since that is not capital's concern … the modern economists have turned themselves into such sycophants of the bourgeois that they want to demonstrate to the latter that it is productive labour when somebody picks the lice out of his hair, or strokes his tail, because for example the latter activity will make his fat head – blockhead – clearer the next day in the office. (1973 [1858]: 272–3)

Playing on this, one might suggest that if my blowing my nose in public suggests to a wandering entrepreneur that there is a market for nasal spray, then we are engaged in an act of 'co-creation' involving a labour that is freely exploited and *directly* produces surplus value. In other words, I 'consume' the tissue into which I blow my noise and 'produce' snot (exchange value) that provides capital with 'information' embodied in the nasal spray. Miraculously, the labour force employed to design, manufacture and market the nasal spray, a nasal app, is somehow bypassed, as if snot alone can be sold directly to market, perhaps into the face of a willing dupe. Blocked nose, blockhead, we are being exploited simply by reacting to this foul air. It is no wonder that unemployment levels are so high.

With this rather distasteful image in mind, let us examine specific prosumer examples: the self-scanning of products by consumers at supermarkets and the disposal of happy meals by properly socialised children at McDonalds (cf. Ritzer and Jurgenson, 2010). These 'new' actions by consumers *may* reduce the need for labour but they do not produce surplus value. No value is added by the consumer, as there is no additional profit to be made either by scanning an item or by disposing of waste. A self-scanner's 'concrete' labour would only be 'abstracted' if the customer paid for the opportunity to self-scan, or more precisely if the customer-scanned product was not bought but returned to the supermarket shelf and then sold at a higher price because value was added. The fundamental problem with the prosumer claim is that while there is concrete labour involved in scanning the items before paying for them it is not *abstracted* by capital. Self-scanning consumers cannot go on strike, they can only take their business elsewhere. Perhaps it is because we are habituated to the checkout operator that this example appears as evidence of exploitation. A child that, for example, puts the remnants of a happy meal in the bin at McDonalds is no more producing surplus value than they would be by clearing away the mess after consuming it at home. Moreover, retailers are just as likely to employ workers to do things that consumers would in the past have done for themselves, such as packing groceries in supermarkets or gift-wrapping products before money is exchanged for them. Are we to suggest, then, that those who insist on packing their own groceries or, because the service is not available, wrap gifts at home are producing nothing but surplus value? Ritzer and Jurgenson, who also suggest that Marx neglected consumption in favour of a productivist logic, seem to think so:

> From the capitalist's point of view (especially in terms of low-skilled work), the only thing better than a low-paid worker is someone (the consumer as prosumer) who does the work for no pay at all. In Marxian terms, while the worker produces a great deal of surplus value, the consumer who 'works' produces nothing but surplus value. (2010: 26)

Readers can probably think of many activities they do from which capital can in such respects benefit. Perhaps, in view of my earlier description, the consumer is being indirectly exploited but to conflate this with surplus value or the equivalent of exploitation of paid labour is to confuse the process by which capital generates profit and render the relation, and thereby the notion of capitalism itself, meaningless.

For many, including Tapscott and Williams, who wrote the bestseller *Wikinomics* (2006), prosumption is now central to the economy and also of universal benefit. By such lights, we are no longer alienated – and yet our alienated labour is still required for us to afford such technologies, and those technologies themselves, whether hardware or software, are produced by alienated labour. Not only is there no fundamental change in the relationship between capital and labour, prosumer activities in such respects are still by and large marginal to capital.

While on the theme of prosumption, let us consider Facebook as an example before discussing social media in general. The site was recently floated on the stock exchange, the value of its shares affected by the number of users. Employees design and administer applications while consumers design and administer content. Without the latter's input Facebook would be worthless. Nevertheless, the user is not typically producing content in order to sell it on to other consumers nor is the content they produce directly translatable into profit. Much like a busy thoroughfare in which commerce is prohibited, Facebook, irrespective of the number of users, would be worthless if the means for generating profit, such as from advertising, were not available. Facebook is no autonomous machine. As the armies of 'knowledge' workers administering the site, sorting advertising deals and scanning for marketing opportunities on behalf of shareholders, will testify, there is a material economy behind the virtual veneer. While the consumer may well have the power, as Firat and Venkatesh suggest, 'to seduce and signify, create her/his own simulations to articulate his/her own visions of life' (1995: 260), they will require, as a potter requires a wheel and clay, the purchase and regular updating of hardware and software. As Edward Comor puts it, 'the prosumer's dependency on the corporations that own, design and run the essential infrastructures through which people work and consume leaves little room for genuinely autonomous development' (2010: 451).

In the final analysis, claims about the changes that prosumption have brought about are based on a narrow conception of Marx's labour theory of value, and a separation in thought of work and consumption which are specific and relational moments in the circuit of capital as Marx originally saw them.

The subject, according to Althusser, misrecognises itself as the addressee of ideology and thereby identifies its own subjectivity with the ideological state apparatus in which the idea is generated. My suggestion here is that we can discern how the subject imagines itself and is interpellated by a culture industry now embedded in the human psyche from the way people represent themselves with the camera and, more pertinently, from the ideals in the global media which 'selfies' are desperately trying to imitate. The subject is interpellated by the DIY procedures that new media in particular invite. The objects engendered by such procedures give rise to a craft consciousness, a consciousness of the capacity for creation without necessarily any recognition of the underlying forces and relations that both enable and give form to such creations. The culture industry is biopolitical in this, the aforementioned ways, and as follows.

Social Media and the Craft Consciousness

Operating like a time sponge that soaks from the mental reservoir whatever energy has not already been spent on labour, or is insufficient for alienated work and consumption, social media is in many respects a machine of mass distraction. It is a repository into which energies, vitiated in daily life, are further drained and dissipated as we surf and seek distractions from the pressures of biopolitical administration. Social media can be thought of as an idiot-making machine, a machine for the production of a narcissistic individual fetishised by the same alienated narcissist. It is a non-space in which a craft consciousness arises, the craft of an isolated individual whose creativity is affirmed on the premise that by inputting text on a screen, playing around with images and uploading footage from concerts seen through mobile phone eyes, they are somehow writer and artist, photographer and director, poet and performer. The subject becomes active in its own style of anti-production, in the production of lack, by the endless additions of content in the form of words, sounds and images never quite of the standard one hoped for and that require ever larger storage capacities to hold – you never know, that image, idea or clever phrase might one day prove useful. In sum, the content itself is generally of poorer stock than what more traditional forms of media had to offer. Cultural investment is arguably shallow because what is invested in is of little merit, requires little thought or skill and, as Jonathan Crary claims, further encloses time into commodity production and acquisition:

> no individual can ever be shopping, gaming, working, blogging, downloading, or texting 24/7. However, since no moment, place, or situation now exists in which one can *not* shop, consume, or exploit networked resources, there is a relentless incursion of the non-time of 24/7 into every aspect of social or personal life. (2013: 30)

There is an entire book to be written about the ideological implications of social media; some of the negative aspects are merely summarised here.

The first point underlines the biopolitical production of subjectivity through the use of open media. Libido is invested in the production of affects that can be represented and captured by media conglomerates operating by the industrial and standardising principles of the culture industry (which they help author). This aids a further differentiation of commodities that speak even more directly to the subject than hitherto possible. By tracking 'trending' interests, culture industries, not to be confused with 'culture industry' which for Adorno and Horkheimer does not refer to a literal business, are able to shorten the 'turnover' time from registering desires and commodifying them through to the manufacture of new hardware and software that capture a 'zeitgeist'. Our use of social media can itself be considered a form of reflexive exploitation in that new skills are developed, new contacts are formed and knowledge is acquired for enhancing employability.

The second point about social media is the further disconnect of the subject from others, through their increasingly only appearing in 'virtual' form and through the personalisation of commodities that appear only to speak to one particular individual. While it could be claimed that social media produces the opposite effect by bringing people who would otherwise have no connection to one another together, at best this can be considered a form of compensation for what has been lost to social life. Dating sites are a case in point. They are increasingly necessary if we think of the difficulty people now have in forming relationships because of constraints on time and the colonisation of space by processes of commodification, but they reduce love to a series of generic tick-boxes that do 'violence' to the fuller subject that seeks love.

This brings us to the third point, the transposition of a happy consciousness. Instead of discovering an identity in fridges, the 'new' happy consciousness discovers an identity in their own posts and apps. The app consciousness, or to use a pun, the appy consciousness, can be satisfied that, against the grain of everything they know about the world and protest about, when up-thumbing another exposé posted on Facebook, they are independent of the broader mass industrial forces that the happy consciousness described by Marcuse is ideologically beholden to. The older happy consciousness is residual or becomes simply a description of those who are not media savvy. Jodi Dean's (2012) criticism of 'communicative capitalism', the phenomenon whereby the circulation of information irrespective of whether it is read or enacted on is itself fetishised, is relevant here. The monopoly of corporations over the means of dissemination has not so much ended as been augmented by the new reality principle of social media, the principle of virtual communication to which so much of life and the prospects for success are staked.

The fourth point about social media is that pseudo-individualisation is operationalised simultaneously with pseudo-socialisation – pseudo-individuals pseudo-socialise. While pseudo-individualisation describes the identification of the subject with the miniscule variations of fetishised commodities, pseudo-socialisation describes the identification of (members of) a group with enervated online communities as substitutes for communities that exist in the offline world. Related then to the point above, the more we rely on virtual media as a source of social activity, the more material life is emptied of its social content and the more alienated from society we are. The appearance of protest camps organised through social media does to an extent negate this, but they are disproportionately small when compared to how social life is deprived of the many nuances of human interaction in the increasingly dominant sphere of digitised communication in which culture is experienced in more atomised ways. The digital sphere becomes enmeshed in and 'augments' the physical one in which we tweet, email, produce selfies and instagrams. It provides a virtual veneer that masks the ugliness of and our disconnection from the inhabited environment in order to guide us through dense commodified forests in which the subject is lost.

The fifth point concerns a more generalised and intense culture of narcissism. In the construction of dating profiles, Facebook images and so forth, the biopolitical culture industry encourages, if not feelings of grandiosity, then the management of identity to evoke a superiority of attitude and lifestyle. The generation that has grown up with social media and has no experience of life prior to the embedding of neoliberal ideology throughout society is perhaps the most narcissistic to have inhabited the earth. Individual narcissism is strengthened by the narcissism of the virtually assembled group, becoming a social narcissism, an inflated sense of a group's power, self-importance and social impact.

It should be stressed that I see none of these points as 'totalising'. They are, after all, observations that, without comprehensive evidence impossible to obtain even by armies of market researchers, must in the final analysis be considered 'more' or 'less' generalisable. As with all cultural and technological developments, the universe for political action is never fully closed and at the hard core of empirical observation one is able to discover the obdurate kernel that warrants hope. If biopolitics denotes both an active administration of the body as a site for exploitation and dialectically, as Hardt and Negri suggest, the production of a subjectivity with the power to contest neoliberalism and exceed or negate a neoliberalised self, then the culture industry is biopolitical by inviting the subject to adapt itself but is unable to fully determine what this subject does with the networks it has established, the knowledge it has acquired, or the affects that can and sometimes do spill over into a political domain. The open-ended nature of many products today signal or at least invite creation. That such tools become another means for capital to extract value, either by harnessing the skills the user develops for the workplace or mining knowledge for the production of new commodities for purchase, does not preclude more emancipatory uses including the contestation of ideology and the exposure of egregious practices of states and corporations. That the US government closely monitors Web 2.0 suggests that they at least recognise such potential.[6] As Foster points out:

> consumer agency is a source of disruption, of unruly overflowings that escape capture and can even destroy value – notably, the value of brands, favourite targets of no logo-style corporate 'anti-globalization' activists. This disruption stems from consumer agency's capacity – admittedly uneven and never guaranteed, but surely amplified by new communication technologies – to assemble publics around matters of concern. (2007: 726)

When all is said and done, shit can still be used for manure providing a fertile soil on which a thousand flowers can bloom.

The Culture Industry Comes Full Circle

Thanks to the fascination of popular culture with all things American, many of us, whether from the United States or not, are now familiar with the phenomenon that is called Black Friday. This is the first day after Thanksgiving when US retailers heavily discount their goods. A typical, widely reported, scene, reminiscent of New Year sales in the UK, is of shoppers rushing into the store to grab bargains, often from one another, in a violent frenzy. In 2013, ABC News claimed that 97 million Americans descended upon shopping malls with numbers swelling over the weekend to 140 million.[7] The scenes evoke those in nuclear holocaust movies such as *The Day After* and *Threads* – the latter is surely the bleakest and most disturbing post-apocalyptic movie ever made and essential viewing for those who fantasise about the end of the world – where upon hearing the five-minute warning, shoppers scramble violently for food stock. Shopper frenzy would appear to be evidence for Freud's point that when the superego law is suspended dangerous primitive forces are unleashed. The battlefields of Europe are displaced onto the battlefields of the shopping mall where the subject as such disappears from view. As Baudrillard put it, the subject

is dying out. The subject that is an agency of will, freedom and representation, the Subject of power, knowledge and history is vanishing, giving way to a diffuse, floating, insubstantial subjectivity that is an immense reverberation surface for a disembodied, empty consciousness. As a result, everything now radiates out from an objectless subjectivity, with each monad and molecule caught in the trap of a definitive narcissism, a perpetual image-playback. This is the image of an end-of-the-world subjectivity, from which the subject as such has disappeared, a victim of that fatal twist to which, in a sense, nothing stands opposed any longer – neither object, nor Real, nor Other. (2010: 45)

Such disembodiment becomes more literal in the holographic images of dead pop stars performing an undying role as if holding the key to our own immortality. Tupac Shaker enjoyed such a comeback in 2012 by performing alongside Dr Dre and Snoop Dog at the Coachella music festival in Los Angeles.[8] Al Gore was also resurrected from the 'dead' of failed presidential contenders when appearing in holographic form at the Live Earth event on '7/7/7'. Celebrities whose stalled careers that never really were are redeemed by shows such as 'I'm a Celebrity Get Me Out of Here' and 'Celebrity Big Brother'. The 'Zero' unknown celebrity confirms their narcissistic dream of entitlement through appearances on reality TV. The numbers that appear at interviews and auditions for such shows greatly exceed the number of those selected. As one commentator writes:

> When you are rejected from reality TV it is the absence of notification that notifies you. You are, simply, not worth watching. The 7 p.m. deadline comes and goes without a phone call to tell you that they want you, that people would turn on the TV for you. When you are rejected from reality TV it is not because you lack the educational qualifications for the position; there are none. It's not because you can't perform the job functions; there are none. When you're not picked it's simply because you're not interesting enough or pretty enough or exciting enough. You're not enough.[9]

Failure, especially at the margins of celebrity, is the kind of disembodiment the pop culture cynic enjoys. The cynic is cultivated and catered for by a culture industry that trades on displays of personal abasement, typically of the lower classes, that go viral on YouTube. One of the more striking examples is the girl-next-door made famous, Rebecca Black, who earned notoriety in 2011 with the song and pop video 'Friday'. Produced by a company specialising in pop culture facsimile to order for parents as gifts to their narcissistic children, Black became an instant celebrity when the video, posted on YouTube, went viral. The hook line was the lyric 'tomorrow is Saturday and Sunday comes afterwards'. The unintentional banality of the line became the joke shared with over 160 million on one post and many more when the song was commercially released due to popular demand, signalling that perhaps the irony may have been lost after all. The enjoyment of pop culture abasement is itself, through the thin alibi of ironic self-awareness, an example of the wilful self-loathing pleasure described by Adorno above. The attitude of the knowing dupe, or unknowing – we cannot be certain – that Adorno wrote of is empirically supported by the numbers of viewers and also, remarkably, in Google's own statistics on the most searched words in a given year. In 2011, the year of Occupy, the Arab Spring and Fukushima, 'Rebecca Black' was the most searched word on the site. When regimes are overthrown, tsunamis rip through cities and global social movements contest ideology, lightness and fun prevail. The joke is on us. Being a knowing dupe amounts to the same thing as being duped, a point that Žižek frequently elucidates through his interpretation of ideology as having a libidinal component or non-ideological feature. As

Fabio Vighi explains, 'it follows that we are never fully aware of the extent of our subjection' (2012: 3).

The culture industry is naturalised and internalised through a process of telemorphosis. It is a biopolitical culture industry in so far as the subject, whose desires are already framed by a culture industry, does the job of pseudo-individualisation and through its creations reveals a craft consciousness most notably in social media. We come full circle as the points Adorno made in the 1960s are empirically substantiated in many examples, too exhaustive to cite here, that attest to and build on the original and revisited thesis. Another feature, originally discussed in *Capitalism's New Clothes*, but worth expanding on here, is the culture-of-crisis industry.

Inverted Fetishism

If the Puritan took pleasure in abstinence, the critic of consumerism takes pleasure in condemning others for their choices and habits, as if whatever disposable income a person happens to have should somehow be burned. Money has to go somewhere, and if not into the pockets of Apple then to another brand, another device, another product sold on the premise that it is good for us, for others less fortunate, or for Mother Nature. There is no escaping the logic of capital. Satisfaction in our ethical and ecological choices is much the same as that of the archetypal housewife of the 1950s, whose agency was confirmed when deciding which branded soap powder gets the whites whiter. Better, it seems, to buy from one capitalist than another, as long as we disavow the complex relations of exploitation that make our miserable gestures of compassion possible. As Stiegler puts it, 'Not merely insofar as we are living beings, but also insofar as we are social beings, that is, economic beings, we consume, we have consumed, and we will consume' (2011: 34). In this inescapable logic – first of life, later appropriated by capital – joy is snatched in the joyless; so much of what counts as an ethical or ecological product is, to many a palate, about as pleasurable as sucking on lemons. Yet, aside from the aesthetic merits of 'alternative' produce, the key issue is how these alternatives are marketed and become substitutes for a more radical politics that if enacted would negatively impact surplus value.

The shift from a commodity that mystifies class relations to one that markets them is an inverted fetishism. What it reveals in part it disguises in totality. In other words, the part is fetishised while the totality that the part stands in for is mystified, shifting the onus of the impact of consumption onto the individual consumer. The ideological effect is to obscure the class relation and thereby invoke everyone, irrespective of circumstance, as individual cause and solution. We are never employable enough so we can never consume enough and so we can never be ethical enough.

A now established genre of popular books that in various ways denounce capitalism reinforces the ideology, providing the 'shock' statistics, vignettes and general information on the cycles of production. They typically propose solutions that invariably involve some kind of change of lifestyle and the call for governments and corporations to adopt more ethical and sustainable codes of practice. Fred Pearce's best selling *Confessions of an Eco-Sinner* is one of many examples:

> Companies like Cafedirect are on the side of the angels, fighting the global giants who constantly attempt to drive down prices ... the fault is with us, the consumers, not the people of Cafedirect. The critical question is how much extra we consumers are prepared to pay, as we peruse the coffee packets on display in the supermarket, in order to feel good about our coffee. So far, we are not prepared to pay very much. We want our ethics on the cheap. If we convince ourselves that we are paying a fair price, giving the coffee farmers a proper return, then we are deluding ourselves. (2008: 28)

This scolding takes no account of the material circumstance of many consumers, or the fact that such actions as buying the most expensive coffee we can find achieve nothing except to make us feel good about ourselves, or that there is no compelling evidence that even at the most rudimentary level farmers get a 'better deal'. When purchasing Fairtrade we tend not to think of the fairness of the conditions under which the checkout operator works. Trying to alleviate the symptoms of capitalism in no way means being critical of or seeking an alternative to capitalism as such. These diatribes play in the same key as Bill Gates' charity pronouncements and Richard Branson's aforementioned anti-capitalist manifesto, worth quoting from again:

> This book has been seven years in the making. It's the story of my seven-year journey towards realising that, while business has been a great

vehicle for growth in the world, neither Virgin nor many other businesses have been doing anywhere near enough to stop the downward spiral we all find ourselves in; and that in many cases, as demonstrated by the recent financial crises in the world, we have actually been causing that spiral to turn ever faster. We are all part of the problem: we waste, we squander and, to put it bluntly, we screw up. Natural resources are being exhausted faster than they can be replenished. In fact, not to put too fine a point on it, many natural resources – such as oil, forests and minerals – can never be replenished. Once they're gone, they're gone. (2011: 20)

The effect of campaigns that generate 'awareness' while at the same time proffer solutions on the market model is to aestheticise poverty, global warming and so on and thereby establish an affective relationship to commodities beyond what Walter Benjamin at the beginning of the twentieth century could have imagined. As Esther Leslie, writing on Benjamin, explains:

Empathy spans both the relationship between people and the past and the relation between people and products, in commodity-producing society. Empathy is promoted between the mass and ruling class ideology and between producer-consumers and exchange value. The self adopts the position of the commodity. Consumers sympathize with commodity objects. (2000: 194)

If the techniques of the culture industry were not already in evidence, we could find, in recent attempts by campaigners to provide market-style incentives, a perfect symmetry with Deleuze's point in 'Societies of Control' that disciplinary regimes are scrambled. One such example is 'gamification' where the achievement-oriented principles and cooperative gameplay of video games such as Minecraft are adapted by charities to get young people involved in money-raising activities.[10] While perhaps a realistic way to engage people in voluntary action, such methods reinforce market logic in terms of both its reward structure and the idea that these are meaningful ways of transforming the social landscape.

The advertising campaign of the chocolate brand *Divine*, discussed in *Capitalism's New Clothes*, further illustrates the point. One advertisement carried the image of a black African woman in traditional dress holding a piece of chocolate with the slogan 'It's not just the TASTE that makes you FEEL GOOD'. The additive – the *objet petit a* – is the ethics, the USP of the brand. Where a choice is available to purchase either the usual brand or an ethically marketed product, guilt, such as it has already been evoked and manipulated, can be gotten rid of in the act of exchange and consumption of the ethically marketed product. Without the choice, to purchase the ethical brand or not, there is no compulsion to act, nothing to feel good or bad about. Guilt is elevated as a thing-like commodity to be exchanged for the product and gifted to the other that the product speaks on behalf of. Guilt in this respect is fetishised, a 'guilt fetishism'. It is an Oedipalised injunction tactically aligned with leftist concerns though wholly at odds with any political project that aims in any substantive way to address them. A Culture of Crisis Industry evokes and manipulates anxieties about the world in order to sell products, and is operationalised by the many examples, often brought to the surface by ethical marketing, of real life tragedy, disaster, exploitation and environmental degradation. If not through advertising then in the many films, television shows, YouTube clips and so on in which social concerns are raised, commerce is able to identify a market and embellish its products to sell to those worried about conditions which they themselves, without any commercial intention, advertise. As Jacques Rancière puts it, 'we are still prone to believe that the reproduction in resin of a commercial idol will make us resist the empire of the "spectacle" or that the photography of some atrocity will mobilise us against injustice' (2009: 61). But, he writes, 'There is no straightforward road from the fact of looking at a spectacle to the fact of understanding the state of the world; no direct road from intellectual awareness to political action' (2009: 75).

It is moot whether the appeal of images and the desire for products and the lifestyles they evoke is a result of a sense of powerlessness and desire to 'do something' even though we know it to have no tangible effect, or whether it is because, by purchasing them or adopting the lifestyles they evoke, we can defer any consequential engagement. Žižek is unsympathetic to the false choices we make and any value that can be derived from them. He writes:

> The exemplary figures of evil today are not ordinary consumers who
> pollute the environment and live in a violent world of disintegrating
> social links, but those who, while fully engaged in creating the conditions

for such universal devastation and pollution, buy their way out of their own activity, living in gated communities, eating organic food, taking holidays in wildlife preserves, and so on. (2008: 23)

It is not by consuming organic food that we are complicit; the 'evil' as such lies in those who trade on such behaviour and market their choices to others who are either implicitly or explicitly excoriated for not doing the same. While the capitalist can be forgiven for their empty ethical gestures on the basis that – unless they are engaged in a suicide pact by siding with the proletariat – their relation to production means they cannot do otherwise, those without such investments, 'the ordinary consumers', deserve no such sympathy.

Colin Beavan – the self-styled 'No Impact Man'[11] – is an exemplary figure of such 'evil'. The no impact project 'not-for-profit' environmental movement has a mission 'to empower citizens to make choices which better their lives and lower their environmental impact through lifestyle change, community action, and participation in environmental politics'. Colin Beavan fronted the enterprise. He wrote a blog, published a book and made a film chronicling 'his family's year-long experiment living a zero-waste lifestyle in New York'. The website contains tips on how to live a sustainable life and provides campaign tools and information on public events. By leading a lifestyle – for just a year – which relied on the very materials, infrastructure, tools, appliances and so on that are created under capitalism, Beavan illustrated the absurdity of such gestures. This example also illustrates Rancière's point that knowledge of environmental degradation or, in a different register, poverty and extreme exploitation, does not necessarily coincide with an understanding of structural relations or a desire to do anything about it. For this, we need Marx, without whom, as appears the case here, we really do believe that products magically appear on shelves, houses pop up from nowhere and Fairtrade products are teleported to their destination: the mouth of a hungry campaigner.

No Impact Man type thinking is embodied in the everyday practices of well-meaning individuals who self-consciously reinforce ethical and eco-myths to friends, family and colleagues. It is embodied in sociologists such as Ulrich Beck, John Urry and Anthony Giddens who identify, in 'self-reflexive' businesses, CEOs and consumers, the potential for a managed solution to climate change.

The political imagination is stymied by subtle invocations of capitalist realism, that there is no alternative to the market and perhaps no need for one because market-based solutions to widely documented problems are available. In so far as the reality of consumer life is indeed destructive in the many ways that campaigners are correct to document, all eyes turn on the consumer who, if not in this world then in another, has to pay the consequences. As Lacan put it, 'one can be guilty' for 'having given ground relative to one's desire'. Moreover, 'Doing things in the name of the good, and even more in the name of the good of the other, is something that is far from protecting us not only from guilt but also from all kinds of inner catastrophes' (1992 [1959–60]: 319).

If consumption among the most affluent classes is a measure of the kind of society envisaged for all, then it is clear that no such society is possible. Ultimately what gives way is the consumer dream (see Ivanova, 2011). Costas Panayotakis, for example, writes:

Since the travelling habits of many of today's anti-capitalist intellectuals and activists (and I include myself in that group) could not become universalised to include every single person on this planet, it is clear that in a post-capitalist society, which respected natural limits while giving everybody an equal chance to travel, the aspirations of people to travel might exceed the possibility of doing so. (2011: 29)

The problem with this is that it assumes a desire symptomatic of the current material condition will be static. In actuality, under a different mode of production, travel would be of less economic value and also less seductive when the inhabited space is no longer alienating. Needs and desires are mediated by a material culture. That people want LED televisions today is no indicator of what, under different circumstances, people will want tomorrow. Marcuse's point that lifestyles would have to change, that expectations will indeed need to be diminished to accommodate the more pressing needs of a global populace, does not need stating when the libidinal economy would necessarily change with a transformation in the mode of production. It is inconceivable that in a society emancipated from the logic of surplus value there would be a culture industry to stoke desires for lifestyles that the more affluent classes currently enjoy. Nor would it be possible under a mode of production no longer geared to the profit motive to choose such a lifestyle.

There is no point in speculating on the reduced means to indulge our desires in a post-capitalist world because by then the American dream of consumerism would truly be at an end. The liberation of desire first requires an end to alienated labour, after which the Oedipalised apparatus of the reality principle (evoked in Adorno's description of the culture industry) can be dismantled, and only then will the kind of becoming that Deleuze and Guattari envisage be possible.

Alienated Socialism

> I'd rather be atomised than communised.
>
> Eisenhower

Atomisation was achieved without the bomb. Atoms form molecules, and molecules, recognisable objects. The problem of subjectivity is not individualism. We arrive in this chapter at the logical conclusion of the argument. The problem is socialism: social-ism of an alienated subject – a 'socialism in one country'. Let us put this in perspective by way of a succinct definition of individualism by Jeremy Gilbert:

> individualism is not primarily a moral or ethical category, but an ontological, phenomenal and epistemological one. It understands the singular human being as the basic unit of all experience, and in naming that being 'individual' it makes a particular set of assumptions about its nature and its relationship to the world and to others ... Properly speaking, the term 'individual' not only expresses the singular uniqueness of the person (or object) it describes, but also implies that that uniqueness is dependent upon its indivisible nature, hence upon something which is absolutely intrinsic to it and not at all a function of its relations with others. (2014: 310)

As a concept, individualism is of limited explanatory value. Alienation, in both the Marxist and Lacanian senses, offers a better explanation for the processes by which we are individuated and come to regard ourselves as socially disconnected. By stressing the -ism, Gilbert is clear that what we are talking about is not an actual state of being but rather an ideological mystification. Perhaps, to paraphrase Žižek (1989), what we do not know is that in the belief that we are independent in thought, desire and action from others, still we orient thought, desire and action towards others, whose company we seek and in whose opinions we gain validation. We want brands in order to belong, apps in order to be connected. We fine-tune objects in the harmonics of others. The superego injunction to enjoy – in other words to be yourself, take command of your own destiny, make the most of the opportunities available to you, be enterprising and so on – demands sociability: it demands that we achieve success in the image of what in neoliberalism success is characterised by; it demands team players; it demands connectivity; it demands tolerance; it demands recognition of the harms inflicted on others; it demands involvement in campaigns to ameliorate that harm; it demands that singles become couples, have a 'healthy' sex life, a fit body and so on. A lonely crowd, as David Riesman (2001 [1961]) would have observed.

Gilbert (2014: 183) endorses what John Protevi calls the 'joyous affect', that all joy, all pleasure, is the experience of 'sociality-as-empowerment'. He relates this to Spinoza's notion of an augmentation and diminution of a body's capacity to act, influencing Deleuze's theories on the exceeding of bodily capacities through relations of affect. The problem with this concept is that it fails to account for the material circumstances in which an affective sociality occurs, something Deleuze and Guattari did of course recognise in the Oedipalised apparatus of capture. Sociality, where it does not aim to negate abstract individualism, where affect does not lift the status of the individual to that of a political force with the aim of an unalienated sociability, can in the most part be oppressive, debilitating, joyless, giving rise to mass stupidity and cultural nihilism. Returning to Žižek, it is important in this respect to traverse the fantasy or ideological form that structures reality, the form of sociability that the desires of materially alienated subjects are conditioned by, invested in and dependent on. The next chapter elaborates on the point that consumption signals a utopian impulse to overcome alienation.

6

Banquets of Worlds

This chapter examines the idea and the possibility of utopia; utopia as an impulse and, more importantly, as a basis for developing propositions that can inspire revolutionary desire and hope. The title of the chapter is taken from something Mikhail Bakhtin once wrote that nicely summarises the class basis of our current privations. In the novels of Rabelais, Bakhtin said, the peasantry celebrated the end of the harvest with a banquet for all the world. Their produce resulted from the collective efforts of an entire community, a common wealth exceeding the harvest of individual labour. The banquet celebrated a body that had transgressed its own material limits. By contrast the banquets of bourgeois literature celebrated:

> the contentment and satiety of the selfish individual, his personal enjoyment, and not the triumph of the people as a whole ... it is no longer the 'banquet for all the world', in which all take part, but an intimate feast with beggars at the door. (Bakhtin, 1984 [1941]: 302)

The banquets of modern times are concretised in newly constructed cityscapes visible for the world to see. A little over 20 years ago, the Pudong district of Shanghai was mostly farmland. Today it boasts three 'supertall' skyscrapers and the majestic Oriental Pearl tower, together forming a visually stunning tableau that evokes China's ascendancy to the rank of economic superpower. As if to underline this fact, each tower and all the adjacent buildings (themselves of heights greater than in most cities), are lit at night in a dazzling array of colours some of which are enveloped with advertising clips. Whereas China has a practically infinite supply of cheap labour from the hinterland to build these cities, Qatar, the hosts of the 2022 football World Cup finals, relies on immigrant labour, and the rising death toll on its building sites is a reminder of the human cost of these global extravaganzas. Much like the Parisian arcades in which Benjamin wandered, these bourgeois banquets are a concrete expression of what collective labour is capable of and how the potential to channel it for a more utopian purpose is squandered – a banquet for some with billions of beggars at the door.

Ernst Bloch (1986 [1947]) described a 'utopian impulse' as a universal longing for an end to (at least one's own) hunger and a recovery of the losses born from alienation. There is a shared, though perhaps unconscious, sense that life is *not yet*, that there is something profoundly lacking in lived experience. As Samuel Beckett once wrote, 'Do you believe in the life to come? Mine was always that.' A utopian imagination asserts itself in the gap between how life really is and how it ought to be. The impulse as such can be described an invariant of a history of dispossession, material scarcity and alienation. The 'warm stream' of subjective passion (as Bloch put it) to overcome lack is the *not yet* conscious that acquires political force through the 'cold stream' of Marxist analysis.

The idea of 'utopia' classically divides into two camps; on the right, as Jameson (2004) notes, the word denotes totalitarian oppression, and on the left it denotes communism, conflated in the eyes of many with the static and sterile image of the Soviet Empire. Ralf Dahrendorf is typical in this respect, claiming that 'In almost every Utopia ... one sees handsome but characterless buildings, symmetrical and perfect cultivations, and a multitude of people, healthy, happy, beautifully dressed, but without personal distinction whatever' (quoted in Kaleb, 1971: 10). If utopia is regarded as an impossible dream it is because the logic that there is no alternative to the market has become hegemonic. In order to repoliticise the idea of utopia, the logic must be refuted. This needs to be followed by the more difficult task of articulating concrete propositions on alternatives to existing relations and, not least, consideration of the available means to achieve them.

A pessimistic and, by this light, anti-utopian consciousness today prevails in a range of mutually reinforcing claims: that there are not enough natural resources for humanity to survive; that the human condition is one of violence and self-aggrandisement; that individualism, despite the many examples of communal association, can no longer be transcended; that there really is no alternative to current market arrangements; or that corporations are now so powerful and the state so fundamentally corrupted that even if a shared wealth were theoretically conceivable, it is now impossible to obtain politically. If there is one truth, it is that, given the rapidly deteriorating ecological conditions on which all of humanity depends, the window of possibility for transforming society is now sufficiently narrow that for a utopian idea to be realised it has to be acted on soon. The obstacles are more formidable than ever, but as Marcuse reminds us:

> The fact is, that we find ourselves up against a system that from the very beginning of the fascist period to the present has disavowed through its acts the idea of historical progress, a system whose internal contradictions repeatedly manifest themselves in inhuman and unnecessary wars and whose growing productivity is growing destruction and growing waste. *Such a system is not immune.* (1970: 94, my emphasis)

A one-sided analysis would suggest that we have indeed passed a tipping point, that we are now so atomised from one another that any prospect of change, however desirable, is no longer possible: that, in other words, the class war is over. But, if not in name then in actions, the class war is fought on a daily basis as states develop increasingly sophisticated systems of surveillance and control while dismantling whatever obstacles remain that prevent business and individual investors from making a quick profit. The NSA revelations and increasingly authoritarian policing methods expose a fear in those who have profited through the years of neoliberalism that their gains may yet be short-lived.

Even as our energies are absorbed into the machinery of abstraction, they are never fully expended. *Jouissance* is an unquenchable drive for the lost objects, though, in Lacanian terms, it is simply derailing rather than registering the possibility of a world that is not yet. More optimistically, for Deleuze and Guattari, desire is conceived as a vital force actualised in an endless process of exceeding the abstract machine and Oedipal mechanisms of capitalism (more on which later). What this misses, for Žižek and others, is the negative dialectics that render palpable the gap between ideas and reality, a negativity that invokes antagonism both as a condition of life and a relation according to which changes are enacted. Marcuse is perhaps the most recognisable Marxist since Bloch to have embraced the utopian category; he saw in the 'dialectic' of civilisation the prospect of a self-conscious resublimation of pleasure and the desublimation and dismantling of the institutions of the reality principle. What Marcuse opposed was not repression per se but what he called surplus repression, operationalised through the performance principle that demands the diversion of sexual energies into unsatisfactory false needs that commerce trades on and which binds us to alienating labour. The point that a degree of individual repression is always necessary to prevent chaos is not, I shall argue below, so far removed from Deleuze and Guattari, who stressed the importance of what they call 'molar assemblages' such as classes, institutions or identities in giving form to molecular processes of social transformation and ensuring that the more derailing or revolutionary lines of flight do not simply bring about wanton destruction.

Siding with Marx, who was weary of utopian models on the grounds that they distracted us from important material analysis of the current situation, the point is to devise not a blueprint but rather a placeholder, what in linguistic terms is called a vanishing mediator, an idea around which people can rally and which 'dissolves' when there are real breakthroughs and the horizons of possibility have changed. This necessarily involves a realistic analysis of the current strengths and weaknesses of the forces arranged against capital and the prospects immanent to the actual situation, subjective, institutional and organisational, of changing the course of history – a discussion reserved for the next chapter, 'Clash of Axioms'.

This chapter is organised into four parts that together map utopia as an impulse, an idea and a (possible) reality beyond certain obstacles. The first part, 'No Man's Land', revisits some of the theoretical ideas on utopia to ground the analysis. Part two, 'Relics of the Past', considers loss as an abstract category for describing that which is absent in lived experience and the concretely actual loss or potential loss of a cherished thing. I aim to show that nostalgia is a useful concept for thinking about what is currently at stake. Nostalgia can be reactive when willing a return to an imaginary past. But if we conceive of what is now present and which would in the future be nostalgically mourned were it destroyed, we get a clearer sense of what we would like to preserve or salvage from the present and take with us into that future. This can be kept in mind alongside more speculative ideas of 'other worlds' that can tangibly be fought for. Part three, 'Utopian Space and Time', eschews the more reactive rural and enclave utopias envisaged by some, and underlines the importance of urban theory in utopian thinking. Changes to the urban environment are central to the material basis for utopian possibilities, as cities are where the majority of the world's population live. The chapter concludes, in part four, 'The World

Without Capitalism', by framing utopia simultaneously as a 'minimal' idea or project to moderate capital and as a 'maximal' idea or project to which the former must be aligned, to rid the world of capitalism. The terms are used to critique Eric Olin Wright's utopian formulations as well as prepare the ground for the manifesto of the final chapter, 'Clash of Axioms'.

No Man's Land

> The critique of utopianism is based on the idea that technology has not advanced sufficiently. No one can maintain that today. Today we have the pure contradiction between the forces and relations of production.
>
> Adorno in conversation with Horkheimer in 1956 (2010: 54)

> As the more perceptive critics of the concept of the 'end of history' have pointed out, there can be no end to history without an end to modern natural science and technology. Not only are we not at an end of science and technology; we appear to be at the cusp of one of the most momentous periods of technological advance in history.
>
> Francis Fukuyama (2002: 15)

The term utopia was first coined by Thomas More (2012 [1551]) through a playful synthesis of two Greek words: 'outopos', meaning 'no place', and 'eutopos' meaning 'good place'. For capital there is no good place of utopia because all utopias, conceived as dreams, are a 'no man's land' impossible to traverse. Utopia departs from the no place of fantasy and becomes an empirical possibility in Marcuse's recognition that the material and technological forces of production are now sufficiently developed that scarcity can, theoretically at least, be overcome. The institutions of the reality principle discipline us to accept privation as a natural condition and recognise work in its alienating form as necessary to our survival. In these miserable circumstances the chief respite is the limited pleasure afforded to consumption in which Eros is typically ensnared. To liberate the human faculties from the binds described in the previous chapters, the institutions of the reality principle would have to be dismantled and transformed. With production oriented to the satisfaction of our social needs, not only would scarcity be overcome but the societal requirement of labour would be significantly reduced. With a change in *both* forces and relations of production, work becomes what it is not yet, life-enhancing rather than alienating, with reason and happiness converging in a 'rationality of gratification'. This was a position informing Marcuse's politics from the 1950s when he wrote *Eros and Civilisation* through to the more pessimistic *Counter-Revolution and Revolt* published in 1972. In the lecture 'The End of Utopia' Marcuse said:

> All the material and intellectual forces which could be put to work for the realisation of a free society are at hand. That they are not used for that purpose is to be attributed to the total mobilisation of existing society against its own potential for liberation. But this situation in no way makes the idea of radical transformation itself a utopia.[1]

Against the more sterile and ascetic visions now common within strains of ecological utopianism, Marcuse stressed the importance of sensuous needs that in practical terms can only be liberated if the industrial forces of production are utilised, though transformed rather than abandoned. As he put it, 'The senses are not only the basis for the *epistemological* constitution of reality, but also for its *transformation*, its *subversion* in the interest of liberation' (1972: 71). Eros is a dialectical force: under conditions of individualism and alienation, it operates unconsciously to perpetuate capitalism's own destructive drive through exploited labour and consumption, but when self-conscious *and* collective, Eros becomes a force for liberation, poetry and play. In Marcuse's utopia, language becomes song and work play, the life of Orpheus the poet and creator. It is also one of beauty and contemplation, the life of Narcissus. These 'Orphic-Narcissistic images are those of the Great Refusal... a refusal aims at liberation – at the reunion of what has become separated.' (2006 [1955]: 170–1). The dismissal of the possibility of *realising* utopia underlined by the claim that there is no alternative to free-market capitalism is what Marcuse challenges when calling for an 'end of utopia': 'the refutation of those ideas and theories that use the concept of utopia to denounce certain socio-historical possibilities' (1970: 62).

If there is a general yardstick for the necessity of utopian thinking it is the degree to which we are alienated or, inversely, the degree to which we have determination over the forces of production including our own labour. I have argued in Chapters 3 to 5 that alienation has both intensified and become more extended in time and space. Against fashionable ideas on prosumption, I have argued that activities related to new technologies, media and such like become indirect sources of profit and at worst further alienate and pacify. Furthermore, the superficial communities that are created online compensate for more profound losses experienced in the real economy and help generalise group narcissism. For Bloch, alienation is more of a subjective experience of lack amid a cultural surplus that is in large part inaccessible but constantly strived for. It 'becomes clear', he wrote, 'that this very [cultural] surplus is produced by nothing other than *the effect of the utopian function* in the ideological creations of the cultural side' (quoted in Levitas, 2011 [1990]: 106). While Bloch himself rejected psychoanalytic theory, there are obvious connotations with unconscious utopian impulses or libidinal passions for objects that are lost and lacking. Putting it in psychoanalytic terms, we might say that hope lies in the fact that libido is an unquenchable force, antagonistic and/or excessive, that has to go somewhere, potentially on a utopian trajectory.

The invariant of desire hits against the obstacle of a repressive apparatus that it seeks to traverse and, for this reason if for no other, the system, as Marcuse said, is not immune. At first blush, both the writings of Marcuse, though stressing a dialectical 'determinate negation', and those of Deleuze and Guattari, appear to suggest that revolution is simply a matter of liberating desire from its Oedipal constraints. If this were the case, we would have to regard the more abstract forms of social control that appear on the surface to have reduced the moral force of the superego as a step in the right direction. Both sets of thinkers stress the dangers of a socially disconnected desire. Deleuze and Guattari, in particular, provide a useful set of tools for qualifying utopian impulses, ideas and practices.

While Deleuze and Guattari (2003b [1980]) appear to invite us to embark on 'lines of flight' from established molar formations of class and identity, they place more stress on the subtle modulations or molecular loosening of the ties that bind. To grasp the nuances of their theory, which at times is so abstract as to appear impenetrable, and its value to utopian thought, we can trace it through the common experience of being born into the 'wrong' class. For all the claims about meritocracy, the lives of many people brought up under conditions of deprivation trace a predictable path. Crudely, a 'molar' line begins with gender assignment through Oedipalisation, which then further crystallises in schooling that boxes affect along pathways to low-skilled labour, marriage and the reproduction of another generation of workers and consumers. But while this is typical, there are many instances in which those from such backgrounds escape this fate by tracing 'molecular' lines and, in more radical ways, by embarking on 'lines of flight'. A child, for example, might enter a 'zone of proximity' with another body, perhaps a teacher who inspires them to exceed institutional limits. The affective capacities of both bodies are augmented and exceed the molar lines prescribed by society. In another example, a male who once sought to overcome feelings of inadequacy by asserting his authority over women, exceeds his masculine and, in patriarchy, dominant (majoritarian) identity by entering into a proximity with micro-femininity. The affects of 'becoming-woman' negate his Oedipalised identity not, say, by his wearing a dress but rather by his loosening his ties to patriarchy, by which action he gains the strength to take lines of flight from a molar lineage, for instance, by challenging patriarchal norms and aligning with feminist movements for equality. There is always the danger that such lines of escape put us at odds with the world in which we still need to survive. A person who in isolation takes lines of flight from labour is likely to become unemployable and marginalised. Then there is the familiar story of how elements of the student movement in the late 1960s, embarking on their own lines of flight from the molarity of bureaucratic conformity, made use of the hard won freedoms to feather their own nests as 'informational' entrepreneurs. In this instance, lines of flight pave the way for 'micro-fascisms', namely ascendant groups that establish new molar orders of domination.

Let us take another example, Ken Loach's film *Kes*, a classic story of a boy's struggle to escape the molar line of his working-class position in a Yorkshire mining community. Flight is symbolised by a wild kestrel that Billy, played by David Bradley, trains by reading books on husbandry. His eyes trace the bird as it soars into the sky, first tethered to a string, later freed of any constraint. To his family and many of his teachers, he is a hopeless and poorly disciplined child, though he discovers an ally in one teacher who encourages him to 'take flight' through his proximity to the bird. We can observe through this process what Deleuze and Guattari call becoming-animal or in this case becoming-Kestrel. The bond that Billy and the bird form with one another produces effects that enable them both to exceed their natures, or rather what the environment has prescribed for them. Through the bird, Billy embarks on lines of flight from his brutal surroundings. They are not dreams of escape, he really does exceed his molar identity and would in due course have traced a different line to that of his family and peers – were it not for his brother killing the bird in an act of revenge and resentment. We witness Billy's own despair, his hopes crushed, his journey ended, the narrative remaining open as to the consequences this will have for his life, whether he will trace another line of flight (knowing how to now, having found the first) or be sucked into a black hole of abjection.

This simple tale of molar formations, molecular modifications and lines of flight helps us conceive the materiality, possibilities and dangers of utopian impulses, ideas and practices. As Deleuze and Guattari explain, underlining both the dangers and the utopian potentialities of lines of flight in the dialectic of capitalist encoding and decoding:

> The difference between the two poles is great, even, and especially, from the point of view of death: the line of flight that creates, or turns into a line of destruction; the plane of consistency that constitutes itself, even piece by piece, or turns into a plan(e) of organization and domination. We are constantly reminded that there is communication between these two lines or planes, that each takes nourishment from the other, borrows from the other: the worst of the world war machines reconstitutes a smooth space to surround and enclose the earth. But the earth asserts its own powers of deterritorialization, its lines of flight, its smooth spaces that live and blaze their way for a new earth. (2003b: 423)

The molar line is the institutionalised idea that the existing system is the best of all possible worlds, modulated by piecemeal molecular reforms. The utopian idea acquires force through the pact that the abstract machine attempts to capture by institutionalising and commodifying ideas, say through the superficial politics of recognition policed by micro-fascists who impose a new set of norms as the criteria for inclusion in the workplace, or their self-important cliques that transpose those demands into markets for new products. Not only do we need to be mindful of the micro-fascist within, but also of how utopian ideas are often themselves variations of the molar line and seek only to establish new orders of domination. This can happen through the state science's appropriation of lines of flight and the establishment of enclave utopias that cannot be universally extended. More importantly, ideas that reject the molar organisations and hierarchies that give form, leadership and direction to revolutionary movements, including socialist parties, trade unions and parliamentary and institutional allies, lack the strength and consistency to oppose the state war machine. Moreover, there is no movement that does not, informally at least, establish its own hierarchies that in more subtle ways discipline the group and give ground to micro-fascists. Such antagonisms lend support to Žižek's more dialectical approach that regards negativity as the basis for ongoing struggle. Nevertheless, as suggested elsewhere, the situation can be approached negatively in how things really exist and positively in terms of how libidinal forces can produce effects greater than and as such in negation of that which capital is able to capture. We return to these points when examining the situation of the left in the next chapter.

For Deleuze and Guattari, virtual becomings of different intensities, molecular lines and lines of flight, actualise in temporary molar formations or assemblages which become repressive when preventing further becomings. We can approach utopian ideas as bodies that enter into proximity with the effects of different assemblages of people (and objects) inspired by and acting on them. The idea itself gives us the strength to exceed the molar line, as the books on husbandry did for Billy in *Kes*, actualised at various moments of rest and becoming in which we gather breath and reflect on where we are before antagonistically continuing a journey that extends the horizon of possibility.

Deleuze and Guattari do not formulate anything like a programme or idea of utopia for which we might strive. This is not their aim. Like Marx, they provide a conceptual tool for others to utilise and adapt as necessary. Prescriptions are not blueprints, programmes are not instructions: by thinking of ideas as assemblages, relays or vanishing mediators that open new horizons of possibility, utopia has practical relevance. A tangible set of goals is required, a politics *with* demands, if there is to be any hope of inspiring those who the left struggle to involve. Ideas can operate in tandem, as a set of what Žižek calls minimal demands, those that are quite feasible under existing conditions though impossible from the point of view of the established political ideology. A minimal utopian prescription might, for example, be defined by policies such as a guaranteed basic income, free and universal healthcare, full employment and wages adequate to living costs, and an end to hunger. These policies are beyond the pale, of course, for existing parliamentary politics in many nation-state formations, although they are entirely reasonable even by the normative standards of the current molar order. A true reformist agenda – one that goes beyond the tokenism of a 'humanitarian' politics, Fairtrade and so forth – can be posited simultaneously with a revolutionary one, a minimal and a maximal set of demands: a weak and strong utopian form as will be elaborated below. Ultimately, if world hunger and the spiralling effects of global warming were to be addressed, then we would need to include a maximal prescription to end existing class relations and the alienation central to them – the ultimate objective of a utopia worth fighting for.

Susan Buck-Morss writes that,

Of course, daydreams are salutary; we could not live without them. But when their logic, in compensating for the disappointments of today, becomes a 'plan' that locks in future meaning, time's indeterminacy and openness is colonised, and the utopian dream becomes a reality of oppression. (2002: 67)

Any plan can be closed if locked in by an authoritarian state to cement its legitimacy or if it does not include alternatives to the present put forward by those currently excluded from decision-making. A thunderous proclamation concretised in the collective determination of history of those currently without a voice is a fundamental non-negotiable aim of any plan worthy of the utopian name. Fredric Jameson's (2002 [1981]) work is perhaps too all-encompassing in its claim that the unity of the collective, all class consciousness *of whatever type*, is utopian. By whatever type we can infer anything from communist agitation through to anti-Semite fascism and even a football crowd finding common purpose in supporting their team. Deleuze and Guattari are useful in this regard by helping us to formulate the difference between utopias that are molar in origin and fascistic in effect and those that are progressive, even antagonistic, in idea and action.

Fantasy is the empty form in which a utopian desire is lodged. Popular culture evokes and manipulates fantasy providing its own content in commodities. The culture industry denies the possibility of common transcendence, offering up only the possibility of an individualistic one. Does internet communication act as a countervailing force that re-educates and embeds a different phantasmal frame? Arguably it exacerbates the disconnectedness of the subject from society, the dialogic virtual space being a poor substitute for the closure of real life utopias. Virtual interlocutors can be chosen or deleted. The people we contingently encounter in physical, perhaps occupied, spaces cannot. Approaching culture dialectically, Jameson writes:

> if the ideological function of mass culture is understood as a process whereby otherwise dangerous and protopolitical impulses are 'managed' and defused, rechanneled and offered spurious objects, then some preliminary step must also be theorised in which these same impulses – the raw material upon which the process works – are initially awakened within the very text that seeks to still them. (2002 [1981]: 277)

In a complex situation such as ours, Jameson claims, oversimplifications about the wrongs people encounter become necessary. They produce a 'clarion call to remove and extirpate [the] specific root of all evil from which all others spring'. It is thus 'a mistake to approach Utopias with positive expectations, as though they offered visions of happy worlds, spaces of fulfilment and cooperation, representations which correspond generically to the idyll or the pastoral rather than the utopia' (2007: 12). What Jameson is rightly opposing here are the partial or 'enclave' utopias such as those in the many experiments in 'self-sustainable' living of a privileged class that owns pieces of privatised turf.

David Harvey has developed perhaps the most detailed and persuasive synthesis of materialist analysis and cultural critique; his discussions on the former have informed my own analysis of capital in the previous chapters. As Ruth Levitas points out, Harvey's utopianism is more spatio-temporally oriented than Jameson's.

> Harvey takes issue with those writers [for example, Jameson] who want to keep choices about the future endlessly open, or want to keep their own hands free of prescription. Eternal openness leaves utopia as 'a pure signifier of hope destined never to acquire a material referent.' It is politically evasive. It 'entails a failure to recognise that the materialisation of anything requires, at least for a time, closure around a particular set of institutional arrangements and a particular spatial form and that the act of closure is in itself a material statement that carries its own authority in human affairs.' (2013: 124)

It is not enough to posit utopia as a kind of ideal-type in a Weberian sense. The difficult work and the most pressing is not that of philosophising on the concept but rather of fleshing out alternative proposals that can be experimented on in the here and now and be concretised in (ideas on) different institutional arrangements. They can be moderated, questioned, advanced and enacted through assessments according to the three lines described by Deleuze and Guattari (molar, molecular and flight lines).

Returning to the 'cultural text' through materialist interpretation, the next part of this chapter will invoke nostalgia to ascertain the stakes in current struggles to defend the limited gains from earlier victories of the working class and to expand the possibility for advancing them. Against the apocalyptic fantasy of an end to all antagonisms as a result of total destruction, against the anti-human primitivism that views human achievements entirely in the negative, the point is to assert the positive in the dialectic of history as a way to emphasise a more humane vision of alternatives: the first step of a salvaging project.

Relics of the Past

Houellebecq nodded, opening his arms as if he were entering a tantric trance; he was, more probably, drunk, and trying to keep his balance on the kitchen stool where he'd crouched. When he spoke again his voice was soft and deep, filled with naïve emotion. 'In my life as a consumer,' he said, 'I've known three perfect products: Paraboot walking boots, the Canon Libris laptop-printer combination, and the Camel Legend parka. I loved these products, with a passion; I would've spent my life in their presence, buying regularly, with natural wastage, identical products. A perfect and faithful relationship has been established, making me a happy consumer. I wasn't completely happy in all aspects of life, but at least I had that: I could, at regular intervals, buy a pair of my favourite boots. It's not much but it's something, especially when you've quite a poor private life. Ah yes, that joy, that simple joy, has been denied me. My favourite products, after a few years, have disappeared from the shelves, their manufacture has stopped purely and simply – and in the case of my poor Camel Legend parka, no doubt the most beautiful parka ever made, it will have lived for only one season...' He slowly began to cry, big tears streaming down his face, and served himself another glass of wine. 'It's brutal, you know, it's terribly brutal. While the most insignificant animal species take thousands, sometimes millions of years to disappear, manufactured products are wiped off the surface of the globe in a few days; they're never given a second chance, they can only suffer, powerless, the irresponsible and fascistic diktat of product line managers who of course know better than anyone else what the customer wants, who claim to capture an *expectation of novelty* in the consumer, and who in reality just turns his life into one exhausting and desperate quest, an endless wandering between eternally modified product lines.

Michel Houellebecq (2011: 109)

The current obsession with retro signals the sense of loss Houellebecq the character feels in this quote, and the desire to recover something of what is fondly remembered as a better time. The popularity of instagrams that drain photographs of their colour to produce a nostalgic effect is testament to this longing. They can be seen in terms of what Svetlana Boym calls a reflective nostalgia, 'a form of deep mourning that performs a labour of grief both through pondering pain and through play that points to the future' (2001: 55). It is mourning at once personal and social. Relics of the past such as those remnants of the British car industry that enthusiasts maintain and drive, the Triumphs, Austins and Hillmans, are now reimagined in updated Minis and Fiat 500s, the latter a car I drive and love for its retro curves and shiny red dashboard. Strangers frequently approach me to express their love for this machine, often describing their own experience of driving the original. In this accelerated time, such ghostly reminders of a love lost are evoked in new objects hot off the production line. In the not so distant future, iPhones – with their sleek and, in some respects, retro design, evoking a timeless aesthetic – are likely to be mourned by future generations where the current one, retroactively, invents a past by processing photographs in sepia tone. The loss becomes more palpable as such products, because of diminishing means, become harder to own, representing perhaps more affluent times. Enjoyment of them is barred by market forces, a structural violence that, as Buck-Morss explains, excludes people from 'capitalism's dreamworlds' (2002: 188); yet the individual feels responsible for their predicament, and their fate compounds into one of social ostracism. Houellebecq mourns a loss of his favourite commodities at the hands of commerce, the 'squeezed middle' mourn a loss they still hope to recover, while the poor mourn what history has denied them, their dream one of nostalgia for what might have been rather than giving rise to hope and political action.

Nostalgia is often thought to be reactionary, an image of the past that never existed, or at its worst a political project to restore a former state. But it is difficult not to be sympathetic to those who yearn for a time when industrial manufacturing was central to the British economy, and when people had reasonably secure jobs and enjoyed a sense of belonging through them. Women had limited opportunities, but nostalgia does not ask for people to give up what they now have and enjoy; it mourns the benefits of the past and sometimes invokes a politics, often reactive, to transform the present. This kind of nostalgia is evident in an example Susan Stewart (2007 [1993]: 145) provides of an empty factory in Flint Michigan which is now a tourist site. Similar examples exist in Britain: abandoned mines now open for tourists, entire villages such as Beamish in the North East that replicate the Victorian age, and guided tours of cities that bring life back to the streets through narratives on the historical importance of the buildings that survive in them. As Boym writes, 'the stronger the loss, the more it is overcompensated with commemorations, the starker the distance from the past, and the more it is prone to idealisations' (2001: 17). My own nostalgia has become more pronounced in Aotearoa, where conversations among British émigrés frequently centre on objects and experiences that are now unavailable, a 'decent' curry, the visceral pleasure of reading a hard copy of the *Guardian* in cafés, wandering around cities rich in history and architecture, and the exhilaration, though often oppressive, of being among crowds. In this internet age, we mourn a past when albums were thumbed in record shops and information was sought in physical books and journals. As information is increasingly virtualised, as cultural artefacts are downloaded almost instantaneously and communication processed through social media, whether positively or negatively, the accessibility of a virtual past may temper the kind of nostalgia described here. When nostalgia is no longer possible there will be nothing left to mourn and there will remain only a superficial appreciation of what is at stake in this apocalyptic age. Is there anything in the present worth defending? To answer in the affirmative means recovering the positive in concrete experience from the negatives of the abstract one.

Today, in this glittering spectacle, there is gold, a hint of utopia to be preserved, extended and transformed when no longer tied to the commodity form. The present, as Benjamin reminds us, is made up of past defeats, relics that haunt the imagination conjuring up a multitude of what-ifs. What if the new German Republic announced by Karl Liebknecht in 1919 had survived? What if the mass protests and occupations throughout France in 1968 had led to a genuine revolution? What if the British miners in 1984–5 had not split and the trade union movement had fully supported them? As Benjamin wrote:

> To articulate what is past does not mean to recognize 'how it really was.' It means to take control of a memory, as it flashes in a moment of danger. For historical materialism it is a question of holding fast to a picture of the past, just as if it had unexpectedly thrust itself, in a moment of danger, on the historical subject.[2]

Events such as May '68 remind us not only of what has been lost but also of what is still possible, that in different moments in history, some more desperate than now, people can and often do put aside their differences and fight a common cause if only to preserve the small victories of struggles past.

It is important that we recognise and fight for what is already existent, to acknowledge that despite its limitations the 'politics of recognition' has at least addressed certain aspects of institutional racism, homophobia and exclusion based on gender. For environmentalists, fighting for what we have means protecting the forests, biodiversity and so on; for urban heritage conservationists it means protecting the social environment when the character of towns and cities is at risk from property developers and chain stores. From the no-place of extinction we can recognise the real place of human creations that are worth defending, worth a struggle that necessarily involves eliminating the plague that threatens them. This was a perspective informed by the threat of nuclear war that Carl Sagan imagined in the classic television series *Cosmos*. 'The Cosmos may be densely populated with intelligent beings', he wrote, but 'the Darwinian lesson is clear: There will be no humans elsewhere. Only here. Only on this small planet. We are a rare as well as an endangered species' (2012 [1981]: 370).

The 'international bestseller' *The World Without Us* imagines a world in which humans have suddenly disappeared. It shows, with the help of scholars in different fields, how quickly the relics of humankind would be consumed by nature. Alan Weisman writes:

Suppose that the worst has happened. Human extinction is a fait accompli. Not by nuclear calamity, asteroid collision, or anything ruinous enough to wipe out most everything else, leaving whatever remained in some radically altered, reduced state. Nor some grim eco-scenario in which we agonisingly fade, dragging many more species with us in the process.

Instead picture a world from which we all suddenly vanished. Tomorrow. (2008: 3–4)

Sagan noted that when the Great Library of Alexandria was razed to the ground, of Sophocles' 123 plays only seven survived. One of the true greats in cinema history, Dreyer's *The Passion of Joan of Arc*, was at one time thought lost. Every play, every work of prose, every piece of music, every masterpiece of cinema, reduced to a cinder – all virtual information erased by electro-magnetic bombs – this is what it means to live in a world without us. And perhaps the clearest expression of such loss, both of culture and of human life itself, is the shell of the Hiroshima town hall that reminds us, Boym (2001) says, of an apocalypse that may yet come to pass. Rather than imagining the loss of our species with the dehumanising effect of reducing us to a biological category, making what is currently at stake for culture and society tangible helps put post-apocalyptic fantasies in perspective. The apocalypticism of our time presents us with an all-or-nothing situation: either revolution or extinction. We need the idea of culture, not as industry or postmodernity, least of all as commodity, but as something perhaps intangible and at the same time essential to what it means to be human; we need to think and reflect on this idea in order to be reminded of what, beyond our bodily existence, we as a species are fighting for.

If not a reminder, every object is a remainder of labour lost: to be recovered in fragments through our enjoyment of it. The CV itself documents the capacity for self-transformation, albeit in the register of a capitalist big Other. The object of consumption, as Bloch claimed, signals a yearning for the end of alienation. Likewise the object of employability, that is, the impossible point when capital no longer judges us because there is no such other as this to answer to. The utopian object of employability is one that is owned and embodied, of being employable by dint of being human. Only through collective possession of the meaning of employability can we be liberated from employability and embark on 'lines of flight' that collectively generate new earths, new peoples, other worlds. Only through common ownership of the means of production can consumption be liberated from the commodity form and the capacity inherent in all of us to realise a different kind of subject for a more just and humane society, a subject not of this world but of another.

Every act involved in making ourselves exploitable signals a utopian desire, unconscious in the present, but coming into consciousness as the labour force begins to recognise the bind it is in and that the only way to achieve its object of being included in society's great project is to change that society. The same obtains for the consumer, for whom the attempted liberation of Eros is redolent in every purchase, today at the cost of its enslavement, tomorrow the sacrifice of surplus value. Along the way, new potentialities emerge that do not in their actuality guarantee any escape from this logic. They require, as Benjamin noted, a human imagination to make the connection and build upon them 'in an act of freedom', that, as Buck-Morss explains, 'attends to the utopian possibilities latent within the technically transformed, material world' (in Douzinas and Žižek, eds., 2010: 74).

A better thought-experiment than Weisman's would be to imagine, with the help of Marxist theorists, a world without capitalism. Such a book is surely needed.

An anticipatory loss that echoes the actual losses enveloped in the different thicknesses of nostalgic mist gives concrete expression to what is at stake that in turn provokes new passions, new fascisms, that it would be perilous to ignore. Nostalgia, dystopian fears and apocalypticism are never neutral, which is why a left utopianism that posits alternatives grounded in and reflective on, rather than in denial of, the material, ideological and libidinal condition is required. A line needs to be drawn under the pastoral idylls of a reactive utopianism that wants to deny the existence of cities where over half the world's population now live and what the subject active within them is capable of. The future of society rests on the city, the chief battleground for the future and the site of any utopianism worth entertaining.

Utopian Space and Time

Wander around any of the world's great cities and pause for a moment to reflect on how any of it is possible. There is harmony in the immense flows of people and traffic, in the commercial thoroughfares and in the places where people meet to chat and replenish their energies. The State is a metronome that establishes the rhythm of capital through which great cities arise. As Marx and Engels put it in *The Communist Manifesto*, the bourgeoisie 'has been the first to show what man's activity can bring about. It has accomplished wonders far surpassing Egyptian pyramids, Roman aqueducts and Gothic cathedrals; it has conducted expeditions that put in the shade all former Exoduses of nations and crusades' (1985 [1848]: 83). Measured by metropolitan area, Tokyo, with over 32 million inhabitants, is by far the most populous city in the world. Seoul, its nearest rival, has a population of over 20 million. Tokyo belongs in the Taiheiyo Belt Megalopolis stretching for 1,200 km which also includes Yokohama, Nagoya, Osaka and Kobe. The combined population is over 82 million. Economic activity in the region makes up approximately 8 per cent of global economic output. Tokyo is also the largest metropolitan economy in the world and the most vulnerable to natural disaster. Any realistic and humane utopian project must account for the needs of people living in such highly concentrated and vulnerable centres of human activity. As David Harvey writes:

> Any movement toward socialism that does not confront the urbanisation of capital and its consequences is bound to fail. The construction of a distinctively socialist form of urbanisation is as necessary to the transition to socialism as the rise of the capitalist city was to the sustenance of capitalism. Thinking through the paths to socialist urbanisation is to chart the way to the socialist alternative itself. (1989: 58)

In a world of 7 billion people and rising, over half of which live in cities, one thing is certain, our future hinges on what happens in them. They are the economies of scale where interdependences are greatest and the connection to nature is most abstract. Localised alternatives fashionable among environmentalists and elements of the left are not much use in densely populated spaces where mass production and complex distribution networks are necessary to ensure people have access to provisions. Utopian ideas must in this respect be grounded in the world as it is encountered and in the subjectivities this world has given rise to. The idea of utopia, if it is to have any political traction, must be on a scale equivalent to, and able to meet, the sort of problems a post-capitalist society would encounter. If our utopia rests on procedures to ensure group consensus, decentralised and non-hierarchical forms of economic management, organic produce and renewable energy that excludes nuclear power, then we are simply dreaming and at worst paving the way for great famines, civil strive and chaos. If this were our only alternative, capitalism really would be the only game in town.

The space of utopia is one in which ideas are contested, played with, experimented on and developed. It is a time that is out of joint with a fully fleshed utopia, an untimely present in which seeds are planted in hardened soils, seeds of which most will perish before there is a more benign climate under which they could germinate. In the city, contradictions are amplified, new forms of surveillance are established as dissent grows, and commodities sneak their way into areas once relatively free of commerce that urban movements challenge. As Jameson put it, 'Utopian space is an imaginary enclave within real social space, in other words, ... the very possibility of Utopian space is itself a result of spatial and social differentiation' (2007: 15).

Notwithstanding the tongue-in-cheek sign as you enter stating that it is twinned with 'Narnia', the Devonshire town of Totnes boasts of its status as a top ten 'non-competitive' town. This is measured by the number of independent shops and the absence of coffee chains. Of course, as the *Guardian* reports, this is stock in trade for an alternative green economy and, while signalling an intention to keep global commerce at bay, it underlines the consumerist logic of enclave utopias that affluent communities indulge in.[3] The region itself is a black hole of unemployment, and this, if anything, is a more accurate measure of its status as 'non-competitive'. Cynicism comes cheap, but it is difficult to derive from such examples their relevance to any but a few people who inhabit them and who draw comfort in their pyrrhic victories over coffee chains, as their neighbours suffer the consequences of spatial and social differentiation. Such divisions are amplified in cities that, as Graham and Marvin (2008 [2001]) note, have become 'secessionary networked spaces' of 'packaged developments' made up of shopping and entertainment malls, business parks and affluent housing complexes separated from the poor by motorways and securitised gated communities. The city is splintered between affluent zones plugged into global networks and the poor who, because of their immobility, are excluded from both those zones and their global connections. Los Angeles exemplifies such divisions, as Mike Davis explains:

In the original Burgess diagram, 'pie slices' or 'half moons' representing ethnic enclaves ('Deutschland,' 'Little Sicily,' or 'the Black Belt') and specialized architectural ecologies ('residential hotels' or 'the two-flat area') are wedged into the city's concentric socioeconomic structure. In contemporary metropolitan Los Angeles, new species of enclaves are emerging in sympathy with the militarization of the landscape. For want of any generally accepted name, we might call them 'social control districts'. (1998: 383)

As David Harvey notes, urban space is an active site of production rather than passive reproduction, and so it is the principal terrain of capitalist accumulation and class struggle, the 'twin themes of a metropolitan dialectic' that absorbs capital and labour surpluses. The privatisation of urban space continues its advance, leading to further enclosures, through property development and the privatisation of public spaces such as Gunwharf Quays in Portsmouth, owned by Land Securities, or Bishops Square in London, sold to JP Morgan asset management in 2010.[4] It includes Spitalfields Market where, incidentally, before going to university I rented a stall to hawk homemade candles. The image of the future city is at its most dystopian, in a J.G. Ballard sort of way, on the outskirts of Chengdu in south-west China which boasts the world's largest standalone building comprising shopping malls, cinemas and a 20,000 capacity indoor swimming pool with '400 metres of "coastline" and a fake beach the size of 10 football pitches complete with its own seaside village'.[5] The 34-acre gated community of Paseo Cayala in Guatemala City, where the cheapest apartments sell for over 70 times the average Guatemalan's annual income, is one example of what Deleuze and Guattari meant when they said the first and third world is scrambled.[6] All is not lost, though! For as the BBC reports:

China, like several other countries, is exploring the creation of sustainable urban areas, or 'ecocities' as they are known. Around the world, ecocities are beginning to emerge from the drawing board, from Masdar City in Abu Dhabi to PlanIT Valley in Portugal. Aimed at being the world's largest of its type, Tianjin Eco-city is a collaborative project between the Chinese and Singaporean government that will house 350,000 people in a low-carbon, green environment around half the size of Manhattan by 2020. All going well, the team hope its model for building a sustainable city will provide the blueprint for future urbanization efforts in China, and other countries.[7]

By contrast, with 10,000 inhabitants, the Nanjiecun commune in China models itself on Mao's idea of a common wealth where tokens are used to buy food and the inequalities of larger cities are largely absent, but like elsewhere it is subject to market penetration and privatisation.[8] The utopian ideal is here marginal to the rest of China and in the case of the sustainable city enclosed, the obvious contradiction of the environmental cost in building it notwithstanding.

Echoing the life of the *flâneur*, Deleuze and Guattari write that 'it is possible to live striated on the deserts, steppes, or seas; it is possible to live smooth even in the cities, to be an urban nomad' (2003b [1980]: 482). The revolutionary class is urban, says Henri Lefebvre. It is a point we are reminded of in the recent spate of revolutions in the Arab world, the protest camps inspired by them, the ongoing struggles in Athens and Madrid and the battles to protect public space in Istanbul. Urbanism, though, as Guy Debord explains,

> is the modern method for solving the ongoing problem of safeguarding class power by atomising the workers who have been dangerously *brought together* by the conditions of urban production ... The efforts of all the established powers since the French Revolution to increase the means of maintaining law and order in the streets have finally culminated in the suppression of the street itself. (In McDonough, ed., 2009: 172)

Writing on Lefebvre, Andy Merrifield distinguishes between 'urbanism', which is concretely experienced in everyday life as use values, and 'urbanisation', which is an abstract phenomenon linked to capitalist development. With respect to the prospect for an urban utopia, Lefebvre writes, 'Socialism (the new society, the new life) can only be defined *concretely* on the level of everyday life, as a system of changes in what can be called lived experience.' Moreover:

> The street is a place to play and learn. The street is disorder. All the elements of urban life, which are fixed and redundant elsewhere, are free to fill the streets and through the streets flow to the centres, where they

meet and interact, torn from their fixed abode. This disorder is alive. It informs. It surprises. (2003 [1970]: 18)

David Pinder advocates an everyday utopia that aims to expand the potentialities of the present. Quoting Michael Gardiner, he emphasises the possibilities in the present situation, of

> 'how the ordinary can become extraordinary not by eclipsing the everyday, or imagining we can leap beyond it arbitrarily to some "higher" level of cognition, knowledge or action, but by fully appropriating and activating the possibilities that lie hidden, typically repressed, within it. Such an enriched experience can then be redirected back to daily life in order to transform it.' (In Gordon et al., 2010: 209)

Unless the dialogues that open up within our cities cohere into a future-oriented political project, our journey into dystopia will not be reversed. We need to imagine a world without capitalism and enact a politics to bring it about. The clearest articulation of what an urban utopia looks like is the one that Marxist scholarship frequently returns to, that of the 1871 Paris Commune. Utopian programmes can be formulated from examples such as these.

The World Without Capitalism

In reality this dilemma is, to my mind, the most urgent task that confronts Marxism today. I have said before that the so called crisis in Marxism is not a crisis in Marxist science, which has never been richer, but rather a crisis in Marxist ideology. If ideology to give it a somewhat different definition is a vision of the future that grips the masses, we have to admit that, save in a few ongoing collective experiments, such as those in Cuba and in Yugoslavia, no Marxist or Socialist party or movement anywhere has the slightest conception of what socialism or communism as a social system ought to be and can be expected to look like. That vision will not be purely economic, although the Marxist economists are as deficient as the rest of us in their failure to address this Utopian problem in any serious way. It is, as well, supremely social and cultural, involving the task

of trying to imagine how a society without hierarchy, a society of free
people, a society that has at once repudiated the economic mechanisms
of the market, can possibly cohere.

Fredric Jameson (1988: 5)

Marx on occasion gave into the temptation of imagining a non-alienated
society. A pinch of irony salted his and Engels' pastoral ideal of people free
to do one thing today and another tomorrow without ever becoming solely
'a hunter, fisherman, herdsman or critic' (1989 [1845–6]: 54). We might
respond that this has now been now realised: we hold down one part-time
job in the morning, another in the afternoon and study in the evening,
without ever being a bartender, a waiter, a campaign manager or a student.
Marx's description of communism in *The Civil War in France* differs in that
it describes an actual state of affairs. He writes:

> The Commune, they exclaim, intends to abolish property, the basis of
> all civilisation! Yes, gentlemen, the Commune intended to abolish that
> class-property which makes the labour of the many the wealth of the
> few. It aimed at the expropriation of the expropriators. It wanted to make
> individual property a truth by transforming the means of production,
> land and capital, now chiefly the means of enslaving and exploiting
> labour, into mere instruments of free and associated labour. But this is
> Communism, 'impossible' Communism! ... If co-operative production is
> not to remain a sham and a snare; if it is to supersede the Capitalist system;
> if united co-operative societies are to regulate national production upon
> a common plan, thus taking it under their own control, and putting an
> end to the constant anarchy and periodical convulsions which are the
> fatality of Capitalist production – what else, gentlemen, would it be but
> Communism, 'possible' Communism? (In McLellan, 1990: 545)

The Paris Commune is arguably the closest example in recent history of
actually existing communism within an urban setting of a mature capitalist
economy. Lefebvre is also worth quoting at length here:

> We will see why and how the scattered and divided city became
> a community of action and how, in the course of the Festival, the
> community became a communion at the vastest scale imaginable. And

how the people acclaimed the symbols of unalienated and unalienating labour, the fall of oppressive power, and the end of alienation. And how it proclaimed the world of labour, that is to say labour as world and creator of worlds. And how, in the course of this immense festival, something here and there pierced through the opaque veils of customary social life, ascended from the lower depths, passed through the accumulated layers of inertia and gloom, saw the light of day, and opened out. (In McDonough, ed., 2009: 174)

The forces of production liberated from their bourgeois owners, cooperation, planning and experiments in popular democracy, are the stuff from which future utopias are fashioned in the mind. A cognitive map is constructed from fiction and reality, an image of a form other than capitalism that is plausible. There are two forms of communist utopia to stress here, a weak form that grounds ideas in the current state of affairs and which aims to substantially reform existing relations, and a strong form that aims to abolish private property, to envisage a world without capitalism. The idea of utopia must, if it is to have a chance of being realised, be composed of the two, striated and smooth, molecular lines and lines of flight.

The idea of utopia is structured by the form in which it appears, what in psychoanalytic terms is called the fantasy frame of desire. In the weak utopian form ideas are delimited by a realistic appraisal of the current material, ideological and libidinal horizons of possibility with regard to which minimal demands are made. A minimal utopia envisages, for example, an end to mass unemployment and the creation of a wage economy adequate to living costs. In the strong utopian form, ideas are no longer delimited by the current state of affairs, they signify for the particular moment what is an invariant of history: a desire to end hunger, alienation, exploitation, disenfranchisement and war, in short to abolish private property. This maximal utopia, signified in many names, is the condition for the possibility of a minimal utopia and vice versa. The maximal is the measure, trajectory and force of the minimal that operates as various points in a relay of real breaks or flight from existing relations towards realising that end. The force of ideas is the bedrock of political programmes. The utopian idea is politicised when translated into programmes and demands. Minimal demands, as Trotsky said of classical social democracy, are limited to changes within the form of bourgeois society and put on hold indefinitely the possibility of a maximal utopia. Luxemburg put it differently: 'For us there is no minimal or maximal programme; socialism is one and the same thing: this is the minimum we have to realise.'[9] What Trotsky called for was a transitional set of demands that acts as a bridge between reform and 'the conquest of power by the proletariat'. What I am suggesting here is that a minimal and maximal utopia operate in tandem and, providing they are not isolated either in thought or practice, can avoid the problems Trotsky associated with social democracy and empty radicalism. As he reminds those who peg their politics to a revolutionary purity: 'A program is formulated not for the editorial board or for the leaders of discussion clubs, but for the revolutionary action of millions.'[10]

A minimal idea that relates to concrete experience has the potential to enlist many supporters. When that idea hits against the obstacle of an opposing class, it can go in one of two directions: inwardly as melancholic resignation and cynicism, or outwardly as resentment. A maximal idea articulates the need for and possibility of a change in form and in doing so liberates utopia from the history framed in bourgeois ideology. The minimal idea is a waypoint or vanishing mediator that draws people into the orbit of a maximal idea articulated through Marxist analysis. In other words, the one exposes us to the other, whose initial aim is to maintain the momentum of ideas and actions and give structure to them. The problem with Erik Olin Wright's vision of 'real utopias' is precisely in its separation of the two. What I refer to here as a 'maximal utopia' he pejoratively calls 'fantasy':

> morally inspired designs for social life unconstrained by realistic considerations of human psychology and social feasibility. Realists eschew such fantasies. What we need are hard-nosed proposals for pragmatically improving our institutions. Instead of indulging in utopian dreams we must accommodate to practical realities. (2010: 5–6)

A 'proper' diagnosis of the existing condition will in actual fact reveal that ending capitalism is the only viable means of preventing further immiseration and eventual catastrophe. The fantasy is the belief that the interests of capital can be accommodated in a way that is socially, economically and ecologically sustainable. A 'hard-nosed pragmatism' is only required in the first instance as a tactical manoeuvre to overcome the formidable obstacles, including in 'human psychology', in bringing about a change in form. This is the role of the minimal utopia, to pave the way and prepare the ground for the realisation of the maximal one. Without the idea of and agitation for a maximal utopia, our horizons are limited to partial reforms that if realised are easily reversed as soon as there are new crises of accumulation, as recent history has shown. By the same token, without a minimal utopia to aim towards, there are only the hollow cries for revolution that echo with diminishing intensity as they are met with state violence and are absorbed in societies of control. Wright identifies 'real' utopias in micro-communities and shares, with their members, the fantasy that somehow these bypass the state. It is a vision that has divorced itself from the need for industrial production and economic planning because, in truth, the utopia so described is the banquet of the privileged individual.

What Wright does provide us with, as Levitas (2013) acknowledges, is a useful framework or methodology for thinking about utopia. There are three components to his method. The first is a diagnosis and critique of existing relations centring on issues of social and political justice, which constitute the reasons why we desire change. The second concerns the practical or viable alternatives according to which utopian visions are formulated. The third, which I take up in the next chapter, is the question of how we transition from the existing situation to another. The first stage of diagnosis is critical in order to determine what is understood as 'viable' and, in turn, how we can formulate strategies to realise alternatives. But we should be careful not to underestimate the role that ideology has to play in shaping our vision of utopia, irrespective of the method deployed or the sophistication of our analysis based on statistical data.

According to Patrick Hayden and Chamsy el-Ojeili:

> To be utopian … is the stuff of [sociology], and it first involves subjecting the [society] of the present to critique. Secondly, it involves imagining human communities that do not yet exist and, thirdly, it involves thinking and acting so as to prevent the foreclosure of social possibilities in the present and future. (Quoted in Levitas, 2013: 102)

By thinking of utopia in terms of form, the limits of what is possible can be anticipated and an idea corresponding to, as well as exceeding, those limits developed. Utopian ideas work at a practical level when they relate to content, to concrete ideas, programmes and demands. By appearing reasonable and practicable, typically offering a solution to a broadly acknowledged problem, minimal utopias are more effective at exposing the limits of current politics and stimulating a demand for alternatives.

We are essentially dealing with two incompatible forms of utopia: that of capitalism, in which anything that disrupts the production of surplus value is unthinkable, and that of communism, in which property relations are unthinkable. This clash of 'axioms' is the topic of the final chapter.

7

Clash of Axioms

A generation's messianic power demands the historical convergence of two ruptures. The first, albeit man-made, is objective. It is the moment of economic, military or ecological crisis, the 'shock' and 'awe' that endangers the continuity of biographically lived time, the history of the individual. The second rupture concerns the hidden potentialities of the present, the untimeliness of our time that demands in response a rupture in collective imagination, a transforming rescue of the tradition that is the antithesis of reactive return.

Susan Buck-Morss (in Douzinas and Žižek eds., 2010: 77)

The point is that Marx alone sought to combine a politics of revolt with the 'poetry of the future' and applied himself to demonstrate that socialism was more modern than capitalism and more productive. To recover that futurism and that excitement is surely the fundamental task of any left 'discursive struggle' today.

Fredric Jameson (2012: 90)

Our diagnosis centres on several interrelated issues. Foremost is the deteriorating socio-economic and ecological conditions in which we live and, through our labours and consumption, have no choice other than to accelerate. The neoliberal model is socially, institutionally and, perhaps of greater political implication, psychically embedded. It forces people to prioritise their own interests over the needs of society and is largely naturalised in thought and action, giving rise to an individualistic, atomised and narcissistic subject, a subject without politics and culturally desensitised. In so far as there is a political ethics today, it is one that business can readily appropriate into the workplace and in commodities. As systems of surveillance are augmented through new managerial apparatus of control, the state brandishes its weapons, first abroad, now at home. Make no mistake: this is a class war if not in name then in practice. While the bourgeoisie has gotten the upper hand, it is a war it cannot win. It needs class divisions in order to exist and as long as there are class divisions there will be war. Only the proletariat, by ending class divisions, can win this war. To paraphrase Marcuse, the end of capitalism is necessary and inevitable, and communism, 'the *real* movement that abolishes the present state of things' (Marx and Engels, 1989 [1845–6]: 57), is necessary and, crucially, *not* inevitable.

The axiom of capital is surplus value. It is a global axiomatic. The axiom of communism is common ownership of the means of production. It is a timeless axiomatic. At this historic juncture we are potentially faced with two possible communisms: a post-apocalyptic and dystopian primitive communism or a utopian communism in which existing apparatuses, industry, technologies and scientific knowledge are put to work for the benefit of all. The collective refusal of a barbarous reality principle that the axiom of capital demands is a necessary step towards the establishment of a global communist axiomatic, a new reality principle. We know what is at stake. This concluding chapter addresses the practical task of ridding the world once and for all of an historical, perverse and now monstrous anomaly.

Before proceeding, let us briefly recap on the substantive points of the book so far. The central argument in Chapter 1, 'Materially Determined Apocalypse', is that converging and amplifying crises, attributable in large part to capital, coupled with the impact of neoliberalism on organised labour, have given rise to a fatalistic apocalyptical attitude. Strands of leftist critique hold out hope of a capitalist apocalypse lifting the veil on existing relations and emptying out the space for alternatives. There are no grounds for supposing a counter-hegemonic project would follow, given that circumstances will hardly be conducive to the flourishing of human life. Even a collapse of the political system is no guarantee that a path to the future will henceforth shine brightly. Without an organised foundation on which to build, a bourgeois class acting for itself will quickly overwhelm a proletarian class existing only in itself.

Chapter 2, 'The Three Orders of Apocalypse', approached the apocalyptic age through the Lacanian Real, Symbolic and Imaginary: really existing apocalypse is framed by fantasy and represented by clips and images taken by those in the midst of catastrophe. Cine-correspondents subconsciously reproduce culture industry spectacle by framing actual events for popular consumption. They author real life in the optics of the hyper-real. The image hits home. If, in the past, film put people in touch with things happening at a distance, film today is the means by which people gain a distance from the actual events they are physically involved in. It is a world seen through mobile phone eyes. The hyper-imaginary co-evolves with cinematic techniques that create verisimilitude, perhaps desensitising us to the real impact of crises and what is at stake in them.

Chapter 3, 'The Double Helix of Dissatisfaction', laid the groundwork for the subsequent two chapters on the draining of libidinal energy into work and consumption, as different and relational parts of the capitalist totality. The concept of alienation was expanded on to encompass those that are not strictly contributing value because their labour power is not actively used. This was the basis for redefining, or rather underlining, class as encompassing all those with essentially nothing to sell except their labour power irrespective of whether or not they have a paid job. The force of desire, species being and so on, is knotted one way or another into the circuit of capital and sutured by ideologies consistent with hegemonic myths that human desires are essentially destructive and therefore must be repressed. Austerity is today's reality principle, an ideology of different hues embraced across the political spectrum, typically, although not exclusively, on the right with respect to the economy and the left with respect to ecology.

Chapter 4, 'Production Spiral', argued against the presumption that we live in a consumer society. The consumer society claim rightly identifies the fetishisation of consumption in contemporary life, but typically and problematically does so by underplaying the central role of work in relation to economy *and* identity. The injunction to be employable is crucial to understanding the ideological separation of the thought of labour from the act of labour – by which I mean everything a person does in order to find and maintain themselves in employment, the binding of identities to CVs and so on. It is not one particular employer that our thoughts and actions are oriented to but rather capital as such, a big Other – a big Boss – imagined every time a line is added to the CV. The subject is invested in the big Other that gifts little pieces of *jouissance* whenever worth is recognised by employers. We want to be exploited because the alternative to exploitation is worse. The fear of unemployment is apparent in the efforts we make to become the privileged object of exchange. The poorest among us, those without a job and those always on the threshold of redundancy as 'surplus labour' contributing no value, cannot refuse what is already out of their reach: they cannot withdraw their labour or even boycott consumer goods. The marginal are politically marginalised.

Chapter 5, 'Consumption Spiral', turned to consumption and questioned the extent to which consumer practices are individuated. It revisited the culture industry thesis, accounting for changes brought about through new technologies and the internet in particular. It is frequently claimed that by utilising internet tools consumers become active non-alienated producers. While perhaps compensating for feelings of alienation, use of social media also underlines our alienation and loss of social connectedness. An outlet for creative expression in a society as alienated and atomised as ours begets 'pro-active' personalisation as minimal as that of culture industry production yet ideologically more compelling because seemingly originating from the self rather than media industries. Narcissism is also socialised in networked groups that speak to themselves and appear to be outside the purview of state and capital; they are enclosures of individuated individuals, hundreds and thousands of micro-fascists. There is an affinity, parodied by Spike Jonze in the 2013 film *Her*, between the subject and its apps, a (happy) app consciousness satisfied by the choice of cheap downloads and the freedoms they enable. As Occupy has shown, though, the internet does enable disconnected individuals to organise protests and seize, if only momentarily, an actual space for open dialogue. As do leafleting, posters and public announcements. The fact that the internet is so valued by the left – fetishised even – is, if anything, a consequence of our social disconnection, a disconnection that internet communication has arguably accelerated. Technologies are dumb. Humans are smart. In societies of control, technologies become 'smart' and humans 'dumb', and this is reversed when protest spills from the screens onto the streets.

Chapter 6, 'Banquets of Worlds', stressed the importance of utopian thinking and practice, recognising also a utopian impulse in humanity, described by Ernst Bloch, that acquires political force when self-consciously aligned with Marxist analysis and critique. Drawing on Deleuze and Guattari's philosophy of becoming, utopian ideas and practices were defined and criticised according to three interrelated lines: molar, molecular and lines of flight. There is a micro-fascist tendency within those groups who seek to separate themselves into enclaves and who embrace a utopianism disconnected from the actual struggles and needs of those inhabiting urban spaces where populations are densely concentrated. If utopian ideas are to have any salience they must, as urban theorists recognise, be practicable in these principal sites of contestation. In its weak form, utopian thinking is limited to the horizons of what is theoretically possible under capitalism and, in its strong form, what is theoretically impossible under capitalism. The former is of political relevance only if supplemented by the latter as the ultimate aim of utopian projects, the aim of abolishing property relations. It is from this proposition that the arguments regarding the contestation of state power will be developed in this chapter.

We begin where 'Banquets of Worlds' ended, with communism as an historical 'invariant' that, unlike utopia, refers to the concrete class struggle that aims to end property relations and thereby the commodity form.

State of Contestation

Politics is a strong and slow boring of hard boards. It takes both passion and perspective. Certainly all historical experience confirms the truth – that man would not have attained the possible unless time and again he had reached out for the impossible. But to do that a man must be a leader, and not only a leader but a hero as well, in a very sober sense of the word. And even those who are neither leaders nor heroes must arm themselves with that steadfastness of heart which can brave even the crumbling of all hopes. This is necessary right now, or else men will not be able to attain even that which is possible today. Only he has the calling for politics who is sure that he shall not crumble when the world from his point of view is too stupid or too base for what he wants to offer. Only he who in the face of all this can say 'In spite of all!' has the calling for politics.

Max Weber (1946 [1921])

Defeats have given rise to a speculative leftism that, as Bruno Bosteels writes, 'comes to represent an uncompromising purification of the notion of communism, not so much as the abolition but rather the complete tabula rasa of the present state of things, including all classes, parties, and ideological apparatuses of the State' (2011: 24). A left whose hopes lie in contingent events can afford to be idle when it comes to the more difficult task of thinking through strategies to raise class consciousness and for organisational forms and tactics that exert real pressure on states. They offer no tangible ideas as to how production might be organised to ensure that even our biological needs can be met. Stuck in an ideological realm in which popular apocalypticism also finds its home, the capitalist class is unlikely to be troubled by the finer points of, and aristocratic discourses on, 'being and becoming', when such discourses echoed by others omit these immediate issues.

Occupy Wall Street signified a refusal of this logic. What can be said about the movement and those it inspired is that, as Žižek (2012b) claims, they popularised the idea that capitalism is not the only game in town and opened a space for counter-hegemonic re-inscription. Experiments in consensual politics, discussions on tactics, and the inclusion of those formerly without a voice to engage in critical dialogue are important, but in Occupy they largely failed in establishing a durable movement to contest state power through strategic alignments with the working class. The mobilisation of protestors in support of dockworkers in Portland, Oregon, leading to the port's closure, was one of the few examples that had real consequences for the circulation of capital. While short-lived, it illustrated, as did May '68 in France, the potency of movements that are tactically aligned to the class struggle, however it is named. But, to emphasise, a politics from below is empty without hierarchical and centralised decision-making nodes – without them, it is largely incapable of progressing a revolutionary project in the face of the formidable, organised and unified power of capital unencumbered by the niceties of procedural politics.

The 'horizontal' procedural forms of decision-making embraced by Occupy and the refusal of 'vertical' command structures opened a void in which more charismatic and articulate participants could assert their authority over their fellows, without their influence being recognised or checked. Moreover, pre-figurative democratic procedures that supposedly gave a voice to everyone crippled attempts to develop a coordinated strategy of resistance that could impact on surplus value. If practice was made to fit theory it was theory that emanated from the anarchist tradition. The fetishisation of a flattened commons is apparent in Hardt and Negri's work. In *Labour of Dionysus* they say:

Communism has no need of agents external to the productivity of cooperative, immaterial, living labour. The transition has no need of the

State. The critical Marxism of the 1970s gave only one response to the problem of the transition: there is nothing by which to transfer, there is only the force of construction, constituent power. (1994: 288)

Hardt and Negri claim that power is dispersed and that capital as such is everywhere present though nowhere concentrated, thereby vulnerable at every point to 'biopolitical' struggles. They explain in *Multitude* that:

The global cycle of struggle develops in the form of a distributed network. Each local struggle functions as a node that communicates with all the other nodes without any hub or centre of intelligence. Each struggle remains singular and tied to its local conditions but at the same time is immersed in the common web. (2004: 17)

By their logic communism is already immanent in our situation, it is a communism of the general intellect that operates outside of the state apparatus and with regard to which capital is reduced to a leach. What seems forgotten from their reading of Deleuze and Guattari are the micro-fascisms of identity politics, the kind in which ascendant groups assert their power over those they leave behind, and that networked flows are precisely what capital thrives on. They pay scant attention to the striations of state science, not just international striations but also – more pertinently for struggle, and largely absent in Deleuze and Guattari's work too – national striations. There is nothing to say about the different histories and legacies of every state formation, to which every political movement is ineluctably attuned, whether or not it is acknowledged. Through the laws that are established and policed, the state is present, as is capital, in different and highly uneven ways in each nation through time and in space. Rather than regard communism to already be existent according to some vague idea of an effective war machine going smooth within the striations of state science, of greater political purchase is to conceive of communism as scrambled with the capitalist axiomatic, the communism of the welfare state echoing in the desire of liberals for a more humanitarian capitalism and in organisations – the 'communism of capital'[1] – that not without irony dehumanise in their demand for humans, not machines, to be extracting whatever residue of the species being is left that has not been instrumentalised.

The clash of axioms reaches its apogee on the terrain of state power, the principal site of contestation. A thousand McDonald's can burn, but capital will not be ended without an appropriation of Law, without wresting what Althusser called the repressive state apparatus – the police, the military – from those who utilise them to guarantee the smooth circulation of capital. As Gramsci wrote:

> If political science means science of the State, and the State is the entire complex of practical activities with which the ruling class not only justifies and maintains its dominance, but manages to win the active consent of those over whom it rules, then it is obvious that all the essential questions of sociology are nothing other than the questions of political science. (2003 [1929–35]: 244)

Eric Hobsbawm writes that:

> the basic problem of the revolution is how to make a hitherto subaltern class capable of hegemony, believe in itself as a potential ruling class and be credible as such to other classes ... the struggle to turn the working class into a potential ruling class, the struggle for hegemony, must be waged *before* the transition of power, as well as during and after it. (2011: 324–7)

This can begin, as Gramsci said, with an ideological struggle in civil society, in the streets and on the squares of our great cities, through various communication networks and media outlets, in the workplace, the school and the university. It is a struggle for hegemony and a tactical alignment of anti-capitalist forces operating independently of the parliamentary regime and also within it.

I want to stress, before proceeding with an argument likely to incur the wrath of popular elements of the 'anti-capitalist' movement, something Erich Fromm once called for which was a minimal of centralisation and a maximal of decentralisation. In the vein of Marcuse, who called for a socially sufficient repression in contrast to surplus repression, the 'minimal' required is a politically sufficient centralisation, in contrast to surplus centralisation and the micro-fascisms of a politically inoperative decentralised form of isolated resistance.

Communism for Alain Badiou is an historical invariant and hypothetical Idea that runs counter to, and is operationalised against, the 'market economy ... parliamentary democracy – the form of state suited to capitalism – and the inevitable and "natural" character of the most monstrous of inequalities' (Badiou, 2008: 98). It is politics with no 'organic relationship with existing parties or the electoral and institutional system that sustains them' (Badiou, 2010: 99). There is no programme, demand or strategy, nothing as such to concretely aim for except perhaps emancipation, whatever that assumes. Much like the divine power of the market to bring about the collapse of capitalism, the inexistent for Badiou, those without determination or voice, will bear the truth of communism through an endless process of becoming when a contingent event ruptures the established world of capitalism. Accordingly, the subject does not pre-exist the event she declares, because until such time she is a mere individual defined by identity, counted as value and reduced to a condition of animality. In defence of Badiou, Bosteels writes:

> Far from remaining a utopian principle, communism would ... be what allows for the historical inscription of politics in the concrete situation. It is what operates in the space in-between the local and the universal, the singular and the eternal, the interested individual and the disinterested subject of a cause greater than him or herself. In this sense, communism actually would be able to avoid the pitfalls of speculative leftism thanks to the triangulation of history, politics and subjectivity enabled by the Idea. (2011: 29–30)

By regarding the party as a function of parliamentary democracy and the state, and by the same token, as an apparatus wholly appropriated in the interests of the bourgeois, and by refusing any definition of communism except in the most abstract of terms, it is difficult to see what Badiou offers other than to open a space for thinking about communism – which is, to be clear, of immense value to the left when the word has been so abased. While revolutionary events transform the political horizons, they happen at least in part because of procedures enacted by individuals who are not, by Badiou's lights, subjects to truth. The success of any revolutionary procedure depends on the pre-existing organisational forms and leaderships vital in defeating the forces of reaction and nurturing a post-revolutionary situation that can bear the weight of responsibility to ensure everyone is fed. These are not simply tactical steps, they involve parties and alliances of different kinds made up of various 'organic intellectuals' (Gramsci) and not necessarily philosophers who Badiou regards central to a political articulation – an aristocratic politics if ever there was.

Rather than disengage from the state, I want to argue that, in this moment at least, strategic alignments with leftist parties vying for power are crucial. Whatever its failings, it was the vote that brought Hugo Chávez to power and thereby transformed the political landscape in Latin America after 500 years of extreme violence, exploitation and plunder. While there are important socio-economic and historical differences between Latin America and Europe, reforms in the former can point to possibilities in the latter. Reformist governments can themselves provoke unintended revolutionary consequences. It is unlikely, for example, that Gorbachev envisaged the dissolution of the Soviet Empire when introducing the policies of *Glasnost* and *Perestroika*. Nicos Poulantzas is worth quoting at length on the question of engagement with the state, this issue of utmost strategic importance:

> Now, (a) We know that political strategy must be grounded on the autonomy of the organisations of the popular masses. But the attainment of such autonomy does not involve the political organisations in leaving the strategic field of the relationship of forces that is the power-State, any more than it involves other organisations such as the trade unions in taking up a position outside the corresponding power mechanisms. To believe that this is even possible is an old illusion of anarchism (in the best sense of the term). Moreover, in neither case does self-organisa- tion on the terrain of power imply that these organisations must directly insert themselves in the physical space of the respective institutions (this will depend on the conjuncture), nor *a fortiori* that they must embrace the materiality of these institutions (quite the contrary). (b) We also know that, alongside their possible presence in the physical space of the state apparatuses, the popular masses must constantly maintain and deploy centres and networks at a distance from these apparatuses: I am referring, of course, to movements for direct, rank-and-file democracy and to self-management networks. But although these take up political objectives, they are not located outside the State or, in any case, outside power – contrary to the illusions of anti-institutional purity. What is

more, to place oneself at any cost outside the State in the thought that one is thereby situated outside power (which is impossible) can often be the best means of *leaving the field open for statism*: in short, it often involves a retreat in the face of the enemy precisely on this strategically crucial terrain. (2000 [1978]: 153)

In contrast, two positions on the left exemplify the problem of putting oneself at a distance from state power. The first, a typical outline of which can be found in *The Coming Insurrection* (The Invisible Committee, 2009), is the strategy of disengagement from the capitalist state and the view that an autonomous liberated space, prefiguring global communism, can be created outside of it. The second, underlined by Badiou's stance towards elections, is that by voting in elections the 'inexistent' capitulate to the bourgeois politics of democratic materialism. Badiou argues:

The government, which would not be very different if it were chosen by lottery, declares that it has been mandated by the choice of the citizens and can act in the name of this choice. Voting thus produces a singular illusion, which passes this disorientation through the fallacious filter of a choice. (2008: 17)

And, with reference to the 'unknown elector': 'Throughout the bourgeois centuries has she too not been instrumentalized and deceived, and had her voice sacrificed on the alter of a "democracy" where she is in fact stripped, by her very vote, of any iota of power?' (Badiou, 2012: 83). While there are nuances to Badiou's politics, such repeated assertions invite a one-sided perspective on power that cannot account for the particulars of and possibilities inherent in the socio-economic, political and historical circumstances of a given nation-state formation. Poulantzas does not fetishise the vote, either in terms of what can be gained from it or what can be achieved by refusing it. Given the materially embedded nature of the capitalist state – that, as Poulantzas points out, condenses the broader social relations and ideologies that emanate from different spheres of influence, and essentially the class struggle itself – it is a crucial terrain of contestation. The state can neither be left alone nor can it be seized as if it exists separately from the relations that it embeds within itself and importantly, in terms of class struggle, the relations by which it is characterised. While the language has changed, what Poulantzas said in the 1970s has contemporary relevance:

> the current road to socialism, the current situation in Europe, presents a number of peculiarities: these concern at one and the same time the new social relations, the state form that has been established, and the precise character of the crisis of the State. For certain European countries, these particularities constitute so many chances – probably unique in world history – for the success of a democratic socialist experience, articulating transformed representative democracy and direct, rank-and-file democracy. This entails the elaboration of a new strategy with respect both to the capture of state power by the popular masses and their organisations, and to the transformations of the State designated by the term 'democratic road to socialism.' (2000 [1978]: 257)

In Greece, Syriza (Coalition of the Radical Left) is in many respects a mirror of the movements on the ground, an alliance of disparate groupings each with their own specific agendas. Its taking of power, a realistic possibility at time of writing, would potentially have real political consequences for Europe and beyond, especially if, like Chávez in Venezuela, it supported those movements which enabled it to assume power. Just as it is mistaken to dismiss revolutionary politics on the basis that every revolution has ended in failure, so, as Venezuela has proven, it is mistaken to dismiss engagement in parliamentary politics because, for example, of what happened to democratic socialism in Chile in 1973. As Leo Panitch, writing in the *Guardian*, says,

> The left used to beat itself up, sometimes quite literally, with debates over reform v revolution, parliamentarianism v extra-parliamentarianism, party v movement – as if one ruled out the other. The question for the 21st century is not reform v revolution, but rather what kinds of reforms, with what kinds of popular movements behind them engaging in the kinds of mobilisations that can inspire similar developments elsewhere, can prove revolutionary enough to withstand the pressures of capitalism.[2]

The important difference in Venezuela is that the movements that brought Chávez to power remained an active determinant in the political struggle for social transformation, attested to by the decisive role they played in bringing Chávez back to power after the (homologous to Chile) US backed coup of 2002. Contrasting the democratic discourse of inclusion to that of Chávez, Žižek's point here has broader significance:

> Chávez is not including the excluded in a pre-existing liberal-democratic framework; he is, on the contrary, taking the 'excluded' dwellers of favelas as his *base* and then reorganising political space and political forms of organisation so that the latter will 'fit' the excluded. Pedantic and abstract as it may appear, this difference – between 'bourgeois democracy' and 'dictatorship of the proletariat' – is crucial. (2009: 102)

Very few of the 'excluded' in Europe are strictly slum dwellers. The excluded here are the swelling numbers of surplus labour, and the 'precariat' inclusive of salaried labour, protesting because they know their futures are vulnerable. Unemployment, the threat thereof, and the likely prospect that, for all our efforts, potential use values will not be realised in exchange for a satisfactory job, or even any job at all, is what connects many of us. The possibility of a genuine act occuring as part of a coordinated strategy of political significance depends on what happens over the coming years with regard to tactical decisions on the terrain of state power. As Poulantzas emphasises:

> At any event, to shift the relationship of forces within the State does not mean to win successive reforms in an unbroken chain, to conquer the state machinery piece by piece, or simply to occupy the positions of government. It denotes nothing other than a *stage of real breaks*, the climax of which – and there has to be one – is reached when the relationship of forces on the strategic terrain of the State swings over to the side of the popular masses. (2000 [1978]: 258)

Those currently 'traversing the fantasy' of their disavowed fetishistic enjoyment of capital by fully acknowledging their place in it and acting accordingly to bring about change are too small in number or marginalised from the accumulation process to effect change. Their presence becomes more significant as those still invested in capital (not only wage labourers) get politically involved through their actions and current sense of outrage at the injustices of austerity programmes, global finance and so on. In short, 'anti-capitalists' can present a critical mass that establishes the grounds for a dialogue expanding the capacity of movements to force shifts in policy that in turn strengthen the possibility of popular struggle.

A politics with demands is required if those who claim to speak for the 99 per cent are to expand the popular base to a numerical level capable of arresting the circuit of capital. Every demand speaks to another potential anti-capitalist, and that potential subject does not have to be from the class that currently holds power nor reached via the mass media that can to a greater or lesser extent be bypassed using internet communication technologies. The demand, to use Rancière's elegant phrase, speaks to the part of no part that is not engaged in a political dialogue and that is conspicuously absent in the many protest camps that have emerged since 2008. A demand addresses the empty place: the constituent that is not represented but which parliamentary politics aims to capture, the constituent who is not on a protest camp but which those who claim the whole world is watching imagine to be on the other side of the screen. It addresses those caught in the matrix of hegemonic reaction yet to be persuaded by a leftist counter-hegemonic project. As many on the left have claimed, we need a new manifesto fashioned by demands of global relevance and adaptive to the concrete situation of more localised struggles taking place under different historical conditions as they unfold.

The weak form of utopia constitutes ideas in a relay towards the final objective of ending capitalism. They are 'superstructural' in the sense that they focus on alternatives to neoliberal ideology and practice that could theoretically be implemented by a leftist reformist government and by such token are minimal. They are abstract because unthinkable from the perspective of established political discourse. By registering what experience recognises to be a human and social need, and what is known to be possible because of what existed in the past or exists elsewhere, they are politically operative if translated into tangible demands. This would constitute what Gramsci calls a 'war of position', working under existing institutional relationships to establish a hegemonic ideology with enough force and persuasion to bring about real social transformations that expand the political horizon towards a final stage in the class struggle, namely a 'war of manoeuvre' when the state-form can finally be challenged by a revolutionary movement capable of ending property relations.

Manifesto

What can be done from the State in function of this communist horizon? To support as much as possible the unfolding of society's autonomous organisational capacities. This is as far as it is possible to go in terms of what a leftist State, a revolutionary State, can do. To broaden the workers' base and the autonomy of the workers' world, to potentialise forms of communitarian economy wherever there are more communitarian networks, articulations, and projects.

Alvaro García Linera (quoted in Borsteels, 2011: 247)

Labour connects all of us whether we have a job, make up the unpaid armies that reproduce future workforces, or are surplus to capital. It is both the primary cause of alienation, insecurity, frustration, hardship and dispossession, and vital to society, to wellbeing, dignity, satisfaction and belonging. Labour is the source of value, in so-called post-industrial societies more disorganised than ever and throughout the world, and, whether minimal or maximal, ideas, strategies, tactics, demands and politics must focus on this relation. The state will bare its teeth whenever there are genuine threats to the flow of capital, when occupying the city, shopping malls, ports and factories, and in every instance where this happens our bodies are the soft targets for state violence. The refusal of work, the withdrawal or subtraction of our labour, puts us, relatively at least, out of harm's way. We cannot refuse, though, something that is not in our possession or proffered to us. Demands can be made about creating full and secure employment, repealing anti-trade-union legislation and, as Alvaro García Linera, the Bolivian vice-president, argues, utilising the state to nurture and support the 'unfolding of societies organisational capacities'. If there is a slogan that applies to a revolutionary left in all circumstances it is this: the circuit of capital must be broken!

As Žižek explains, 'the situation becomes politicised when this particular demand starts to function as a metaphoric condensation of the global opposition against Them, those in power, so that the protest is no longer actually just about that demand, but about the universal dimension that resonates in that particular demand' (2000: 204). Harvey makes a concrete suggestion on how such a demand could be conceived when he writes: 'In the same way that Marx depicted restriction on the length of the working day as a first step down a revolutionary path, so claiming back the right for everyone to live in a decent house in a decent living environment can be seen as the first step towards a more comprehensive revolutionary movement' (2012: 137).

The idea of a basic income is often flaunted as a progressive step in ending the insecurity that many of us contend with. It proposes a flat payment to everyone irrespective of whether they have a job, as the baseline for a standard of living adequate to needs. As with the minimum wage, however, if implemented it would likely be pegged at such a level that it would have minimal impact on our lives while providing a subsidy to capital to reduce labour costs and perhaps increase demand for its commodities. It would not restrict capital's ability to extract surplus value or to circulate. The problem lies in the underlying form of production that characterises the form of welfare, the cause rather than the emollient, and in regard to which a reformist agenda *with revolutionary consequences* must be formulated. Basic income is the panacea of a left that wistfully recalls those lazy Sunday afternoons when mommy cooked the roast and washed the dishes. It is a left that imagines the rate will be pegged so high that an idle life can return, when we need to think concretely about the reorganisation of labour to ensure that everyone can play a role in establishing a new social compact. Labour is fundamental to human existence and survival, it is the transformation of work not welfare that needs to exercise the imagination.

Lazzarato (2012) claims that politics can be radicalised through campaigns centring on debt. While the elimination of debt is an important step in relieving the labour force from its future enslavement to creditors, debt is an ineluctable aspect of capitalist production and as such transcends any class division. Without the socialisation of housing, workers will need access to credit to pay their mortgages and debt is required to compensate for low wages if there is no substantive redistribution of wealth. The demand to scrap individual debt is nevertheless a useful rallying point given its effect on so many people, and so it is included in the propositions below in a qualified way, since getting rid of individual debt does not end the necessity for credit.

There are many books like this one, but few that make concrete propositions, develop programmes or list a set of demands that, adapted and prioritised according to conditions in each nation-state formation, can serve as vanishing mediators or universal anchoring points in regard to which protestors can rally and popular counter-hegemonic movements flourish. Many if not all the propositions I make here have been recommended at various times and places, by revolutionaries, intellectuals, scholars, committees and parties too numerous to cite and, while they are not exhaustive, they would, I believe, impact on capital's ability to extract surplus value. They are formulated with this in mind. They are not addressed to the state or the media but rather to the politically active and disenfranchised, the uncounted and those vulnerable to fascist persuasion as a result of their isolation and anger.

Let us begin with the ultimate and underlying aim of the leftist struggle that must inform every minimal programme, idea or demand, in slogan form: abolish all private property! Now to a minimal programme or set of demands. These are listed in no particular order; and to stress, they are not intended to be exhaustive or detailed and would necessarily be subject to debate and disagreement.

1. (Re)Nationalise essential industries and services

Return to public ownership those state assets that have been sold during the neoliberal phase. Whatever problems there are with nationalisation, it is a vital step in blocking and reversing the encroachment of capital into all aspects of life. At a minimum, where these are not already in national ownership, it would include the (re)nationalisation of transport infrastructure, water and energy, healthcare, education, repressive apparatuses such as the military and the prison-industrial complex, welfare services and the banking system. Slogan: Common ownership of vital industries and services!

2. Workers management

Democratic inclusion of all employees in the management of all companies and institutions, whether publicly or privately owned, with the aim of ending managerialism and shareholder domination, to give voice and shift power to those currently exploited. Establish local autonomy over the provision of education, among other services now under strict managerial control, and progressively distribute corporate gains to the entire workforce. Slogan: Collective determination in the workplace!

3. Decommodify services

Return to public management and ownership those state services, including waste disposal, catering, consulting and so on, which are currently parcelled out to private contractors or under the control of private interests. Slogan: Public ownership of vital services!

4. Tax the rich

Enact a massive redistribution of wealth through heavy taxation of the rich, seizure of their superfluous assets and closure of all tax loopholes. Slogan: Tax the rich!

5. Decommodify the future

This includes an end to student fees to be replaced by non-repayable grants with the effect of liberating those in education from low-paid labour to fund their studies, the gradual elimination of mortgages for those whose homes are not superfluous to their needs, and the elimination of consumer debt, a policy effective only in tandem with other propositions. Slogan: End debt!

6. Free time

The minimisation and even distribution of necessary labour, as per Marcuse, to qualify the principle 'from each according to his or her abilities to each according to his or her needs', as per Marx. Slogan: Minimise labour, maximise the equitable distribution of wealth!

7. Full and secure employment

Related to point 6, full employment to be established by reducing working hours, the introduction of new labour regulations to create job security, and the repeal of anti-trade-union legislation. Slogan: Full employment and unionisation for all workers!

8. Free the City

Enact the redistribution of wealth and power to the regions; control and, where possible, re-appropriate space from commerce, including shopping malls and residential landlords; and re-prioritise principal sites of social activity given over to business. Maximise public transport, minimise private transport. Slogan: Free the city!

9. Free information

Unleash the power of the internet as a positive force for change through common ownership of the principal sites of communication. Dismantle the surveillance society. Make intellectual production, patents, pharmaceuticals, academic journals and so forth freely accessible to all with the exception of knowledge and materials that cause harm, for example weapons science and child porn. Expand library services and open new spaces for public dialogue. Media and entertainment industries to be brought under local control in order to dismantle the global culture industry. Slogan: Free the mind, free information, free culture!

10. Localise to globalise

Industrial-scale farming is necessary to ensure that everyone has enough to eat, but organised to provision the vital needs of regional populations and minimise, where not impacting the needs of others, its global distribution in order to reduce carbon emissions. End foreign ownership of supermarket chains, end their monopolisation, and eventually bring them under public control. Relatedly and concomitant with the above demands, end foreign ownership of housing stock, land, commercial properties and key services. Slogan: Local produce for local people, surpluses to the world!

11. Stop the leaches

Bring financial provision under regional control, heavily tax financial trading, and transfer second homes to public bodies. Slogan: Our homes, our property. Socialise all essential housing stock!

12. Free the nations

Self-determination of all peoples, control over local resources, end imperialist warfare in whichever guise, economic, political and cultural, return all remaining colonies to the control of the people and address the legacies of colonisation in post-colonial states through economic reforms that address indigenous issues and which are shaped, in view of universal needs, by indigenous peoples. End all residues of monarchical power. Slogan: Free the nations!

13. End incarceration

Prisons do not work, they dehumanise the prison population, which becomes a source of free or cheap labour. Prison to be an option of last resort until new means are devised to control and punish sex offenders, murderers, state and corporate criminals and so forth. Slogan: End incarceration!

14. End waste

Curtail built-in obsolescence, produce things in order to last, enact strict regulations on all producers to minimise industrial waste. Dismantle the culture industry to bring about the transformation of needs, wants and desires. Slogan: End waste!

15. Protect the environment

Exploitation of all resources vital to the health of the global ecosystem and biodiversity reduced to sustainable levels; forests, water supplies and so forth brought under the stewardship of a global authority with compensations to nations and peoples affected by ecological regulations. Slogan: Liberate the commons!

If enacted, even partially, each one of these measures would impact surplus value and the circulation of capital and, together with a shift in power towards extra-parliamentary movements, open the way for an eventual end to property relations. The devil as they say is in the detail. These are mere points of departure that would need fleshing out through dialogues at local, national, regional and global levels when timely to do so. They rearticulate aspects of Marx and Engels' programme in the *Communist Manifesto*, Trotsky's transitional programme, policies and proposals of leftist states past and present, heterodox economists, scholars, activists, movements and revolutionary councils.

What then is the minimum necessary centralisation to achieve the maximal practicable decentralisation? This is a huge and complex issue that, in the final analysis, can only be resolved through open dialogue and in the midst of political action. In current movements there is a hegemonic contingent in favour of horizontal dispersions of power. Where revolutionary movements have in the past taken this approach, the Spartacists in Germany, the Anarcho-syndicalists in Spain, they were soon crushed. Centralised administrations and vanguard-style parties have faired better but in all cases were isolated and, without empowering the masses, eventually corrupted. It is not a choice between one or the other, between autonomy and authoritarianism, but a mixture, balanced by circumstance, of horizontal and vertical pre- and post-revolutionary organisational forms such as that described by Linera above. Žižek variously, and Jodi Dean in

The Communist Horizon, have recently advocated a more Leninist politics, emphasising the importance of the party. As Dean writes:

> The communist party politicises the part that is not a part, claiming the gap constitutive of the people and subjectifying it as the collective desire of the collectivity. Its task is not to fulfil or satisfy this desire (an impossibility), but to maintain it, to cultivate it as a desire. (2012: 245)

The issue I take with this is the presumption that tactical engagements with the existing form of democracy amount to a commodification of sorts. I have stressed the importance of Nicos Poulantzas' contribution on this crucial issue, which does not need repeating.

In *Counter-Revolution and Revolt*, Marcuse called for decentralised forms of organisation to combat the monopoly of state violence, that become the nuclei of social change *only* if they are given political direction and organisation. In respect of this, revolutionary councils need to overcome the fetishism of the 'below' where there are reactionary tendencies. Students, Marcuse claimed, have a key role to play in revolutionary struggle. Universities are an important base for radical activity and training grounds in which to become equipped for the task of political action and the 'long march through the institutions' involving the development of counter-institutions. This strikes me as a solid set of propositions to work with, to refine and develop in view of earlier points. Students, workers and protest movements need to put aside their differences and prejudices about 'vertical' or 'horizontal' organisation and think through the most effective ways to engage the masses, establishing the organisational foundations, strategies and tactics that can effect real change and which have a chance of ensuring that whether by revolution, economic collapse, political disintegration or catastrophe, they have the capacity to sustain a future worth living.

In the final part of the chapter, I return to the idea of full employment and a refusal of the employability injunction, of greater significance in the most advanced capitalist nations of the world.

The Verdict

The strategic task of the next period – prerevolutionary period of agitation, propaganda and organization – consists in overcoming the contradiction between the maturity of the objective revolutionary conditions and the immaturity of the proletariat and its vanguard (the confusion and disappointment of the older generation, the inexperience of the younger generation). It is necessary to help the masses in the process of the daily struggle to find the bridge between present demand and the socialist program of the revolution. This bridge should include a system of transitional demands, stemming from today's conditions and from today's consciousness of wide layers of the working class and unalterably leading to one final conclusion: the conquest of power by the proletariat.

Leon Trotsky, *The Transitional Programme*[3]

World history would indeed be very easy to make if the struggle were taken up only on condition of infallibly favourable chances. It would on the other hand be of a very mystical nature, if 'accidents' played no part. These accidents naturally form part of the general course of development and are compensated by other accidents. But acceleration and decay are very much dependent on such 'accidents', including the 'accident' of the character of the people who first head the movement.

Marx to Kugelmann, 17 April 1871 (in McLellan 1990: 593)

What kind of subject does politics address? A subject whose libidinal economy is likely to mirror that of the capitalist economy, and, at present, after 30 years or so of neoliberalism, possessive individualism, self-aggrandisement and narcissism, a subject who sees the world through neoliberal eyes, through the eyes of the culture industry. It is a subject to be emptied of its commoditised substance, not in this world but in another.

According to Žižek, a political subtraction from the existing state of affairs operates at the level of phantasy. As Fabio Vighi explains: 'subtraction is always at least minimally traumatic because I subtract first and foremost from my fetishistic enjoyment of what I profess to hate' (2012: 137). Traumas are not something that can be self-induced. The Act, as Žižek (2000: 374) puts it, differs from activity in so far as the phantasmal background by which life acquires meaning is contingently disturbed. In terms of employability, we could think of this as the moment when everything we do to improve our job prospects no longer has any meaning. Not only do we recognise the enjoyment derived from filling in the lack in the Other – imagining ourselves in the place of surplus value (the job vacancy) – but we derive no satisfaction in improving our employability because it would have no symbolic value. When the fantasy of our enjoyment of employability is traversed, the career itself – the CV – is sacrificed. A measure of the strength of movements against capital can be discerned when it is possible to answer the question *Can the career be sacrificed?* in the affirmative.

A contingent change in the situation forces the decision. Moving away from preoccupations with French and Italian political history, the 1984-5 miners' strike and 1989 Hillsborough stadium disaster can be thought of as English instances of this: trauma necessitating a decision that reconstitutes the subject caught up in the moment. In both cases, what may have been theoretically acknowledged became concrete reality: that the police really are a brutal weapon of state oppression; that the mass media – for example, the BBC and mass circulation newspapers in their coverage of the Battle of Orgreave and the Hillsborough disaster respectively – are an apparatus of ideological distortion; and that the state in general is an apparatus of class violence. With the fundamental antagonism thus revealed to concrete experience, any symbolic fiction that these things happen only to other people is shattered. Those caught up in such events are forced to take sides and reckon in their very sense of being with a new symbolic reality. Events such as these, however, are rare, and often only affect a relatively small number of people. If the political act is necessarily traumatic and only occurs through a chance sequence of events, the theory of subtraction has no political value. But by separating subtraction into two different forms, corresponding to Marx's and Lacan's different concepts of exploitation, material and libidinal, and recognising that a material subtraction or negation does not have to involve a traumatic emptying out of the subject first, the limitations of a theory that presupposes contingent traumatic breaks can be overcome. Contingencies can be planned for through collective action prior to them.

The commodification of desire has changed the biological constitution of the individual, or rather the libidinal economy, to such an extent that a traumatic event is needed before the individual can be freed. However, it is the political activities of such individuals, ineluctably entwined in the commodity form, that will prove decisive in the current context of struggle. We must contend with the thing in us more than ourselves – the *objet a* or lack that capital produces in regard to which our efforts to gain inclusion are knotted. But we can only do so if there has already been a change in the situation in which those biologically constituted needs are organised. Political action – our own political action – must in the meantime be undertaken in spite of our libidinal attachments to surplus value. In contrast to Žižek, trauma, I want to argue, is not the *a priori* of the political act. Put another way, enjoyment of capital – the *jouissance* knotted into the creation and destruction of value, work and consumption – is not necessarily antithetical to political action – even political action to halt capital – if that enjoyment is identified as symptomatic of a system that itself must change in order for there to be a libidinal subtraction from the commodity form, for desire to be liberated from the interests of capital.

Consider the role of the student in struggles against austerity, finance capital and the neoliberalisation of the university. Here we have the archetypal subject of what Lacan calls the 'university discourse' in which knowledge is modified and counted by its investment in capital from the privileged position of being able to develop credentials that improve employability. Lacan's retort to the heckling students at Vincennes in 1969, quoted in Chapter 4, is worth repeating here:

> You are the product of the university, and you prove that you are the surplus value, even if only in this respect – which you not only consent to, but which you also applaud – and I see no reason to object – which is that you leave here, yourselves equivalent to more or fewer credit points. You come here to gain credit points for yourselves. You leave here stamped, 'credit points.' (2007 [1969]: 201)

The scarcity of jobs and grants is a powerful material and ideological device for justifying repressive submission to the university discourse, irrespective of what we know or politically (self-consciously) desire. In this context it is difficult to deny the fleeting though ultimately dissatisfying *jouissance* spent and stained on the CV. Refusal is not an option until a political struggle reaches a decisive stage when sacrifice would not simply guarantee unemployment and political marginality.

Our relation to politics prior to a traumatic separation can be thought of in terms of Žižek's (1989) classic critique of ideology: that we know full well the 'secret' beneath the commodity – that, for example, goods do not magically appear on supermarket shelves but arrive there by way of exploited labour through the plundering of natural resources, imperialist violence and so forth – yet still in our social activity we act as if such things do not happen, as if the commodity is indeed a magical thing. The fetishistic illusion in this respect enables us to go on living with such knowledge, critiquing the 'system' while disavowing our contributions to it. Yet, inverting the point, even if protestors are only dimly aware of how enjoyment is knotted into the operation they protest against, they are nonetheless protesting: students blockade shopping centres and prise open spaces for critical dialogue, the 'salaried bourgeoisie' go on strike and entrepreneurial slum dwellers disrupt production and prop up leftist regimes. The danger for critical theory is that it gets caught up in abstract ideas of subtraction and ceases to be of political relevance in times when ideas do matter and strategies can be decisive. In the unpromising circumstances of the present, by day we engage in the proletarian struggle and by night work for the bourgeoisie. If the left, then, is to avoid staking its future on a contingent event, it needs over a period of time to develop the organisational capacity for a generalised subtraction from the circuit of capital – strikes, boycotts, intervention, sabotage, blockades – strategies that everyone irrespective of their status within the division of labour, or, up to a point, libidinal investments, can partake in. Our fetishistic enjoyments of capital are an obstacle to emancipation only in so far as at the level of ideology they prevent us from doing the mundane job of taking action and developing the capacity for a generalised, properly political act in the sense referred to by Žižek. In short, critical theory is essential for the ideological tasks of separation and strategy, articulating the problem by explaining how capitalism operates materially, ideologically and libidinally, showing what is at stake and advancing a dialogue on what can be done rather than individualising the problem, which is arguably what happens when everything hinges on traversing the fantasy of our enjoyment of capital. As Gramsci put it:

> To the extent that ideologies are historically necessary, they have a validity which is 'psychological'; they 'organize' human masses, they form the terrain on which men move, acquire consciousness of their position, struggle, etc. To the extent that they are 'arbitrary' they only create individual 'movements', polemics and so on (though even these are not completely useless, since they function like an error which by contrasting with truth, demonstrates it). (2003 [1929–35]: 199)

The master signifier of employability gets to the core of the problem. 'Equality', writes Badiou, 'means that everyone is referred back to their choice, and not to their position. That is what links a political truth to the instance of a decision, which always establishes itself in concrete situations, point by point' (2009: 26). The decision to sacrifice one's career, the refusal of employability, is consistent with the four determinations of what Badiou calls the truths of politics: 'will (against socio-economic necessity), equality (against the established hierarchies of power or wealth), confidence (against anti-popular suspicion or the fear of the masses), authority or terror (against the "natural" free play of competition)' (2009: 27). The inexistent, the indivisible remainder, the part of no part, the surplus as concrete exception, whatever elegant term we care to use, is what presents itself, point by point, in a pre-evental truth procedure that refuses employability, in other words, that develops the capacity to refuse to be counted as use value for the purposes of exchange. A blank essay on 'turnitin' (the preferred online system in academia for ensuring against plagiarism) that nonetheless was written, a blank CV to a prospective employer by a worker who nonetheless fits the job descriptor – 'include me, out!', refusals such as these are a long way from becoming generalised.

A molecular revolution is necessary, perhaps of the kind described by Deleuze and Guattari, but also Gramsci: the idea, as discussed by Peter Thomas (2009), of gradual changes in the material conditions of the subject giving rise to a different kind of subjectivity that wants or is prepared to do things that in its former self it had refused. It is a change that is gradual and unconscious and one that occurs through different circumstances – in the dark age of neoliberalism including after the 2008 crisis, in these apocalyptic 'times', and through the renewed passions of a left that protests against capitalism.

The stakes are high. It is increasingly apparent that a fundamental transformation in both the forces and relations of production are required if there is to be a future world worth inhabiting. But such transformations will not occur in one fell swoop. The idea that a revolution is coming is an opiate in which the disenfranchised may take comfort but has no practical benefit to the immediate task of realising the possibility for social transformation. The struggles that take place in the here and now are never by such lights 'it'. They are never the one battle to end all battles. By this token, because few struggles today in themselves appear to be decisive, it is easy to be half-hearted and defer commitment until such a moment – that may never arrive – when the situation really is a revolutionary one. We go on a 'day of action' and because our duty is done can enjoy further protests by others from the sidelines. History is never made according to such gestures. Every struggle that signifies a part in the totality of the war against surplus value, that concretely links a minimal programme with maximal prescription, must today be fought as if the future depends on victory. One battle can be lost, and recognising when it has been lost is of strategic importance, but *the* struggle is never exhausted and is a continuous one. For those minimal struggles to impact surplus value and thereby relate to a maximal aim they must be fought in a permanent relay as if they are 'it'. The battles against what was to become known as neoliberalism in Europe and throughout the world, the intensity and immersion of miners in the struggle to bring down the Thatcher government in Britain, were fought in this way. If they are not to become mere footnotes of a discontinuous past, that absorption of a collective force in the singularity of a specific aim needs to be carried through into current struggles against war and international finance, and any future struggles that may contingently arise. While the capacity to fight such battles appears to have diminished, it is this spirit, perhaps a *jouissance* of politics proper, that we need to recover and enact, as if every struggle, whether for better working conditions or against urban gentrification or finance capital, is a defining moment in the long march towards social transformation. Sidney Lumet's aptly titled film *The Verdict* underlines the point I want to make. Representing the parents of a victim of medical malpractice, down-on-his-luck lawyer Frank Galvin, played by Paul Newman, is advised at a low point in the trial by his friend and colleague Mickey Morrissey, played by Jack Warden, to resign himself to defeat and save his energies for future cases. Galvin's answer is instructive: 'There are no other cases. This is the case.' Even when appearing hopeless, the case against capital must continually be made, the weaknesses in the defence exposed, victims and witnesses, the self-same person, called upon to win over the jury – themselves victims and witnesses of the self-same relation – the ultimate aim of which is to become both judge and law maker.

While much has been written about the pacifying effects of consumption, it is our relation to production and the capitalist state that has greatest ideological and political significance. Through the lens of psychoanalytic theory, this relation, understood as a libidinal one, reveals the extent to which the subject is bound to capital and what a revolutionary struggle must ultimately entail. The master signifier that draws surplus value and surplus *jouissance* into a society-wide compact is employability, an object without substance, an aim without outcome, and a starting point for re-articulating a demand that hits capital where it hurts, in its capacity to extract surplus value from us. The apocalypse is the already present and the not yet totalised. Necessity weighs heavily upon us though, in the midst of which differences must be put to one side and a political response from those without property, a *proletarian* struggle adequate to the current challenges, engendered. Redemption, the difficult task of salvaging history from the wreckage of capital, is in our hands alone. The means and capacities are available to us. There is still time.

Notes

All online sources accessed September 2014

Introduction

1. www.caritas.org/activities/climate_change/ParadiseLost.html
2. www.telegraph.co.uk/earth/carteret-islands/6771651/The-sea-is-killing-our-island-paradise.html

Chapter 1

1. www.theguardian.com/environment/earth-insight/2014/mar/14/nasa-civilisation-irreversible-collapse-study-scientists
2. http://news.msn.com/rumors/rumor-us-stockpiling-ammunition-for-use-in-civil-unrest
3. www.dailymail.co.uk/news/article-2099714/Meet-preppers-Up-3-MILLION-people-preparing-end-world-know-it.html
4. http://online.wsj.com/news/articles
5. See Inglis (2014) for an excellent critique of such thinkers.
6. 'So lethal was the disease that cases were known of persons going to bed well and dying before they woke, of doctors catching the illness at a bedside and dying before the patient. So rapidly did it spread from one to another that to a French physician, Simon de Covino, it seemed as if one sick person "could infect the whole world"' (Tuchman, 1978: 92).

Chapter 2

1. www.theguardian.com/money/2009/mar/17/fsa-respossessions-arrears-rise
2. www.theguardian.com/money/2012/aug/09/repossessions-fall-18-month-low-cml
3. www.theguardian.com/society/2014/feb/28/man-starved-to-death-after-benefits-cut
4. www.theguardian.com/business/2013/apr/14/poll-gloom-doom-decades-living-standards/print
5. www.theguardian.com/society/2013/oct/12/homes-repossession-shelter-universal-credit
6. www.theguardian.com/society/2014/feb/23/europe-11m-empty-properties-enough-house-homeless-continent-twice

7. http://endoftheamericandream.com/archives/35-statistics-that-show-the-average-american-family-has-been-broke-down-tore-down-beat-down-busted-and-disgusted-by-this-economy
8. http://inthesetimes.com/print/evicting_the_homeless
9. http://theeconomiccollapseblog.com/archives/turn-out-the-lights-the-largest-u-s-cities-are-becoming-cesspools-of-filth-decay-and-wretchedness/turn-out-the-lights-the-largest-us-cities-are-becoming-cesspools-of-filth-decay-and-wretchedness
10. http://inthesetimes.com/article/13467
11. www.nytimes.com/2012/04/15/world/europe/increasingly-in-europe-suicides-by-economic-crisis.html?pagewanted=print&_r=0
12. www.economiaepolitica.it/index.php/distribuzione-e-poverta/economic-recession-and-suicide-in-italy/#.UzfcnoVWhtg
13. www.theguardian.com/world/2012/apr/30/italian-women-husbands-recession-march/print
14. From hereon I use the Maori name for the country more familiarly known by its colonial name New Zealand. An excellent source on the history of the Maori struggle, and perhaps a lesson in guerrilla tactics, is Ranginui Walker's (1990) *Struggle Without End*.
15. www.nbr.co.nz/article/warner-bros-sought-job-law-change-film-the-hobbit-nz-135087
16. www.hobbitontours.com
17. www.nzherald.co.nz/travel/news/article.cfm?c_id=7&objectid=10762234
18. www.theguardian.com/world/2013/jan/09/australian-wildfires-family-defining-photograph
19. www.theguardian.com/commentisfree/2011/oct/21/muammar-gaddafi-death-images-media
20. www.theguardian.com/world/video/2013/jul/30/great-white-shark-south-africa-video
21. I have written about the commodification of the contingent in an article published in 2007 listed in the bibliography.
22. For example, www.youtube.com/watch?v=b9DMiy_DVok
23. www.theguardian.com/world/2012/feb/12/costa-concordia-video-crew-panicking
24. https://www.youtube.com/watch?v=lPhZLYetJ7w
25. www.theguardian.com/commentisfree/2012/apr/29/difference-hobbit-news-not-much

Chapter 3

1. With permission from the editors, selected passages from my essay in Feldner, Vighi and Žižek, eds., *States of Crisis and Post-Capitalist Scenarios* (Cremin 2014), are reproduced here, in the next chapter, and in the final chapter.
2. www.footprintnetwork.org/en/index.php/gfn/page/world_footprint/

3. www.theguardian.com/commentisfree/2012/feb/16/suzanne-moore-disgusted-by-poor

4. www.natcen.ac.uk/our-research/research/public-attitudes-to-poverty-and-welfare-1983-2011

5. www.theguardian.com/politics/2013/may/14/labour-voters-poor-study-solidarity

6. www.monbiot.com/2009/09/29/the-population-myth

7. Of the many statistics on inequality, one worth noting here is that the wealthiest 20 per cent of the US population spends 60 per cent of all income (Angus and Butler, 2011: 149).

8. See, for example, www.nytimes.com/2014/04/20/magazine/its-the-end-of-the-world-as-we-know-it-and-he-feels-fine.html?_r=2. The *Daily Telegraph* notes how Aronofsky's movie *Noah* reifies nature by presenting human life to be an expendable stain on the environment: www.dailytelegraph.com.au/news/opinion/the-noah-film-is-afloat-with-extremism/story-fnj45fva-1226869091537

Chapter 4

1. www.theguardian.com/uk-news/2014/mar/10/rise-zero-hours-contracts

2. www.opendemocracy.net/guy-standing/precariat-why-it-needs-deliberative-democracy

3. Susan George (2010) reports that today the richest 10 per cent of adults own 85 per cent of global household wealth. The poorest half of world population owns barely 1 per cent of the global wealth.

4. An extended essay on consumption can be found in Cremin 2012.

5. My previous book, *Capitalism's New Clothes* (2011), goes into more detail on Foucault's work and the contribution of 'neo' Foucauldians to the study of the labour process.

6. www.theguardian.com/business/2014/jan/20/oxfam-85-richest-people-half-of-the-world

7. www.theguardian.com/business/2013/nov/29/eurozone-youth-unemployment-record-high-under-25s

8. www.telegraph.co.uk/finance/jobs/10584384/Global-unemployment-on-rise-despite-economic-recovery.html

9. www.theguardian.com/world/datablog/2013/jul/02/survey-european-graduates-hopes-fears

10. I give a variation of the critique of employability with more empirical examples in the chapter 'Naked Enterprise' in *Capitalism's New Clothes* (2011).

11. http://talentlist.co.nz/files/trainings/KEEP%20YOURSELF%20BUSY%20WHILE%20UNEMPLOYED.pdf

12. www.firebrandtalent.com

13. www.lovemoney.com/news/the-economy-politics-and-your-job/
your-job/3430/how-to-survive-unemployment
14. http://career-advice.monster.ie/cvs-applications/cv-advice/what-are-my-
unique-selling-points-ie/article.aspx
15. http://career-advice.monster.co.uk/cvs-applications/cv-advice/spring-clean-
your-cv/article.aspx
16. www.theguardian.com/money/2013/apr/22/top-10-things-employers-
looking-for/print

Chapter 5

1. 'Should Bush Tell America to go Shopping Again?', *Wall Street Journal*, 7
October 2008, http://blogs.wsj.com/economics/2008/10/07/should-bush-
tell-america-to-go-shopping-again
2. www.washingtontimes.com/news/2011/aug/17/prepping-debt-plan-obama-
calls-shared-sacrifice/?page=all
3. www.theaustralian.com.au/business/latest/pms-10bn-recession-buster/story-
e6frg90f-1111117754875
4. www.forbes.com/sites/scottdecarlo/2012/09/19/cost-of-living-extremely-
well-index-our-annual-consumer-price-index-billionaire-style
5. www.bbc.co.uk/news/uk-england-london-20943576
6. www.guardian.co.uk/world/2013/jun/06/us-tech-giants-nsa-data
7. https://www.youtube.com/watch?v=RmZlkGqBeNA
8. www.forbes.com/sites/anthonykosner/2012/04/14/hip-hop-resurrection-
dr-dre-to-perform-california-love-with-hologram-of-tupac-at-coachella
9. www.psmag.com/culture/ugly-reality-creating-reality-television-
casting-68538
10. www.marketingweek.co.uk/christian-charity-turns-to-gamification-to-
engage-young/3028925.article
11. See http://noimpactproject.org

Chapter 6

1. H. Marcuse, 'The End of Utopia', cited from www.marxists.org/reference/
archive/marcuse/works/1967/end-utopia.htm
2. W. Benjamin, 'On the Concept of History', cited from www.marxists.org/
reference/archive/benjamin/1940/history.htm
3. www.theguardian.com/sport/2012/may/20/olympic-torch-writers-relay-
day2
4. www.theguardian.com/uk/2012/jun/11/granary-square-privately-owned-
public-space
5. www.guardian.co.uk/society/2012/jan/21/rise-megacity-live

6. www.theguardian.com/world/2013/jan/09/guatemalan-capital-wealthy-haven-city

7. www.bbc.com/future/story/20120503-sustainable-cities-on-the-rise

8. www.theguardian.com/world/2013/dec/26/nanjiecun-commune-capitalism

9. R. Luxemburg, 'Our Program and the Political Situation', cited from http://www.marxists.org/archive/luxemburg/1918/12/31.htm

10. L. Trotsky, 'The Transitional Programme', cited from 'http://www.marxist.net/trotsky/programme/p2frame.htm?opportunism.htm

Chapter 7

1. See the special 2013 issue of the journal *Ephemera: Theory and Politics in Organizations* on the theme of the 'Communism of Capital'.

2. www.theguardian.com/commentisfree/2014/jan/12/europe-left-capitalism-social-democrats-reforms

3. L. Trotsky, 'The Transitional Programme', cited from www.marxist.net/trotsky/programme

Bibliography

Adorno, T. (2000 [1951]) *Minima Moralia*, London: Verso.

Adorno, T. (2001 [1963]) *The Culture Industry*, London: Routledge.

Adorno, T. (2007 [1966]) *Negative Dialectics*, London: Continuum.

Adorno, T. and Horkheimer, M. (1997 [1947]) *Dialectic of Enlightenment*, London: Verso.

Adorno, T. and Horkheimer, M. (2010 [1956]) 'Towards a New Manifesto?', *New Left Review*, 65, Sept/Oct.

Angus, I. and Butler, S. (2011) *Too Many People: Population, Immigration and the Environmental Crisis*, London: Haymarket Books.

Badiou, A. (2008) *The Meaning of Sarkozy*, London: Verso.

Badiou, A. (2009) *Logics of Worlds: Being and Event 2*, London: Continuum.

Badiou, A. (2010) *The Communist Hypothesis*, London: Verso.

Badiou, A. (2012) *The Rebirth of History: Times of Riots and Uprisings*, London: Verso.

Bakhtin, M. (1984 [1941]) *Rabelais and his World*, Bloomington: University of Indiana Press.

Bataille, G. (1999 [1946–49]) *The Accursed Share*, New York: Zone Books.

Baudrillard, J. (2001) *Impossible Exchange*, London: Verso.

Baudrillard, J. (2003) *The Spirit of Terrorism*, London: Verso.

Baudrillard, J. (2010) *Carnival and Cannibal or the Play of Global Antagonism*, London: Seagull Books.

Bauman, Z. (2004 [1991]) *Modernity and Ambivalence*, Oxford: Blackwell.

Bauman, Z. (2005) *Work, Consumerism and the New Poor*, Berkshire: Open University Press.

Bauman, Z. (2007) *Consuming Life*, Cambridge: Polity Press.

Bauman, Z. (2007) *Liquid Fear*, Cambridge: Polity Press.

Beck, U. (2012 [1986]) *Risk Society: Towards a New Modernity*, London: Sage.

Benjamin, W. (2003 [1927–40]) *The Arcades Project*, London: Harvard University Press.

Berardi, F. (2011) *After the Future*, Edinburgh: AK Press.

Bloch, E. (1986 [1947]) *The Principle of Hope: Volume One*, Cambridge MA: The MIT Press.

Blyth, M. (2013) *Austerity: The History of a Dangerous Idea*, Oxford University Press.

Boltanski, L. and Chiapello, E. (2007) *The New Spirit of Capitalism*, London: Verso.

Bosteels, B. (2011) *The Actuality of Communism*, London: Verso.

Boyer, P. (1992) *When Time Shall Be No More*, Massachusetts: Harvard University Press.

Boym, S. (2001) *The Future of Nostalgia*, New York: Basic Books.

Branson, R. (2011) *Screw Business as Usual*, London: Virgin Books.

Breman, J. (2013) 'A Bogus Concept', *New Left Review*, 84, Nov/Dec.

Buck-Morss, S. (2002) *Dreamworld and Catastrophe: The Passing of Mass Utopia in East and West*, Cambridge MA: The MIT Press.

Calhoun, C. and Derluguian, G. eds, (2011) *Business as Usual: The Roots of the Global Financial Meltdown*, New York: New York University Press.

Cederstrom, C. and Fleming, P. (2012) *Dead Man Working*, Hants: Zer0 Books.

Claeys, G. and Sargent, L., eds., (1999) *The Utopia Reader*, New York: New York University Press.

Clarke, J. and Newman, J. (2012) 'The Alchemy of Austerity', *Critical Social Policy*, 32(3): 299–319.

Comor, E. (2010) 'Digital Prosumption and Alienation', *Ephemera: Theory & Politics in Organization*, 10(3/4): 439–54.

Crary, J. (2013) *24/7*, London: Verso.

Cremin, C. (2007) 'Living and Really Living: The Gap Year and the Commodification of the Contingent', *Ephemera: Theory and Politics in Organisations*, 7(4), Nov.

Cremin, C. (2011) *Capitalism's New Clothes: Enterprise, Ethics and Enjoyment in Times of Crises*, London: Pluto Press.

Cremin, C. (2012) *iCommunism*, Hants: Zer0 Books.

Cremin, C. (2014) 'Getting its Act Together: What Chance Subtraction under Conditions of Scarcity?' in Feldner, H. Vighi, F. and Žižek, S., eds., *States of Crisis and Post-Capitalist Scenarios*, Farnham: Ashgate.

Davis, M. (1998) *Ecology of Fear: Los Angeles and the Imagination of Disaster*, New York: Metropolitan Books.

Davis, M. (2002) *Dead Cities*, New York: The New Press.

Dean, J. (2009) *Democracy and Other Neoliberal Fantasies*, Durham: Duke University Press.

Dean, J. (2012) *The Communist Horizon*, London: Verso.

Deleuze, G. (1986 [1983]) *Cinema 1*, London: Continuum.

Deleuze, G. (1992) 'Postscript on the Societies of Control', *October*, 59: 3–7.

Deleuze, G. and Guattari, F. (2003a [1972]) *Anti-Oedipus: Capitalism and Schizophrenia*, London: Continuum.

Deleuze, G. and Guattari, F. (2003b [1980]) *A Thousand Plateaus: Capitalism and Schizophrenia*, London: Continuum.

Derrida, J. (1984) 'No Apocalypse, Not Now (Full Speed Ahead, Seven Missiles, Seven Missives)', *Diacritics*, 14(2), Nuclear Criticism.

Dixon, W. (2003) *Visions of the Apocalypse: Spectacles of Destruction in American Cinema*, London: Wallflower Press.

Douzinas, C. and Žižek, S., eds., (2010) *The Idea of Communism*, London: Verso.

Engels, F. (2009 [1845]) *The Condition of the Working Class in England*, Oxford: Oxford University Press.

Feltham, O., ed., (2005) *Alain Badiou: Live Theory*, London: Continuum.

Firat, F. and Venkatesh, A. (1995) 'Liberatory Postmodernism and the Reenchantment of Consumption', *Journal of Consumer Research*, 22(3): 239–67.

Fisher, M. (2009) *Capitalist Realism*, Hants: Zer0 Books.

Fleming, P. (2014) 'Review Article: When 'Life Itself' Goes to Work: Reviewing shifts in organisational life through the lens of biopower', *Human Relations*, 67(7): 875–901.

Foster, J. (2000) *Marx's Ecology: Materialism and Nature*, New York: Monthly Review Press.

Foster, R. (2007) 'The Work of the New Economy: Consumers, Brands, and Value Creation', *Cultural Anthropology*, 22(4): 707–31.

Foucault, M. (1977) *Language, Counter-memory, Practice: Selected Interviews and Essays by Michel Foucault*, ed. D. Bouchard, New York: Cornell University Press.

Freud, S. (2010 [1920]) *Beyond the Pleasure Principle*, in Smith, I., ed., *Freud – Complete Works*, available at https://openlibrary.org.

Fukuyama, F. (2002) *Our Posthuman Future: Consequences of the Biotechnology Revolution*, New York: Picador.

Galeano, E. (2009 [1971]) *Open Veins of Latin America: The Five Centuries of the Pillage of a Continent*, London: Profile Books.

George, S. (2010) *Whose Crisis, Whose Future?* Cambridge: Polity Press.

Gilbert, J. (2014) *Common Ground: Democracy and Collectivity in an Age of Individualism*, London: Pluto Press.

Gordon, M. Prakash, G. and Tilley, H., eds., (2010) *Utopia–Dystopia: Conditions of Historical Possibility*, Princeton: Princeton University Press.

Gramsci, A. (2003 [1929–35]) *Selections from the Prison Notebooks*, London: Lawrence and Wishart.

Graham, S. and Marvin, S. (2008 [2001]) *Splintering Urbanism: Networked Infrastructures, Technological Mobilities and the Urban Condition*, London: Routledge.

Hardt, M. and Negri, A. (1994) *Labour of Dionysus: A Critique of the State-Form*, Minneapolis: University of Minnesota Press.

Hardt, M. and Negri, A. (2001) *Empire*, Cambridge MA: The MIT Press.

Hardt, M. and Negri, A. (2004) *Multitude*, New York: Penguin.

Hardt, M. and Negri, A. (2009) *Common Wealth*, Cambridge MA: Harvard University Press.

Harvey, D. (1984) *The Limits to Capital*, Oxford: Blackwell.

Harvey, D. (1989) *The Urban Experience*, Baltimore: Johns Hopkins University Press.

Harvey, D. (2005) *A Brief History of Neoliberalism*, Oxford: Oxford University Press.

Harvey, D. (2010a) *A Companion to Marx's Capital*, London: Verso.

Harvey, D. (2010b) *The Enigma of Capital and the Crises of Capitalism*, London: Profile Books.

Harvey, D. (2012) *Rebel Cities: From the Right to the City to the Urban Revolution*, London: Verso.

Hobsbawm, E. (2011) *How to Change the World*, London: Little Brown.

Houellebecq, M. (2011) *The Map and the Territory*, London: William Heinemann.

Inglis, D. (2014) 'What is Worth Defending in Sociology Today? Presentism, Historical Vision and the Uses of Sociology', *Cultural Sociology*, 8(1): 99–118.

Ivanova, M. (2011) 'Consumerism and the Crisis: Wither 'the American Dream?', *Critical Sociology*, 37(3): 329–50.

Jameson, F. (2007) *Archaeologies of the Future: The Desire Called Utopia and Other Science Fictions*, London: Verso.

Jameson, F., (1988) 'Cognitive Mapping', in Nelson, C. and Grossberg, L., eds., *Marxism and the Interpretation of Culture*, Champaign: University of Illinois Press.

Jameson, F. (2002 [1981]) *The Political Unconscious*, London: Routledge.

Jameson, F. (2003) 'Future City', *New Left Review*, 21, May/June.

Jameson, F. (2004) 'The Politics of Utopia', *New Left Review*, 24, Jan/Feb.

Jensen, D. (2006) *Endgame: Volume 1, The Problem of Civilisation*, New York: Seven Stories Press.

Jameson, F. (2011) *Representing Capital: A Reading of Volume One*, London: Verso.

Kaleb, G., ed., (1971) *Utopia*, New York: Atherton Press.

Kay, J.H. (1998) *Asphalt Nation: How the Automobile Took over America and How We Can Take it Back*, Berkeley: University of California Press.

Keller, C. (2004) *Apocalypse Now and Then*, Minneapolis: Augsburg Fortress Publishers.

Kesel, M. (2009) *Eros and Ethics: Reading Jacques Lacan's Seminar VII*, New York: SUNY.

Lacan, J. (1992 [1959–60]) *The Ethics of Psychoanalysis: Book VII*, London: Routledge.

Lacan, J. (2007 [1969]) *The Other Side of Psychoanalysis: Book XVII*, London: Routledge.

Lefebvre, H. (2003 [1970]) *The Urban Revolution*, Minneapolis: University of Minnesota Press.

Lazzarato, M. (2012) *The Making of the Indebted Man*, Los Angeles: Semiotext(e).

Lemke, T. (2002) 'Foucault, Governmentality, and Critique', *Rethinking Marxism*, 14(3), Fall.

Leslie, E. (2000) *Walter Benjamin: Overpowering Conformism*, London: Pluto Press.

Levitas, R. (2011 [1990]) *The Concept of Utopia*, Oxford: Peter Lang.

Levitas, R. (2013) *Utopia as Method*, London: Palgrave Macmillan.

Luxemburg, R. (2003 [1913]) *The Accumulation of Capital*, London: Routledge.

Marcuse, H. (1969) *An Essay on Liberation*, Boston: Beacon Press.

Marcuse, H. (1970) *Five Lectures: Psychoanalysis, Politics and Utopia*, London: Penguin.

Marcuse, H. (1972) *Counter-Revolution and Revolt*, Boston: Beacon Press.

Marcuse, H. (2002 [1964]) *One-Dimensional Man*, London: Routledge.

Marcuse, H. (2006 [1955]) *Eros and Civilisation*, London, Routledge.

Marx, K. (1973 [1858]) *Grundrisse: Introduction to the Critique of Political Economy*, London: Pelican.

Marx, K. (2001 [1867]) *Capital: Volume 1*, London: Penguin.

Marx, K. and Engels, F. (1985 [1848]) *The Communist Manifesto*, London: Penguin.

Marx, K. and Engels, F. (1989 [1845–6]) *The German Ideology*, London: Lawrence & Wishart.

Matthewman, S. (2015) *Everyday Disasters*, Basingstoke: Palgrave MacMillan.

McDonough, T., ed., (2009) *The Situationists and the City*, London: Verso.

McLellan, D., ed., (1990) *Karl Marx: Selected Writings*, Oxford: Oxford University Press.

Milne, E. Mitchell, C. and de Lange, N. (2012) *Handbook of Participatory Video*, Plymouth: Altamira Press.

More, T. (2012 [1551]) *Utopia*, London: Penguin.

Nabokov, V. (2006 [1955]) *Lolita*, London: Penguin.

Noys, B. (2012) *The Persistence of the Negative: A Critique of Contemporary Continental Theory*, Edinburgh: Edinburgh University Press.

Panayotakis, C. (2011) *Remaking Scarcity: From Capitalist Inefficiency to Economic Democracy*, London: Pluto Press.

Pearce, F. (2008) *Confessions of an Eco-Sinner*, Boston: Beacon Press.

Poulantzas, N. (2000 [1978]) *State, Power, Socialism*, London: Verso.

Rancière, J. (2009) *The Emancipated Spectator*, London: Verso.

Riesman, D. (2001 [1961]) *The Lonely Crowd*, New Haven: Yale University Press.

Ritzer, G. (2005) *Enchanting a Disenchanted World*, Thousand Oaks: Pine Forge Press.

Ritzer, G. and Jurgenson, N. (2010) 'Production, Consumption, Prosumption: The Nature of Capitalism in the Age of the Digital "Prosumer"', *Journal of Consumer Culture*, 10(1): 13–36.

Sagan, C. (2012 [1981]) *Cosmos: The Story of Cosmic Evolution, Science and Civilisation*, London: Abacas.

Sayers, S. (2007) 'The Concept of Labour: Marx and His Critics', *Science and Society*, 71(4): 431–54.

Simmel, G. (2004 [1900]) *The Philosophy of Money*, London: Routledge.

Standing, G. (2011) *The Precariat: The New Dangerous Class* , London: Bloomsbury Academic.

Stewart, S. (2007 [1993]) *On Longing: Narratives of the Miniature, the Gigantic, the Souvenir, the Collection*, Durham: Duke University Press.

Streeck, W. (2012) 'Citizens as Customers: Considerations on the New Politics of Consumption', *New Left Review*, 76, July/Aug.

Stiegler, B. (2011) *The Decadence of Industrial Democracies*, Cambridge: Polity Press.

Tapscott, D. and Williams, A. (2006) *Wikinomics*, New York: Penguin.

The Invisible Committee (2009), *The Coming Insurrection*, Los Angeles: Semiotext(e).

Thomas, P. (2009) *The Gramscian Moment: Philosophy, Hegemony and Marxism*, Chicago: Haymarket Books.

Toscano, A. (2010) *Fanaticism: On the Uses of an Idea*, London: Verso.

Treadwell, J. Briggs, D. Winlow, S. and Hall, S. (2013) 'Shopocalypse Now: Consumer Culture and the English Riots of 2011', *British Journal of Criminology*, 53: 1–17.

Tuchman, B. (1978) *A Distant Mirror: The Calamitous 14th Century*, New York: Ballantine Books.

Vaneigem, R. (1979) *Book of Pleasures*, Pending Press.

Vighi, F. (2012) *On Žižek's Dialectics: Surplus, Subtraction, Sublimation*, London: Continuum.

Virilio, P. (2005 [1998]) *The Information Bomb*, London: Verso.

Volonisov, V.N. (1986 [192?]) *Marxism and the Philosophy of Language*, Cambridge MA: Harvard University Press.

Walker, R. (1990) *Ka Whawhai Tonu Matou / Struggle Without End*, London: Penguin.

Weber, M. (1946 [1921]) 'Politics as a Vocation', in H.H. Gerth and C. Wright Mills, eds., *From Max Weber: Essays in Sociology*, New York: Oxford University Press.

Weber, M. (2003 [1904–5]) *The Protestant Ethic and the Spirit of Capitalism*, New York: Dover Publications.

Weeks, K. (2011) *The Problem with Work: Feminism, Marxism, Antiwork Politics and Postwork Imaginaries*, Durham: Duke University Press.

Weisman, A. (2008) *The World Without Us*, London: Virgin Books.

Williams, E.C. (2011) *Combined and Uneven Apocalypse*, Hants: Zer0 Books.

Williams, R. (2005) *Culture and Materialism*, London: Verso.

Wright, E.O. (2010) *Envisioning Real Utopias*, London: Verso.

Žižek, S. (1989) *The Sublime Object of Ideology*, London: Verso.

Žižek, S. (1992) *Looking Awry: An Introduction to Jacques Lacan through Popular Culture*, Cambridge MA: The MIT Press.

Žižek, S. (2000) *The Ticklish Subject: The Absent Centre of Political Ontology*, London: Verso.

Žižek, S. (2004) *Organs Without Bodies: On Deleuze and Consequences*, London: Routledge.

Žižek, S. (2006) *The Parallax View*, Cambridge MA: The MIT Press.

Žižek, S. (2008) *Violence*, London: Profile Books.

Žižek, S. (2009) *First as Tragedy, Then as Farce*, London: Verso.

Žižek, S. (2010) *Living in the End Times*, London: Verso.

Žižek, S. (2012a) *Less than Nothing: Hegel and the Shadow of Dialectical Materialism*, London: Verso.

Žižek, S (2012b) *The Year of Dreaming Dangerously*, London: Verso.

Index

Compiled by Sue Carlton